THE NEW PACIFIC COMMUNITY IN THE 1990s

CENTER FOR ASIA PACIFIC STUDIES, RESEARCH PROJECT NO. 3
PACIFIC STATES UNIVERSITY AND KON-KUK UNIVERSITY

THE NEW PACIFIC COMMUNITY IN THE 1990s

Ruth H. Chung
Charles A. Goldman
Ralph C. Hassig
Edward A. Olsen
Courtney Purrington
Rinn-Sup Shinn
Sheldon W. Simon
Robert G. Sutter
David Winterford
Robert L. Youngblood

Foreword by
Seung Jong Hyun

Young Jeh Kim
editor

An East Gate Book

M.E. Sharpe
Armonk, New York
London, England

An East Gate Book

Library of Congress Cataloging-in-Publication Data

The new Pacific community in the 1990s / Young Jeh Kim, editor.
p.   cm.
"An East gate book."
Includes bibliographical references and index.
ISBN 1-56324-783-6.—ISBN 1-56324-784-4 (pbk.)
1. Pacific Area.
I. Kim, Young Jeh, 1939–
DU17.N48   1996
950′.09823—dc20
96-12784
CIP

Printed in the United States of America

The paper used in this publication meets the minimum requirements of the
American National Standard for Information Sciences—
Permanence of Paper for Printed Library Materials,
ANSI Z 39.48-1984.

∞

BM (c)   10   9   8   7   6   5   4   3   2   1
BM (p)   10   9   8   7   6   5   4   3   2   1

Contents

About the Contributors

Ruth H. Chung (Ph.D., University of California, Santa Barbara) is an assistant professor of psychology and Asian–American studies at Pomona College, Claremont, California. She is a Korean-American counseling psychologist who specializes in cross-cultural psychology. She conducts research on acculturation and ethnic identity, and on the relationship of these factors to psychological problems and attitudes toward seeking psychological help.

Charles A. Goldman (Ph.D., Stanford University) is an economist in the international policy department at RAND, Santa Monica, California. He is the author of six working papers and two professional presentations. He is currently developing a simulation model of the U.S. higher education system in science and engineering disciplines, and he conducts research on aspects of government and corporate policies affecting trade in goods and human capital.

Ralph C. Hassig (Ph.D., University of California, Los Angeles) is a social psychologist who spent five years teaching in Asia for the University of Maryland. He currently teaches consumer psychology and international marketing at California State University, Los Angeles. He also works as a private consultant specializing in U.S.-Asian security affairs, especially with regard to U.S.–South Korean–North Korean relations. He has written reports on cultural matters, including the marketing of U.S. cigarettes to South Korea, and U.S. perceptions of South Korea after the Seoul Olympics.

Edward A. Olsen (Ph.D., University of California, Los Angeles) is professor of Asian Studies in the Department of National Security Affairs, Naval Postgraduate School, Monterey, California. He is the author or editor of eleven books and monographs and numerous scholarly and newspaper articles on East Asian security, with a particular emphasis on Japan-Korea relations. He began his career as an East Asia specialist in the U.S. Department of State, Bureau of Intelligence and Research, Office of Asia-Pacific Affairs.

Courtney Purrington (Ph.D., Harvard University) is a political scientist at the Center for Asia-Pacific Policy, RAND, Santa Monica, California. He is the author of eight professional articles. His academic affiliations include the Edwin Reischauer Institute of Japanese Studies and the Center for International Affairs at Harvard University, Cambridge, Massachusetts; the Institute of World Economy and International Affairs, Moscow; and the Japan Institute of International Affairs, Tokyo.

Rinn-Sup Shinn (M.A., Georgetown University) is a specialist in northeast Asian affairs. He is currently an analyst in Asian affairs in the Foreign Affairs and National Defense Division of the Congressional Research Service (CRS), the U.S. Library of Congress. Prior to his work at CRS, he served as a senior political analyst in Foreign Area Studies of The American University, co-authoring some forty volumes of country studies (including China, Japan, and the two Koreas) under contract with the U.S. Department of the Army. He also serves as an independent consultant and lecturer for other public and private institutions. He has published articles dealing with contemporary North and South Korean affairs.

Sheldon W. Simon (Ph.D., University of Minnesota) is a professor of political science and a faculty associate of the Center for Asian Studies at Arizona State University, Tempe. He is the author or editor of seven books and over seventy-five scholarly articles and book chapters dealing with Asian foreign and security policies. He is a member of the Contemporary Affairs Council of The Asia Society and of the Fulbright award selection committee, and he is a recent past vice president of The International Studies Association. His most recent book is *East Asian Security in the Post–Cold War Era*. He has also served as a consultant to the U.S. Department of State, the U.S. Department of Defense, and the U.S. Information Agency.

Robert G. Sutter (Ph.D., Harvard University) is currently a senior specialist in international policy with the Congressional Research Service (CRS), the U.S. Library of Congress. Since 1984, he has held a variety of research management positions and special assignments at CRS, serving as chief of the eighty-person Foreign Affairs and National Defense Division for five years. Prior to his work at CRS, he served for nine years as an analyst of Chinese foreign policy at the Central Intelligence Agency. Since 1980, he has also held special assignments dealing with U.S.-Asian relations with the U.S. Department of State, the Senate Foreign Relations Committee, and the Central Intelligence Agency. He has published eight books and numerous articles dealing with contemporary China, Japan, Korea, and Indochina and their relations with the United States.

David Winterford (Ph.D., University of British Columbia) is a professor of national security strategy and Asian affairs at the Armed Forces Staff College in Norfolk, Virginia. He has also been for many years a member of the faculties of the Aequus Institute, Claremont, California, and of the National Security Affairs Department, Naval Postgraduate School, Monterey, California, specializing in Southeast Asian security issues. His most recent book, co-authored with Robert Looney, is *The Economic Consequences of Defense Spending in the Middle East and South Asia.* His publications on Asian security issues, U.S.-Asian relations, and Asian economic issues have appeared in a number of leading journals.

Robert L. Youngblood (Ph.D., University of Michigan) is a professor of political science and a faculty associate of the Center for Asian Studies at Arizona State University, Tempe. He is the author or editor of three books and thirty articles dealing with Southeast Asian politics and church-state relations. He has held visiting appointments at the University of the Philippines and Ateneo de Manila University, Quezon City, Philippines; and at Notre Dame of Jolo College, Jolo, Sulu, Philippines.

Young Jeh Kim (Ph.D., University of Tennessee) is president of Pacific States University and director of the Center for Asia Pacific

Studies at Pacific States University, Los Angeles, California. He was a professor of political science for twenty-six years at Alcorn State University. He is the author or editor of five books and twenty-four articles dealing with contemporary China and Korea and their relations with the United States, with particular emphases on Korean unification and on conventional and nuclear issues of the Korean peninsula.

Foreword

This book emerged from a group research project sponsored by the Center for Asia Pacific Studies (CAPS). The Center for Asia Pacific Studies was organized by Kon-Kuk University, Seoul, Korea, and Pacific States University, Los Angeles, California, on May 1, 1994, to study the present and future problems and prospects of Korea and the Asia-Pacific region in the post–Cold War era. The center brought together some of North America's leading academic specialists on the Asia-Pacific region and asked them to articulate the New Pacific Community concept. The first task was to organize five group projects involving ten outstanding specialists on the Asia-Pacific region's political, economic, military, and social-cultural issues. These specialists were asked to define the New Pacific Community from their own perspectives. The second task was a project in which Kon-Kuk University professors dealt with the New Pacific Community in the 1990s from their own perspectives. The third task was the First International Conference on Korea and the Asia-Pacific Region: Political, Security, and Economic Strategies for Globalization and Modernization, which was held on December 9 through 11, 1994, at the Harvard Grand Hotel in Los Angeles. The results of the first task are reported herein. The results of the second task were published by Seoul Press in October 1995 as *Vision of APEC in the 21st Century: Problems and Prospects* (Young Jeh Kim, ed.). The results of the third task were published by Bak Young Sa, Seoul, in October 1995 as *Korean Peninsula and Pacific-Rim Community* (Young Jeh Kim, ed.). The final task was to hold the first annual seminar on Korean and Black Relations: Understanding African-Americans.

Because of the topics presented, this book should appeal to students and scholars in the United States as well as in the countries of the Asia-Pacific region. Observers of the international scene who might be considered to have a more remote interest would certainly include Europeans and South Americans. The 1995 APEC (Asia-Pacific Economic Cooperation) meeting adds another dimension of interest to this book.

As chairman of the Kon-Kuk University Foundation, I am happy to write this foreword because Kon-Kuk University's mandate to implement internationalization includes support for CAPS. I am convinced that *The New Pacific Community in the 1990s* will promote understanding of the concept of the New Pacific Community and of the various aspects of the post–Cold War legacy as well as the new direction of the Asia-Pacific region in the twenty-first century. I would like to extend my sincere thanks to Dr. Young Jeh Kim, director of CAPS at Pacific States University, and to Dr. Sung Wha Hong, co-director of CAPS at Kon-Kuk University, who developed the original plans for the center.

Seung Jong Hyun, Chairman
Kon-Kuk University Foundation
Seoul, Korea
August 1995

Acknowledgments

I would like to thank several individuals at both Kon-Kuk University and Pacific States University for financing and arranging the CAPS projects. At Kon-Kuk University, these individuals include Dr. Hyung-Sub Yoon, President; Dr. Sung Wha Hong, vice president and co-director of CAPS; Dr. Hee Young Song, director of planning; and Dr. Sung Sam Oh, and my assistant, Dr. Woo Yeol Lee, at Pacific States University. These individuals' generous support for the project was instrumental in publishing this book.

I would also like to extend special thanks to Dr. Seung Jong Hyun, Chairman, and Dr. Yeon Soo Kim, Executive Director, of the Kon-Kuk University Foundation, for both financial support and planning assistance. The Center for Asia Pacific Studies is the first joint venture of Kon-Kuk University and Pacific States University that contributes to the intellectual community at the international level.

Finally, the views expressed in this book are solely those of the authors and should not be ascribed to the sponsoring organization.

Young Jeh Kim, Director
Center for Asia Pacific Studies, Pacific States University
Los Angeles, California
August 1995

Introduction

Young Jeh Kim

The New Pacific Community in the 1990s has one unifying thread: U.S. foreign policy and influence in the Asia-Pacific region face a major turning point in the 1990s. As part of a research project undertaken by the Center for Asia Pacific Studies at Pacific States University in Los Angeles, California, and Kon-Kuk University in Seoul, Korea, ten outstanding North American specialists on the Asia-Pacific region have evaluated this region from their own unique perspectives to produce the six thoughtful position papers presented here as Chapters 1 through 6. Each chapter discusses aspects of a new world order in which peace and prosperity could flourish. Influenced by the collapse of the Cold War, the realignment of world trading partnerships, the impact of new immigration patterns, and the reformation of the place of human rights as a cornerstone of U.S. foreign policy, the old world view has been altered markedly. Each author, an international expert in his or her field of study, provides the reader with a provocative glimpse into a handful of major challenges facing the world in the twenty-first century.

The following paragraphs describe some of the major themes and debates presented by the ten authors, highlighting the main ideas that put the future of the Asia-Pacific region in focus.

The first chapter, "Forces Shaping the New Pacific Community in the 1990s," by Courtney Purrington and Charles A. Goldman of the RAND Center for Asia-Pacific Policy, offers a conceptual framework for understanding the most important political and social forces that will shape the New Pacific Community in the 1990s. Purrington and Goldman define the "New Pacific Community" as the free actions of private individuals interacting with each other and with the governments of the region. They argue that the people of the New Pacific Community region and their ideas have created the fastest-growing economies in the world and the most extensive international trade combined with the extremely rapid process of technology transformation in the New Pacific Community region.

According to Purrington and Goldman, a community is composed of people. The relations of people in families, cities, and countries are the basic foundations of the local communities that make up the Pacific Community. The overriding principle in the Pacific Community is that as the community develops economically, birth rates fall and life expectancy increases. All developing and developed countries in the Pacific Community depend on education to improve the productivity of workers and to continue progress toward more sophisticated methods of production. As a developed country, the United States attracts university-level students from all over the world, especially from the Pacific Community. The people of the Pacific Community are linked to each other by a shared natural environment, the rapid spread of information, and information technologies. These general trends can also be seen in other parts of the world.

This chapter divides the most significant forces into the centripetal forces (i.e., Asia-Pacific cooperation) and the centrifugal forces (i.e., Asia-Pacific competition and discord) and regards the consequence of the trends as contradictory. The chapter also examines the domestic politics of regional actors such as China, Japan, and the United States for their varying effects on regional interaction. The determining factor in the future of the Pacific Community will be the evolution of relations between Japan and China, between the United States and Japan, and between the United States and China. The roles of medium and smaller powers in the post–Cold War era are also given special attention by the authors.

In addition, this chapter analyzes the basic trends shaping the community, focusing on three critical bilateral relationships: United States–Japan, Japan–China, and China–United States; and outlines the role of institutions in the Pacific region as well as the results of their influence on the New Pacific Community.

In their conclusion, Purrington and Goldman argue that boundaries, alternatives, and modalities are elusive as definers of the New Pacific Community. Given the complexities of the cultures, economic systems, geography, military capabilities, political systems, and stages of economic development, it would be difficult to define membership criteria. These alternatives include an "Atlantic identity" within North America and a "Pacific identity" in the Asia-Pacific region, a "U.S. identity" in NAFTA and a free trade area in the Western Hemisphere, and a "Pan-Asian" identity within Asia. Regarding modalities, it will be hard to resolve economic, military, political, and social conflicts in the region in terms of evolutionary approach versus dispute-resolution mechanisms and enforcement procedures. The coming twenty-first century will force the world to define the New Pacific Community in terms of a common vision of its destiny.

Under the broad concept of the New Pacific Community, both the second chapter, "Peaceful Cooperation between Asian Countries and the United States in the New Pacific Community of the 1990s," by Robert G. Sutter, and the third chapter, "The United States and the Two Koreas: An Uncertain Triangle," by Rinn-Sup Shinn, analyze the political aspects of the New Pacific Community. Both Sutter and Shinn argue that U.S. policy and influence in the New Pacific Community face an important turning point in the 1990s due to the end of the Cold War, protracted economic difficulties in the United States, and generational changes of leadership in Washington, D.C.

Sutter's basic argument is that challenges for U.S. policy are foreshadowed by the economic dynamism predicted for the New Pacific Community in 2010 in terms of the world's four largest economies: Japan, China, the European Union (EU), and the United States. The fifth will be the Association of Southeast Asian Nations (ASEAN), which probably will include the Indochina peninsula. Thus, three of the five largest economies will be in East and Southeast Asia. In addition, by the year 2010, the U.S. gross national product (GNP), on a purchasing-power parity basis, will be roughly one-third the size of East Asia's. The New Pacific Community will also strengthen its political power in the future. Sutter argues that President Bill Clinton appears to be aware of these economic and political trends and has been a leader in articulating strong U.S. interest in the New Pacific Community. President Clinton introduced the New Pacific Community concept at the Asia Pacific Economic Cooperation (APEC) leaders' meeting in Seattle in November 1993. President Clinton's logic is that the future of America's economic interests rests on closer interaction with the dynamic economies of Asia, and that, in order to preserve and enhance

U.S. interests in the Pacific Community, more political and military cooperation will be necessary.

Sutter's main themes are the evolution of U.S. policy in Asia and the Pacific, U.S. policy after the Vietnam War, post–Cold War developments, and U.S. trends and prospects.

As for the evolution of U.S. policy in Asia and the Pacific, Sutter looks at three sets of objectives: the balance of power, future U.S. economic interests, and the strengthening of democracy and human rights in the New Pacific Community. Results of the U.S. Cold War strategy include Japan's economic growth, the U.S.-China rapprochement, the Washington-Moscow détente in nuclear arms, and the oil crises of the 1970s.

U.S. policy in Asia began to disintegrate after the collapse of the U.S.-backed regimes in South Vietnam and Cambodia in 1975. After the fall of Saigon, there was particular concern that Pyongyang might think the time was right to attack Seoul. President Jimmy Carter seemed determined to change the emphasis of U.S. policy from political realism to morality by participating in the Panama Canal treaty, the Camp David accords, and the de facto recognition of Beijing. President Carter's Asian policy played a significant role in the 1980 presidential campaign. Ronald Reagan attacked not only Carter's emphasis on the human rights issue but also his policies on other foreign affairs issues, citing the failure of Carter's policy on Taiwan. After taking office, President Reagan invited South Korean President Chun Doo Hwan to Washington and thereby demonstrated his opposition to Carter's human rights policy. Reagan formulated his strategy and tactics toward Tokyo to increase Japanese defense spending, to find ways to reconcile his past strong backing of Taiwan, and to ensure closer relations with Beijing. Economically, the 1980s were truly phenomenal for Asian countries, including Japan, China, the newly industrialized countries (NICs), and the ASEAN countries. U.S. trade with these countries surpassed U.S. trade with the Europeans. Sutter concludes that the decline in U.S. economic power relative to Japan and other world economic actors does not mean the United States is entering a period of decline. He argues that U.S. influence in the New Pacific Community in the 1990s will be considerably less than it was before the 1970s. But U.S. cultural influence seems to have had no decline in the New Pacific Community in the 1990s.

Post–Cold War developments in world affairs in general and in East

Asia in particular started in the latter part of the Reagan administration and continued into the Bush administration. These developments included the final collapse of the Soviet Union and a less well defined policy approach that included varying degrees of emphasis on the salient economic, political, and strategic U.S. concerns. The Clinton administration inherited this situation and learned from it, avoiding major pitfalls in developing policy toward the New Pacific Community. Sutter's chapter includes both a useful analysis of underlying East Asian trends toward the United States in the post–Cold War environment and an assessment of President Clinton's policy. East Asian leaders are confident about their economic policies and dynamic growth and less worried about U.S. protectionism. U.S. leaders look at the post–Cold War environment as less of a political-military problem now than it was in the past, when the United States tolerated large trade imbalances with Asian countries in order to maintain a strong united front against Moscow. Asian leaders' nervousness about the security situation continues because a U.S. military presence in Asia will still be necessary in the future as an effective counterweight to possible expansionist ambitions of the stronger nations. In this context, the United States is more trusted than others in the region. The East Asian political trends concern the new definition of political legitimacy in East Asia along with economic development and nation building. Aside from other political issues, human rights and democracy receive the most publicity. The Clinton administration has gone back to the idealistic policies of the Carter administration regarding human rights and democracy in the New Pacific Community. This is a concern for the leaders of the East Asia region, because their economies have developed faster than the political values of human rights and democracy.

U.S. policies have undergone many changes in the post–Cold War environment due to the end of the Cold War and the collapse of the Soviet Union, the protracted U.S. economic difficulties, and the generational change of U.S. leaders. There are three important groups of thinking: preserving U.S. interests (Bush administration), pulling back foreign investments while strengthening investments at home (Ross Perot), and the concept that because of its superpower status the United States is "bound to lead" in the Asia-Pacific region (Joseph Nye).

The Clinton administration's more open and flexible approach has reduced the high level of anxiety over security issues that developed in

East Asia in the post–Cold War setting, except in the case of North Korea. Clinton wants to promote change in foreign policy but not to jeopardize U.S. security and economic interests.

Regarding future prospects, Sutter argues that the success or failure of recent Clinton administration policies in East Asia will be determined by Washington, Tokyo, and Beijing. A new triangular relationship is developing in post–Cold War Asia, and the growing economic, political, and military power of China and Japan reflects their important roles in determining the East Asian political order. According to an optimistic scenario, Japan, China, and the United States will promote their mutual interests in Asian stability and prosperity as a kind of strategic goal. This scenario also has a negative aspect in terms of ineffective U.S. policies that lead to reduced U.S. influence in Asia.

The United States needs to keep a strong influence in the region in order to maintain a meaningful triangular relationship among the three powers. Tokyo and Beijing can move closer together only under the condition of Washington's continued military relationship with Tokyo. If this condition does not exist, the relationships in the triangle will change.

Sutter argues that by being in the new great power triangular relationship, the United States is in the most advantageous and influential position to pursue U.S. security, economic, and political interests in East Asia. The United States has two options. One option is to continue U.S. assertiveness by maintaining the interests of Tokyo and Beijing in good relations with Washington and other sources of influence. This option will antagonize many in Asia and destabilize the region in the short term, but will maintain greater triangular cooperation and regional stability as long as Tokyo and Beijing cooperate with Washington's expectations. The other option is the reverse: pull back some of Washington's more contentious initiatives in the broader interest of promoting stability and prosperity beneficial to a wide circle in East Asia. This option receives support from the domestic constituencies in the United States but does not guarantee to strengthen political, military, and economic policies in the region. Sutter cautions the leaders in Washington to select the right option based on broader, "strategic" trends affecting developments in Asia and meeting longer-term (twenty-first century) U.S. interests.

The third chapter, "The United States and the Two Koreas: An Uncertain Triangle," by Rinn-Sup Shinn, is a case study of Sutter's concept of triangular cooperation in East Asia. Shinn's "uncertain triangle" refers to Washington, Seoul, and Pyongyang in terms of the summer 1994 crisis over North Korea's suspected nuclear arms program, and the three major interrelated issues: the Korean armistice of 1953, the implementation of the Geneva Nuclear Accord, and the ongoing North Korean–South Korean dialogue. Shinn concludes that tripartite cooperation might not readily materialize due to the conflicting inter-Korean approaches to reconciliation, peace, and security, and, depending on how the Geneva Nuclear Accord is received, in the future could become embroiled again in the same old dispute over Pyongyang's refusal to reveal details of North Korea's nuclear program. He also looks at the dispute's potential implications for Washington and Seoul, and analyzes how the triangular relationship has evolved over Washington's Pyongyang policy, the Korean War armistice, Pyongyang's nuclear arms program, and the inter-Korean dialogue. He deals with these issues along with background, the current status, and implications for the future. Shinn argues that the unifying thread through all issues is Pyongyang's long-term, two-stage aims in seeking U.S. military withdrawal from South Korea: to dictate the terms of inter-Korean reconciliation in a bid to gain the high ground and to unify Korea on Pyongyang's terms after the U.S. withdrawal.

In discussing implications for the Korean triangle, Shinn suggests that the two Koreas have something in common in terms of peace and security on their peninsula. Seoul seeks peace and security through constant vigilance, a strong defense buildup, a robust market democracy, and a continued U.S. military presence. Pyongyang, however, regards peace and security as the conditions for the withdrawal of U.S. forces from the South and regards the U.S. presence as tilting the inter-Korean balance of power in favor of the South. The problem is that, through the Geneva Nuclear Accord of October 1994, Pyongyang seems to assume it can write its own rules for dealing with Seoul and Washington even on issues that deeply affect South Korea. According to Shinn, Seoul's security dilemma seems likely to continue in the future due to its relative lack of physical resources. Without the U.S. forces in the South, one can argue that Seoul could not guarantee its own security. Thus, the United States is now faced with the delicate task of dealing with the two Koreas in different ways. The United States must force Pyongyang to adhere to the terms of the Geneva Nuclear Accord: It must mediate Seoul's significant role in building the light-water reactor (LWR) promised to Pyongyang in the Geneva Nuclear Accord; it must also persuade Seoul to increase its share of costs for maintaining U.S. troops in the South. Therefore, the Korean triangle seems assured of ten years of Cold Peace (through 2005), always assuming North Korea's continued rational behavior.

The fourth chapter, "The Military Role of Asian Countries in the New Pacific Community of the 1990s," by Edward A. Olsen and David Winterford, focuses on the mixed feelings in Asia by looking at the strategic context of Asia in terms of both the hard and the soft sides of strategy—military issues as well as geo-economic and assorted diplomatic matters. Both authors argue that powerful economies reside in the New Pacific Community, including the four newly industrialized "tigers" (South Korea, Singapore, Taiwan, and Hong Kong), along with Japan as a transformed power; China as a "takeoff" since 1979; and Malaysia, Thailand, Indonesia, and perhaps Vietnam as the next "tigers." In short, the New Pacific Community is an engine of the global economy and a defining part of the post–Cold War international system.

Olsen and Winterford examine five key themes of the changing role of Asian countries along with economic factors as the driving force for regional optimism: (1) They first examine post–Cold War security concerns in terms of the military prowess of Japan, China, and India, as well as—possibly—a unified Korea's ownership of vital natural resources and its enhanced defense capabilities. (2) Regional military leadership is the next topic, including Japan's military capability and intentions, South Korea's "new military diplomacy" to adapt to the post–Cold War era through economic and political diversification, China's military modernization and its long-term plans for a blue-water navy, New Delhi's robust plans for military modernization, and the prospect of a fledgling great power on the Korean peninsula after the two Koreas are unified. (3) Their discussion of regional conflicts and the new security order covers the problem of China, the future roles of Japan and India, and the nexus of problems on the Korean peninsula, as well as the possible resolution of these conflicts by all the contemporary Asian leaders within the context of a New Pacific Community framework. For example, Indonesia, Brunei, and Singapore have reestablished relations with China. Seoul has established diplomatic relations with Moscow, Beijing, and Hanoi. Pyongyang is exploring its diplomatic relations with Washington and Tokyo. India has extended its interests in Southeast Asia. These examples indicate that a more unpredictable security environment was created by the end of the Cold War. (4) Next comes a discussion of increases in military expenditures and defense modernization in the Asia-Pacific region—increases that have taken place at an "unprecedented rate." For example, defense budgets are considerably higher in Northeast Asia than in Southeast Asia, and they also grow at a faster rate than is common in Southeast Asia. As the authors suggest in the data and analysis in this chapter, from Seoul to Singapore through New Delhi, regional defense planners intend to acquire sophisticated weapons and electronic systems for air, sea, and land combat, along with state-of-the-art long-range missiles. The rationale of these authors is that, with an uncertain role for the United States in maintaining regional security, and given the evolving rivalry for hegemony among Tokyo, Beijing, and New Delhi, Southeast Asian defense planners have almost no option but to enhance their own capabilities to deter conflict. (5) Finally, Olsen and Winterford discuss the prospects and options of the United States and Asian security. They argue that the United States has been adjusting to the post–Cold War era in Asia throughout the Bush and Clinton administrations but has not produced a coherent U.S. security policy for the region. While Asian leaders demand that the United States produce a grand strategy to meet Asian expectations, they must realize that there is a possible new variable in the New Pacific Community balance of power: uncertainties about the long-term U.S. commitment to the region that stem not from foreign, defense, or economic policy but from the inner dynamics of U.S. society. In conclusion, they insist that the New Pacific Community leaders must adjust to the end of the Cold War and its unexpected consequences for the region's peace and security.

In the fifth chapter, "Problems and Prospects of Asian Countries and the United States in the New Pacific Community," Sheldon W. Simon and Robert L. Youngblood argue first that the New Pacific Community is the result of (1) moves away from U.S.-centered bilateralism to a diffuse multilateral structure in terms of market forces rather than politics, and (2) the region's vital importance to the United States because U.S. trade with the Pacific Community is 1.5 times as large as U.S. trade with Europe, because 2.6 million jobs in the United States are dependent on exports to APEC countries, and because 30 percent of U.S. overseas investment is in APEC countries. The political-economic and security components are running on separate tracks. The political-economic track in the Asia-Pacific region has been driven by market forces rather than by politics, as well as by fears that include being shut out of other regions. The United States considers the Asia-Pacific economies as vital national interests.

The United States plans to maintain its important political security and economic positions in the Asia-Pacific region. But the United States has made human rights a condition for economic assistance and favorable political relations; and has realized the decline of its ability to use access to U.S. markets as leverage to force human rights.

Simon analyzes APEC and open regionalism as a process of market-oriented, outward-looking policy reform structure. He looks at sub-regionalism: the ASEAN Free Trade Area (AFTA) and the East Asian Economic Caucus (EAEC) may supersede ASEAN's own free trade area.

The security track of Asia-Pacific regionalism refers to the weak U.S. presence in terms of an insufficient guarantee of security, including territorial disputes, local arms buildups, and ethnic tensions. For example, Seoul's establishment of diplomatic relations with Beijing, Moscow, and Hanoi is an indication of South Korea's gradual buildup of a military capability for regional (not just peninsular) action. Simon argues that the Clinton administration emphasizes democracy and human rights as the top priorities of its global agenda.

Simon looks at trends in defense cooperation within the Association of Southeast Asian Nations (ASEAN) as an optimistic sign based on a discussion of security issues that took place in September 1994. The so-called bilateral defense cooperation pact between Malaysia and the Philippines provides for regular joint military exercises as well as an exchange of military information, and for the countries' joint use of each other's defense locations. Simon considers the ASEAN Regional Forum (ARF) as the old idea of a concert of countries like the Conference on Security and Cooperation in Europe (CSCE) and a venue for the discussion of security transparency and confidence-building measures (CBMs). The ARF is interested in CBMs and preventive diplomacy based on nonaggression and nonintervention agreements. In short, the United States will remain an important player in Asia's political, economic, and security future but will have inexorably declining economic and security roles in the New Pacific Community.

Youngblood compares the U.S. human rights issue as a condition for economic and political relations with President Clinton's decision in May 1994 to renew the most favored nation (MFN) trading privileges of China, and a rigid linking of U.S. trading privileges with East and Southeast Asia. The views and actions of the United States on human rights have been attacked in Asia: the May 1992 riots in Los Angeles have been noted, "solidarity" among Asian leaders has been encouraged, and warnings against "one country's" use of human rights to start political attacks against other nations have been given. The Clinton administration and Congress took steps to diversify sources of pressure on countries with poor human rights records by allocating $500,000 in the 1995 Foreign Assistance Appropriations Bill for human rights and environmental nongovernmental organizations (NGOs) in Indonesia. This bill includes the de-linking of trade and human rights, the discontinuation of the export of medium-range (300-kilometer) M-11 surface-to-surface missiles, and Beijing's approval of the nuclear-free Korean peninsula agreement between Washington and Pyongyang. Youngblood analyzes looming population and environmental challenges, including lessons from the Philippines and China, in terms of the magnitude of Asia's potential population problem (the population of Asia is expected to reach 4.4 billion by the middle of the next century). He cites the Philippines as an example of the debilitating effects of rapid population increase, in terms of slow growth and dwindling resources, and he cites China as a potentially disruptive factor in the Pacific region, with its huge population in the post–Deng Xiaoping period. Besides discussing Tokyo, Seoul, and Taipei, Youngblood argues that population growth and development policies in Southeast Asian countries have resulted in significant environmental damage.

Youngblood considers population and the environment, discussing the implications for U.S. policy as a "big brother" assisting Asian governments in population management in terms of the pro–family planning stance of September 1994 at the United Nations (UN) Conference on Population and Development in Cairo, Egypt, while not losing sight of the consequences of the world's population increasing annually by 94 million. The United States, also concerned about the amount of environmental destruction taking place in Asia, is encouraging enforcement of tough environmental standards, is seeking ways to help industries develop new environment-friendly technologies, and is working within existing international organizations such as the United Nations.

In his concluding observations, Youngblood suggests that the United States faces a dilemma in that it must attempt to resolve differences on human rights, population growth, and environmental degradation through nonacrimonious dialogue, always knowing that confrontation on these issues can hurt U.S. strategic interests in Asia by damaging U.S. prospects for increased trade and investment in the region. The economic stakes for the United States are immense. The U.S. economy of the future will depend on reducing the trade deficit with the New Pacific Community by increasing exports and investments in the same region. This will force the United States to explore alternatives on human rights, population growth, and environmental degradation. In the long term, the best interests of the United States will be served by helping China and the rest of the New Pacific Community to become prosperous, stable, and democratic.

In the last chapter, "Cultural Relations between Korea and the United States in the 1990s," Ralph C. Hassig and Ruth H. Chung define the term "cultural relations" as people's way of life as a consequence of being members of a given society. This is a restrictive term in the field of international relations, where cultural relations exist alongside political and economic relations. These authors explore cultural relations by examining the images that Koreans and Americans have developed of each other through media exposure, and analyze the case of Korean immigrants in the United States as well as the nature of cultural relations between the two countries. The first part of the chapter observes current Korean-American sociocultural relations from an American perspective in terms of U.S. perceptions of Korea, including the history of cultural relations, current events, and personal contacts.

In dealing with the trade dispute, South Korean political events, the perceived threat from North Korea, and the joint effort to respond to Pyongyang's possible threat, the authors use not only an informal content analysis of leading U.S. print media but also psychological principles of social perception that lead to reporting bias. They argue that, to some extent, intercultural contact of an intense and prolonged nature introduces acculturation aspect change in two cultures in a positive direction. They believe that as the two cultures draw closer together, American culture will play a more important role in Korean culture as "tilted" acculturations.

In the second part of the chapter, Hassig and Chung apply models of adaptation and acculturation to the Korean-American relationship. They use the experience of Korean immigrants living in the United States to explore the question of cultural change as a model case in order to project the reciprocal relationships among and between New Pacific Community countries.

Considering the six chapters as a whole, it is evident that there is no uniformly accepted general and working definition of the New Pacific Community among the ten specialists. But reality demands an articulation of the emerging definition of the New Pacific Community in order to find the direction and new vision of the Asia-Pacific region. These ten outstanding scholars introduce their own perspectives on the New Pacific Community. This is a beginning. Knowing the emerging trends in the Asia-Pacific region, these specialists have an intellectual obligation to work on a concept of the New Pacific Community for the policy makers as well as for students of the field.

THE NEW PACIFIC
COMMUNITY
IN THE 1990s

1

Forces Shaping the New
Pacific Community in the 1990s

Courtney Purrington and Charles A. Goldman

Introduction

The Asia-Pacific region is undergoing a remarkable transformation
that is resulting in growing regional prosperity and increasing economic, political, and even social interconnectedness. Foremost among
the major forces shaping the region is economic dynamism, including
intensified flows of capital, goods, services, and technology; rapid economic growth in many countries; and changes in modes of production.
Other important forces include demographic change (aging, population
growth, and urbanization), and the impact of education and information technology on societies. Expanded social linkages among regional
actors are also taking place as a result of intensified intraregional communication, travel, and even labor flows.[1]

Asia-Pacific dynamism is taking place within the overall context of
a less threatening regional security environment. Domestic political
stability, which was an essential precondition for rapid economic
growth in Japan, South Korea, and Taiwan during the Cold War, is
presently a feature of much of the Asia-Pacific landscape. Domestic
insurgencies are no longer a major threat to order in much of Southeast
Asia. While successful management of a triangular balance of power
between China, Japan, and the United States remains a long-run
challenge to regional integration, the threat of conflict among the
major powers in the Asia-Pacific region has at least temporarily re-

ceded. Moreover, an improved security dialogue between China and its neighbors and lessened regional suspicions of Japan have also contributed to a more benign security environment. Indeed, excluding sovereignty disputes involving the two Chinas and the two Koreas, the threat of conflict between most Asia-Pacific states has at least temporarily receded. This is true in part because economic dynamism is reinforcing the incentives for peaceful regional integration.[2]

A relatively benign security environment has allowed Asia-Pacific states to focus not simply on economic development for the purpose of building national power, but also on the improvement of living standards and the resolution of social pressures stemming from economic modernization. Such efforts should improve prospects for stable political transitions to more open, democratic regimes in certain developing states. At the same time, this will also create strong and enduring interests in these states in the maintenance of economic growth by expanding levels of external economic interactions, thereby furthering the development of a Pacific community.

Expanding levels of interaction stemming from regional dynamism are contributing to the formation of a nascent Pacific identity, as shared interests increase the incentives for peaceful interaction.[3] If a Pacific community is ever realized, security will "concern flows of people, ideas, and goods within a context of shared views about how best to organize the participants' economies, societies, and political systems."[4] While such a consensus of views is nowhere yet evident and the potential resort to military force remains central to an understanding of regional security, expanding levels of economic interaction are increasing the demand for novel institutions designed to promote confidence-building measures (CBMs) among potential regional rivals and to manage potential conflicts that could disrupt or even undermine regional economic growth and trade.[5] As a result, the region has witnessed what could be termed "institutional euphoria" after the Cold War, including a strengthening of the scope and membership of existing regional institutions and the creation of embryonic institutions.

Despite such promising regional dynamics, many thoughtful observers remain pessimistic about long-term prospects for peaceful integration and the eventual emergence of a Pacific community, held together by shared interests, common values, and collective responsibilities.[6] Instead, the region's cultural and ethnic diversity, variety of economic and political systems, as well as smoldering historical legacies and rivalries, are all held to impede the emergence of a community like that of Europe. Similarly, demands for more open and participatory regimes by the region's growing middle class could destabilize certain types of regimes and weaken or undermine economic dynamism in the region. In addition, regional dynamism is eroding the influence of the United States, which has historically played an important stabilizing role in the region, in terms of both supplying a large and an open market for regional exports and maintaining a forward-based military presence in East Asia. No other country appears ready (or able) to replace the United States and assume this role. Finally, subregional and extraregional integration also threaten the emergence of a genuine community across the Pacific.

In contrast to an optimistic liberal view that increasing interdependence, in terms of finance, technology, and trade, has both raised the cost of conflict and lowered the incentives for Asia-Pacific states to resort to war, realistic observers note how arms races, differential rates of economic growth, nationalism, territorial conflicts, and prominent relative gains concerns could easily undermine future regional cooperation.[7] Indeed, these observers speculate that the future of the region may even resemble Europe's past, troubled history. The denouement of these contesting visions of the region's future—one projecting the emergence of a Pacific community versus a realistic view of a region that is "ripe for rivalry" and will be propelled "back to the future"—will most likely occur in the next decade.

Accordingly, this chapter presents an overview of the most significant forces that will shape the region in the next decade and affect prospects for the emergence of a Pacific community. The first part of the analysis enumerates the centripetal forces driving regional actors toward enhanced levels of cooperation, as well as the centrifugal forces that could exacerbate interstate competition and discord.

The impact of such trends on prospects for the realization of a Pacific community is expected to be contradictory. For example, intraregional trade creates incentives for cooperation between states as internationally competitive domestic industries lobby for free trade within their governments, while at the same time uncompetitive domestic industries and workers displaced by foreign competition will often demand special protection. Economic growth, while conducive to the overall prosperity of the region, if uneven, could exacerbate relative gains concerns among states, especially if there are no expectations of long-term, peaceful interactions. Moreover, economic growth and movement up the technological ladder can facilitate the acquisition of more lethal and advanced arms by developing countries. This in turn could encourage arms races and exacerbate proliferation concerns. Moreover, interstate competition over the locus of advanced technologies, viewed as the key to national wealth and power in the next century, could lead to heightened interstate tensions between advanced industrial economies, such as Japan and the United States, or between advanced industrial economies and developing economies seeking to move up the technological ladder.

In order to sort out the varying impact of such trends on regional interactions, an examination of specific regional actors becomes necessary. Special attention will be given to the interaction of three of the most significant actors within the region: China, Japan, and the United States. In particular, the future evolution of Japan-China, U.S.-Japan, and U.S.-China relations will be emphasized as playing an important role in determining the future of an Asia-Pacific community. Special attention, however, will also be paid to the role of medium and smaller powers, which have assumed greater importance after the Cold War.

The remainder of this chapter is divided into three sections.[8] The first section examines the basic trends shaping the community. The next section focuses on the key states that will shape the future evolution of the region. The final section outlines the growing role of regional institutions and their potential impact on the nascent Pacific Community. Charles A. Goldman wrote parts of the first section dealing with economic, demographic, educational, environmental, and technological trends in the region, while Courtney Purrington is the author of the remainder of the chapter.

Basic Trends Shaping the New Pacific Community

The community of the Pacific could be analyzed from the perspective of people, cities, provinces, countries, or groups of countries. This section will establish and analyze the basic trends operating at each of these levels of analysis. Specifically, it considers the effects on community of economic growth, international trade, technology transfer, demographics, education, the natural environment, information technology, and security.

In each of these areas, there are reasons to suppose that the basic

Table 1.1

Gross Domestic Product of Principal Countries in the Asia-Pacific Region (1970 and 1991 as a percentage of total world product)

	1970	1991
Americas (not including the United States)	8.1%	7.5%
United States	36.2%	25.9%
Total Americas	44.3%	33.4%
East Asia and Pacific (not including Japan)	6.7%	7.4%
Japan	7.3%	15.5%
Total East Asia and Pacific	14.0%	22.9%
Total Pacific Region	58.3%	56.3%

trends will push people of the region closer together, and reasons such trends will pull the community apart. In general, the discussion here emphasizes the aspects of change that enhance the prospects for community, while recognizing the existence of disintegrating forces.

First, it is necessary to define what the New Pacific Community would include. This very definition is problematic. Should the community be defined strictly by geography, as those countries bordering the Pacific Ocean? Or should the community be defined by economic, cultural, political, or institutional ties? For the purposes of this chapter, a strict definition is not imposed, although it will be useful to consider the community as composed of two major parts: (1) East Asia and the Pacific nations, and (2) North and South America.

Economic Growth, International Trade, and Technology Transfer

The Pacific region is the source of well over half the world's economic output. Surprisingly, that statistic has not changed very much over the past two decades, as shown in Table 1.1.[9] Excluding Japan and the United States, the other countries in the region account for about the same proportion of world product as they did twenty years ago. The United States has declined in importance, as Japan has risen. Over the next decade, expected high growth rates in the Asian countries will most likely raise the importance of Asia.

The Asia-Pacific region includes the fastest-growing economies in the world. Over the 1980s, no fewer than six important Asian economies (China, Taiwan, South Korea, Thailand, Hong Kong, and Singapore) grew at faster than a 6 percent real rate of growth, per year. This rate of growth, compounded year after year, means that these economies approximately doubled in size over the decade of the 1980s. Even relative to the healthy average rate of growth in the world economy over the period (about 3 percent per year), these rates are significant.[10] Other Asian countries, most notably Malaysia and Indonesia, grew nearly as fast as the six named above. By contrast, the best showings in the Americas were made by Puerto Rico, Colombia, and Chile, which grew by about 4 percent per annum over the 1980s. Thus, the best showing in the Americas was little better than the world average, whereas many Asian economies performed at double the world average. If these patterns continue, the Asian side of the Pacific Community will come to dominate the American side in terms of economic output. This economic domination may result in a shift in political power in the same direction, as discussed in later sections of this chapter.

The fundamental sources of this growth are actually not well understood. Growth accounting ordinarily divides growth in output into shares attributable to the growth in various inputs: labor and capital. The remaining share, if any, is termed "growth in productivity" or, technically, "total factor productivity." This type of productivity comes from advances in the state of knowledge in producing goods and services. Over the long run, because the inputs cannot increase without limit (especially the time of workers), most growth arises from these productivity increases.

Paul Krugman, in a recent *Foreign Affairs* article, examined evidence that the growth rates in Asia are due to what he calls growth in inputs, rather than progress in improving technology.[11] Krugman cites rising labor force participation and increased use of capital as definite increases in the inputs. But he also calls an increase in education an increase in inputs. Education makes workers more productive, but this type of productivity is treated as distinct from total factor productivity. Krugman does not consider a rise in educational attainment to be technological progress, even though the educational system is connected to productivity in two fundamental ways. First, the educational system prepares future workers to absorb and apply advanced technology at work. Second, advanced education is connected with advanced research, which generates new ideas for productivity. While this connec-

Table 1.2

Asian Exports, Not Including Japan

Destination	1987	1993
United States and Canada	29.1%	23.0%
Western Europe	16.2%	16.1%
Japan	15.0%	12.4%
Intra-Asia	27.4%	37.1%

tion between research and teaching has been historically practiced in the developed countries, especially the United States, Canada, and Europe, it is increasingly part of the higher education system in developing countries. This section later expands the ramifications of education for the Pacific Community.

The implications for the Pacific Community are profound. If growth in the next century will result from productivity increases, that means that the development and transmission of ideas will be the critical driver of prosperity around the Pacific. Later, this section reviews some trends in information technologies, which are already transforming the nature of work and leisure.

Interlinked with economic growth is international trade. The growth in income in the developing countries of Asia has resulted from an orientation toward exports to the developed world. Especially in the past few years, the trade among Asian nations has been growing dramatically. As Table 1.2 shows, the greatest growth in exports for the Asian economies (not including Japan) has been the other Asian economics.[12] Over a recent six-year period, the share of exports shipped within Asia increased by 10 percentage points, from 27.4 percent to 37.1 percent.

Underlying the rapid growth in international trade is a fundamental transformation of production. Starting in the 1960s, multinational corporations transferred technology to developing countries through foreign direct investment, joint ventures, and licensing. Japan was the first country to adopt foreign technology to stimulate its economy. The four "tigers"—South Korea, Taiwan, Hong Kong, and Singapore—were the next group of countries to follow the pattern.

Today, the next generations are climbing the technology ladder all around the Pacific rim: in China, Malaysia, Thailand, and Mexico. The process of technology transfer brings people and ideas together, fostering a new type of community.

Increasingly, corporations are thinking globally, as distinct from merely internationally. While the term "globalization" is used casually, without definition, we define a truly global corporation as one that consists of a collection of autonomous enterprises around the world, connected by common ties, but without central control. Minoru Makihara, president of Mitsubishi Corporation (the *sogo shosha,* or trading company, of the Mitsubishi group), recently laid out the challenge for multinationals:[13]

> Mitsubishi Corporation is an international, but still Japan-oriented, organization. Most of our management remains Japanese, and management authority, even over overseas offices, remains centered in Tokyo.
>
> Ideally, though, as the name implies, the multinationals of tomorrow will have no single nationality. Rather, I believe they will be viewed as local hubs with worldwide operations, and a corporate part of the local community. It is our challenge, and my challenge, to change our corporate structure and personnel policies to reflect the new realities of the global marketplace, making every effort to transform ourselves into a truly multinational, global corporation.

The major multinationals have their origins in Japan, the United States, and Europe. U.S. firms invested in Asia early, but lost ground to Japanese firms in the 1980s. In the 1990s, U.S. and European firms seem to be increasing their Asian investments, although Japanese investment remains high.

The signing of the North American Free Trade Agreement (NAFTA), linking Canada, Mexico, and the United States into a low-tariff zone, has made Mexico an attractive location for foreign investment by Japanese corporations. The North American side of the Pacific has not developed as rapidly as the Asian side. In many Central and South American countries, excessive government regulation and resistance to foreign ideas has made economic growth difficult. A few countries have made successes in terms of decreasing regulation and promoting economic growth, notably Chile. The notion of reducing government interference in business decisions is spreading, thanks to the publicity of economic performance of the Asian newly industrializing economies (NIEs) and the diffusion of information in the marketplace of ideas.

Overseas operations of multinational corporations are a principal means of bringing people and values from one culture into contact with others. In the course of foreign direct investment, joint ventures, and technology transfer, the New Pacific Community is being formed and defined every day. It is a community defined most of all by the free actions of private individuals interacting with each other and with the governments of the region.

As described above, economic growth and technology transfer are shaping the New Pacific Community. The high rates of growth on the Asian side of the community are already shifting the community's center of gravity toward the Asian economies. But the American economies are also growing.

Demographic Trends and Education

Although this point seems obvious, it is worth remembering that any community is composed of people. The relations of people in families, cities, and countries are the foundation of local communities that make up the Pacific Community. Changes in the population structure of a community will have profound effects on the relations of its members at the individual level, and at the level of nation-states. During the next few decades, the populations of the Pacific region will undergo dramatic structural changes in age distribution and in urbanization. The experience of nations in the Pacific Community illustrates the general principle that, as countries develop economically, birth rates fall and life expectancy increases. These trends can be seen in almost every country of the region.[14]

The Chinese government has attempted to accelerate the fall in birth rates through a strict one-child policy, developed in the 1970s. This policy dictates that most women are limited to having just one child over their lifetimes. Despite exceptions for rural families and members of minority groups, most women adhere to the one-child limit. Women who exceed the limit, or threaten to exceed it, are subject to fines, reductions in wages, and persuasive counseling about undergoing abortion or sterilization.

As a result of general economic development, urbanization, and the one-child policy, in the short span of a generation, China's birth rate has fallen by a factor of three: from 5.9 births per woman in 1960 to less than 2 today.[15] But the policy has had severe side effects on Chinese society. The Chinese cultural preference for male children as heirs and supporters of their parents has led parents to demand ultrasound sex determination in utero and, often, abortions to terminate pregnancies of females. Many newborn girls are abandoned after birth, especially by rural families. Recognizing the horror of this tragic situation, publicity about the plight of these orphaned Chinese girls has motivated concerned citizens of the Pacific nations to come to China in order to adopt one or more of these girls and raise them in their families elsewhere in the region. In a small way, this phenomenon will contribute to the mixing of racial and ethnic groups in the decades to come in the Pacific Community.

As a result of the interaction of Chinese government population policy with Chinese cultural preference for male children, the balance between male and female children in China is wildly different from the balance in other countries. Some 114 males are born for every 100 females.[16] As the current generation of children matures, the imbalance between males and females will mean that many males will find it impossible to marry within China. As these males search for spouses, they may accelerate the process of China's opening to the rest of Asia, to integrate with the communities of Chinese living in Singapore, Taiwan, the United States, and Canada. This overseas Chinese community already has strong ties through family and business relationships. These ties could be enhanced in the twenty-first century, as the large population of mainland China seeks personal and economic opportunities in the outside world.

The Chinese population policy has the effect of raising the average age in society, as fewer children are born each year, but there are more rapidly aging societies than China. The most rapidly aging society in the world is Japan.[17] Japan's aging population may have important effects on world financial markets. According to the life-cycle savings hypothesis, young people save for their retirement and old people consume their savings. If this holds true for Japanese society, an aging population in Japan should reduce Japan's role as a source of finance in world markets. This may hamper the investment boom in the Pacific region if savings in other countries, such as the United States, do not rise to offset the decline in savings in Japan.

As noted above, in the discussion of the sources of economic growth, all developing and developed societies in the Pacific region depend on education to improve the productivity of workers and continue the progress to more and more sophisticated methods of production. But different countries have taken very different approaches to education. Despite the advanced nature of the economies of Japan and the United States, the two countries' education systems share little in common. The Japanese system places most emphasis on primary and secondary education, especially on routine types of learning needed to pass college entrance examinations. Once students pass those examinations, they are not taxed during their undergraduate years. In contrast, the U.S. system places far more demands on college students than on elementary and secondary students. Throughout the U.S. system, there is more emphasis on creative thinking, although there has also been much attention to the deficiencies of U.S. public elementary education in reading, writing, and math.

More immediate concerns in the newly industrializing economies are the growing shortages of technically skilled workers. The vocational education systems in the rapidly developing countries are hard-pressed to keep up with burgeoning demand for labor to operate, maintain, and design machinery. As machinery used in factories becomes ever more sophisticated, this shortage will become more acute, unless these societies invest in appropriate education for their present and future workforces. In Malaysia, for example, universities produce about 5,700 graduate engineers a year. The net demand from Malaysian employers is about 10,000 per year, creating a significant shortfall.[18] The situation in Thailand is no better. A similar shortfall applies to technicians in both countries. As a result, skilled wages are rising dramatically, threatening to cut the comparative advantage of these newly industrializing economies, before they move further up the technology ladder.

Two solutions to these problems are education of qualified students abroad and importation of workers from other countries.

The U.S. higher education system justly attracts students from all over the world. For both graduate and undergraduate study, U.S. institutions are the choice of the world's most motivated and talented students. A significant number of students from China, Taiwan, Japan, and South Korea have studied in the United States, making higher education a potent force for building the New Pacific Community, as students from many societies come in contact with each other. Currently, few U.S. students study in the Asian countries.

The possibility of attracting foreign workers seems to hold additional promise of building the Pacific Community, but ethnic tensions may result if foreign workers experience nativist hostility in their host countries, driving a wedge between the peoples of the Pacific.

From population imbalances to educational needs, the demographic trends cited here hold the promise that complementary needs in the societies of the Asia-Pacific region can be met in a genuine community.

The Natural Environment

The people of the Pacific Community are linked to each other, and to the rest of the world, by a shared natural environment. Decisions made in one city, province, or country necessarily affect other areas through the environment. Although the mechanism and severity of global warming is in scientific dispute, the immediate harmful effects of burning fossil fuels are well established. China's reliance on native soft coal (and petroleum) is leading to pollution that affects the daily lives of billions of people inside China and throughout the Pacific. According to a recent report, as a result of its heavy use of soft coal, China ranks third in the world in carbon dioxide emissions (an important greenhouse gas), "and could soon be first" in the world.[19] The same report cites China's growing needs for energy and the burden those needs place on the natural environment. The critical problems of acid rain from sulfur dioxide and other emissions have already begun to impact Korea and Japan. Pollution affects the oceans, rivers, and streams as well. Major fisheries have been destroyed through pollution and overfishing both inland and at sea.[20]

Questions about the future of the natural environment are most often cast in terms of international conflicts and interstate disagreements, but the environment need not be only a source of conflict for the Pacific Community. U.S. and Japanese companies have developed the most advanced environmental technologies in the world, and are eager to find new markets to implement pollution-saving systems. These firms, of course, are motivated by profits, especially the potential for future profits as developing countries come to a greater appreciation of the natural world and become more willing to pay for environmental conservation. In the meantime, the developed world will not stand by while developing nations sacrifice the common environment for short-term economic gains. Through Official Development Assistance (ODA) and private charitable ventures, the developed world is helping the developing world to work toward cleaner, less intrusive economic growth. The stake of the developed world lies not only in promoting the health of the global environment but also in the desire to promote regional Pacific stability. Rampant pollution is a sure recipe for national conflict in the Pacific Community, but it may be avoided by a combination of public and private efforts.

Information Technology

The spread of information and technologies throughout the Pacific region is transforming what "community" means. Through the Internet, an informal telecommunications network linking computers in almost every country of the world, people from around the world can carry on textual as well as visual conversations almost without regard for culture, nationality, or time zone. The Internet has grown dramatically in the recent past and promises to continue to connect users throughout the Pacific Community. There are now twenty-eight Internet news-groups devoted to subjects related to the society and politics of the Asia-Pacific region, as shown in Table 1.3.[21] As of October 1995, these newsgroups attracted about 50,000 postings per month. In addition, users from all over the world post news articles in thousands of forums on a vast variety of subjects. The Worldwide Web (WWW) allows companies, organizations, and individuals to grant universal access to information, including text, graphics, photographs, sound, and movies. Hong Kong has made notable use of these technologies, disseminating tourist information and, recently, a computer-generated movie of its new airport, which is due to open in 1997.

But much simpler technologies have already had a profound effect on what "community" means to the people of the New Pacific Community. Three relatively simple technologies that have transformed individuals' perceptions of their own societies are telephone, fax, and satellite broadcasting.

The fax machine brought eyewitness news of the events in the spring of 1989 in Tiananmen Square, Beijing, to a worldwide audience of students and political activists. In turn, these activists and students faxed messages of popular support for the students demonstrating in Tiananmen Square.

Satellite television, pocket pagers, and cellular telephones are proliferating quickly through the Asia-Pacific region, notably in China. These technologies share the characteristic of not depending on point-to-point wiring, as in the traditional telephone system. As a result, pagers and cellular telephones are supplementing antiquated low-

Table 1.3

Internet Newsgroups Related to the Asia-Pacific Region

Estimated Monthly Articles	Newsgroup
218	soc.culture.burma
650	soc.culture.cambodia
2,348	soc.culture.chile
4,283	soc.culture.china
1,258	soc.culture.colombia
740	soc.culture.ecuador
4,060	soc.culture.hongkong
2,080	soc.culture.hongkong.entertainment
1,663	soc.culture.indonesia
4,135	soc.culture.japan
1,900	soc.culture.korean
3,155	soc.culture.malaysia
1,553	soc.culture.mexican
478	soc.culture.mexican.american
120	soc.culture.mongolian
223	soc.culture.nepal
1,035	soc.culture.peru
3,573	soc.culture.singapore
3,810	soc.culture.taiwan
1,913	soc.culture.thai
543	soc.culture.uruguay
5,170	soc.culture.usa
803	soc.culture.venezuela
3,858	soc.culture.vietnamese
1,873	talk.politics.china
840	talk.politics.tibet
650	sci.lang.japan
1,235	rec.travel.asia
54,160	Total

capacity telephone networks in rapidly developing countries like China. Motorola reports that China is already its biggest market for pocket pagers. In Hong Kong, despite costs for equipment and service that are higher than in the United States, cellular phones are ubiquitous. Hong Kong people are driven by a need to be "in touch" at all times. Other societies are following close behind in the quest for communication.

Satellite dishes are allowing people throughout Asia to receive video programming from many countries in many languages. As these technologies break down isolation and national barriers, they are a source of concern for certain Asian governments. To the governments of countries such as China and Burma, information technologies pose a mortal threat to the established political and social order, as citizens gain increasing direct access to news, information, and entertainment, all free of state control.

Two networks that are transforming the way people view themselves and their neighbors are Star TV and CNN (Cable News Network). Star TV operates both English- and Chinese-language stations that broadcast over satellite channels to reach hundreds of millions of people in Asia. To communicate program information to an audience that would be poorly served by print media, Star TV makes a weekly program guide available by fax to any caller with access to a fax machine.

CNN broadcasts in English around the globe. Business leaders, consumers, and government officials rely on its presentation of up-to-the-minute news. Even the government of North Korea invited CNN into North Korea's closed society to broadcast scenes from Pyongyang shortly after the death of Kim Il Sung.

All these information technologies are redefining the meaning of "community." The rapid increase in ability to share information means that old institutions and structures, especially those devoted to isolating people, are at grave risk. At the same time, television, telephone, and Internet communication are bringing together individuals from around the Pacific Community according to topical interests that transcend national boundaries.

Basic Security Trends

Although the Asia-Pacific region is the most economically dynamic region in the world economy, it also remains marked by interstate competition over the locus of wealth and power in the international system, ethnic conflict, sovereignty disputes, risks of nuclear proliferation, and increased arms expenditures that could eventually result in destabilizing arms races. Such fissiparous forces threaten to rend asunder regional ties in large part created by burgeoning intraregional trade, foreign direct investment, and technology flows. These forces will be even more difficult for state actors to manage peacefully, since they are taking place within the context of declining U.S. regional leverage and rising Japanese and Chinese influence, and a low level of institutionalization in the region. Such a power transition, along with a low level of institutionalization, presents a number of inherent challenges to regional stability in the next decade.

While such forces represent significant obstacles to the regional integration, the Asia-Pacific region is not necessarily "ripe for rivalry" as some observers have asserted. For example, continued economic growth and increasing levels of interdependence could mitigate or even resolve ethnic tensions and certain forms of interstate rivalry, including territorial conflicts and irredentist claims evident throughout the region.[22] Whether such an assessment is correct will depend in part on whether more positive-sum forms of competition and more intrinsic patterns of interdependence and cooperation emerge, thereby increasing the constraints on the use of force and promoting expectations of long-term, peaceful interactions among Asia-Pacific states. Such a development could in turn strengthen multilateral institutional mechanisms, such as the ASEAN Regional Forum (ARF), designed to address regionwide security problems. Eventually, this process could create more durable forms of security cooperation, as in Europe. While there remain numerous obstacles to peaceful integration, the region is generally moving toward:

> a greater recognition of the primacy of economic goals over ideological aims, pessimism about the utility of warfare and heightened concern for its negative collateral costs, a commitment to expanded regional trade, and an acceptance of the concept of negotiated settlement as the best avenue for settling territorial and border disputes.[23]

Sovereignty Disputes

The Asia-Pacific region is suffused with sovereignty conflicts, both over conflicting territorial claims between states and over legitimacy claims between divided nations that pose a significant threat to regional order. These conflicts are the most likely future flash points for armed actions in the region, especially the conflicts involving Korea, Taiwan, and the South China Sea.

Recently, some of these sovereignty conflicts have been either settled (e.g., conflicts in Cambodia and Hong Kong) or at least temporarily defused (e.g., Chinese border claims with India and Russia). Japan's territorial dispute with Russia over islands in the Southern

Kuriles area is unlikely to result in armed conflict, but nevertheless impedes the signing of a peace treaty and enhanced levels of economic and security cooperation between both countries. Conflicting Chinese, Japanese, and Taiwanese claims to the Senkaku Islands, which are occupied by Japan, are also unlikely to lead to armed conflict as long as the U.S.-Japan alliance persists and Japan remains important to Chinese economic development efforts. The area of potentially large oil reserves of the East China Sea continental shelf, claimed in part by China, Japan, South Korea, and Taiwan, represents a long-term trouble spot, especially given the growing demand for energy in East Asia.

China has settled or shelved its outstanding border conflicts with India, Russia, and Vietnam. Russia and China have settled most of their conflicting border claims, which led to brief skirmishes in 1969. Both states also agreed to establish a 100-kilometer demilitarized zone (DMZ) on either side of their common border in December 1992. The following year, India and China reached an agreement to reduce troop deployments along their common border and shelved their conflicting territorial claims that earlier led to skirmishes. Vietnam and China also agreed not to use force to resolve their conflicting border claims in 1993. These confidence-building measures among the major land powers of Asia represent significant momentum toward settlement of their long-standing territorial disputes.

The most important security problem confronting the Asia-Pacific region in the next decade concerns the future evolution of the Korean peninsula. The Korean peninsula superficially remains the same—a continuing stalemate between North Korea and South Korea—but the end of the Cold War has resulted in unprecedented changes that have made Korean unification imaginable. For example, South Korea—in the Republic of Korea (ROK)—succeeded in establishing full diplomatic relations with China and Russia and is rapidly expanding economic trade with both neighbors. Second, North Korea—the Democratic People's Republic of Korea (DPRK)—lost the Soviet Union as a major patron. Third, both Koreas joined the United Nations. President George Bush announced that all tactical nuclear weapons would be withdrawn from Korea in September 1991. Fourth, after attempting to isolate North Korea as a "renegade state," the United States entered into high-level talks with Pyongyang in 1993, for the first time ever. Fifth, following sixteen months of contentious bargaining over North Korea's nuclear program, the 1994 U.S.-DPRK agreement expanded economic contacts between North Korea and South Korea that could eventually serve as the basis for a "soft landing" for Korean unification. Finally, Kim Young Sam's inauguration as president in February 1993 ended more than thirty years of military rule over South Korea.

Despite such positive developments, the future stability of the North Korean regime remains uncertain. Any post–Kim Il Sung regime, including that currently led by his anointed heir and son, Kim Jong Il, will lack the legitimacy that North Korea's founding father enjoyed. A protracted power struggle could increase the influence of hard-line elements within the North Korean military. Even if no prolonged power struggle takes place, the stagnation of the North Korean economy could eventually lead to a popular explosion and meltdown of the regime. The danger of a meltdown would increase the incentives for North Korea to resort to military adventurism in its dispute with South Korea, or use of nuclear blackmail. Even if a peaceful meltdown took place, absorption of North Korea could be destabilizing to the South's fragile economic and political system.

Taiwan is the second most important source of potential armed conflict in the Asia-Pacific region. It is especially significant since it potentially could involve conflict between the major powers. During the Cold War, both Chinese governments maintained a legal fiction that there was only one China, but recent trends point toward Taiwan's eventual declaration of independence from China. First, native-born Lee Teng-hui became president in 1988, following the recruitment of native Taiwanese into the Kuomintang (KMT). In 1992 Lee issued a decree that restored constitutional rule, which allowed for free elections to Taiwan's legislative and executive bodies. This led to the emergence of the populist and pro-independence Democratic Progressive Party (DPP) and eventually to a split in the KMT, with the New Party formed by former conservative KMT members. Forced to compete electorally with the DPP, the KMT has relaxed its "one-China" claim. In 1993, Lee announced that he would seek United Nations (UN) membership for the 21 million people on Taiwan whom Beijing did not represent. With this decision to seek explicit recognition of its status as a separate entity, Taiwan has moved closer to an actual declaration of independence.

Although several conflict scenarios are imaginable, the most likely would result from Beijing's negative reaction to a Taiwanese declaration of independence, or even the election of a pro-independence DPP candidate at some point. Mitigating such aggressiveness would be China's concern over the reactions of other countries, especially concern over jeopardizing foreign investment in China, as well as uncertainty over how the United States would militarily respond. On the other hand, any further Taiwanese movement toward independence could have a negative impact on a post-Deng succession struggle in Beijing, tilting the balance in favor of conservative and nationalist elements and increasing the influence of the military on Chinese politics.

A third significant source of potential armed conflict in the Asia-Pacific region is territorial disputes in the South China Sea over the Spratly, Paracel, and other islands. Claimants to some or all of these territories include Brunei, China, Indonesia, Malaysia, Philippines, Taiwan, and Vietnam. In February 1992, China claimed both island groups and the Senkaku Islands in a new law establishing its territorial sea. Dealing differently with these conflicts than with its land border conflicts, China has been more willing to press its claims to maritime areas that contain significant natural resources, or are situated at the crossroads of important sea-lanes. In order to buttress its claims, China has carried out large-scale naval exercises in the region, has conducted oil exploration, and is establishing an air and naval base on Woody Island, located in the middle of the Paracel Islands.[24] With its growing naval power, China is increasingly assertive in its claims. Yet, such assertiveness continues to be tempered by a desire to maintain good relations with ASEAN, Japan, and other regional actors that are important sources of foreign direct investment and trade for China and are therefore critical to Chinese economic development.

Nuclear Proliferation

The future efficacy of global nonproliferation efforts and regional stability is closely tied to halting the spread of nuclear weapons in East Asia. This task includes the achievement of a verifiable freeze in North Korea's nuclear development program. In this respect, the U.S.–DPRK agreement was an important step. The signing of the Southeast Asia Nuclear Weapon-Free Zone treaty in December 1995 was a second significant step in this direction. This treaty commits all ASEAN members, along with Cambodia, Laos, and Burma, not to undertake to develop, manufacture, or possess nuclear arms in their respective territories. The unwillingness of China and the United States to sign a supplementary protocol to the treaty, which would obligate them not to use or threaten to use nuclear weapons within the zone, however, somewhat diminishes its utility. A third, largely unrealized task consists of securing China's involvement in future nuclear arms reduction talks, gaining its adherence to a voluntary nuclear testing moratorium and its eventual engagement in negotiations for a comprehensive test ban treaty, and strengthening its adherence to guidelines of the Missile Technology Control Regime.

A final task includes increased transparency in the possession of fissile materials by Japan and other East Asian states. A failure to halt North Korea's nuclear weapons development program could serve as a catalyst for other East Asian states to "go nuclear." Already several East Asian countries, including Japan, South Korea, and Taiwan, possess the technological and material resources necessary to produce nuclear weapons. Indeed, with its advanced missile technology and large stocks of plutonium, Japan could even become a nuclear superpower within a decade. Such an event would in turn encourage Japan's neighbors to acquire nuclear weapons.

Although Japan is a strong supporter of the Nuclear Non-Proliferation Treaty (NPT), its possession of large stocks of plutonium ostensibly for the sole purpose of maintaining energy security has raised doubts about whether it is also hedging on the future possession of nuclear weapons, despite its enunciated three nonnuclear principles. The U.S. nuclear umbrella currently mitigates the need for South Korea and Japan to choose the nuclear option in the event of a failure to halt proliferation in North Korea. However, uncertainty over the future viability of the Japan-U.S. alliance encourages Japan to maintain a nuclear option. In an effort to increase transparency over its production and storage of plutonium, Japan has recently declared the size of its stockpile. It has also delayed construction of a second reprocessing plant and breeder reactor. Japan's continued maintenance of large stockpiles of fissile material, however, weakens the U.S. position on maintenance of tight controls over use of U.S. enriched nuclear fuel by developing countries.

Arms Spending and Arms Races

Although military expenditures in most Asia-Pacific countries as a percentage of gross national product (GNP) have remained roughly the same or even declined in the past decade, an upward trend in overall military spending is taking place in both Northeast Asia and Southeast Asia.[25] Economic dynamism in much of the region has greatly facilitated increasingly sophisticated and expensive arms acquisitions.

In Northeast Asia large increases in overall military spending by China, Japan, South Korea, and Taiwan have taken place since 1990, although spending on weapons procurement has been flat or downward in Japan and South Korea. The level of spending by China is particularly remarkable, with annual increases in defense spending averaging nearly 15 percent since 1990.[26] Such patterns in Chinese military expenditures, if continued unchecked over the next decade, could set off a regional arms race, since Chinese defense spending would eventually exceed that of all other East Asian countries combined. Even more troublesome would be the eventual reaction of Russia.

Overall increases in military expenditures have also taken place in Southeast Asia, except in the Philippines and Vietnam. Nevertheless, overall military expenditures have remained relatively balanced among the Southeast Asian nations. Increased levels of military spending are leading to development of more professional armed forces and more sophisticated force structures, including the acquisition of weapons systems that enhance long-range maritime capabilities. Much of this activity can be attributed to internal security requirements of certain archipelago states; hedging behavior in an uncertain and changing security environment, including the future posture of China toward the region; efforts to upgrade antiquated weapons systems for reasons of prestige; and the business interests of influential political-military elites in certain countries.

Relative Gains Concerns

Differential rates in economic growth between states, which could lead to rising relative gains concerns within the region, constitute a potential impediment to significant levels of regional cooperation. This is especially true of the China-Japan-U.S. triangular relationship. Realist theories of international relations emphasize the importance of relative gains as a source of conflict, while liberal theories emphasize absolute gains under certain conditions.[27] What appears to be critical in determining whether relative gains concerns are prominent in the calculus of states is whether the states believe that differential gains will be eventually used against them. A power transition therefore need not result in conflict between major powers. For example, the United States' overtaking of Britain in the early twentieth century did not result in an Anglo-U.S. war.

Some observers have claimed to have found evidence of U.S. relative gains concerns vis-à-vis Japan during the 1980s,[28] but relative gains concerns expressed at the popular level, within Congress, and among some intellectual quarters have generally not been translated into foreign policy toward Japan. Instead, U.S. diplomacy reflected concern over absolute gains—addressing an inequitable division of benefits arising from an unequal access to Japan's markets; domestic welfare concerns, such as job creation, maintaining competitiveness in advanced technologies critical for long-run economic growth, and lessening damage done to U.S. industrial sectors by Japanese competition; and domestic politics.

Mitigating U.S. relative gains concerns was the Japan-U.S. alliance.[29] The alliance enhanced expectations of long-run, peaceful interactions between two economic competitors, so that neither side expected that differences in economic growth would result in eventual war. In the absence of the alliance, however, or until a genuine Pacific Community develops, relative gains would likely increasingly characterize Japan-U.S. interactions, even though Japan's economic rate of growth has slowed to levels similar to that of the United States. Positive externalities stemming from uncertainty over China's long-term regional objectives could eventually further mitigate relative gains concerns in the US.-Japan relationship, although over the short run China could become a contentious issue.

China's future interactions with Japan and the United States present a much more troublesome picture. Its relations with the preeminent global economic powers could increasingly become characterized by rising relative gains concerns. Unlike the Japan-U.S. relationship, China's relationships with both countries are not anchored by an alliance. In contrast to Japan, which has tended to work in concert with U.S. global objectives as a supporter state, China has not behaved like a status-quo power. Not only has China embarked on a rapid path of military modernization (including the creation of a blue-water navy), aggressively pressed its territorial claims, and continued to engage in nuclear testing, but also it has sometimes flouted U.S. security objectives outside the region (e.g., by making arms sales to the Middle

East). Moreover, when China's rapid economic growth is combined with its sheer size and natural resources, it appears much more threatening to the existing regional order. Indeed, the size of China's economy approaches Japan's, when calculated in terms of purchasing-power parity.[30]

Despite the potential for relative gains to overwhelm cooperation between China and other Asia-Pacific countries, concern over long-run conflictual interactions with China has encouraged its neighbors to seek its enmeshment. Instead of seeking China's containment, these states are seeking to encourage its transformation into a status-quo power within the regional order. The outcome of such a strategy will shape the future evolution of the Asia-Pacific region. A normalized China is an essential prerequisite for peaceful integration and eventual emergence of a Pacific Community. On the other hand, the failure of such a strategy over the long run would resemble the failure of the Lilliputians' attempt to bind Gulliver.

Ironically, it is a U.S. military presence that mitigates relative gains concerns among East Asian states over rising Chinese power. In the absence of a U.S. regional presence, it is not difficult to imagine the development of arms races between China and its neighbors.[31] China's expanding levels of military spending and rapid economic growth would likely set off alarms in East Asia. Similarly, despite lessened historical suspicions of Japan, especially in Southeast Asia, a continued U.S. presence allows it to expand its economic influence, without alarming other Asia-Pacific states.

Shaping the Community

China-Japan-U.S. Triangular Relations

The future stability of the Asia-Pacific region will be strongly influenced by developments in a triangular set of relations involving China, Japan, and the United States. Currently, unlike any other time since the European powers became involved in Asia, the region is not marked by relations of enmity among the great powers. This presents an enormous window of opportunity in the next decade to construct a peaceful regional order.

Before engaging in euphoria over the prospects for an Asia-Pacific Community, however, a cautionary note is necessary.[32] All three countries are currently engaged in a hedging strategy, in case current relations among them deteriorate. China is engaged in a rapid expansion in defense spending, including modernization of its armed forces and expansion of its force projection capabilities. Japan is expanding its economic and political influence among its former colonies and Southeast Asia, upgrading its armed forces with increasingly indigenous efforts, maintaining sizable stocks of plutonium, and reducing its reliance on the North American market. The United States is maintaining its system of alliances in the Western Pacific, while U.S. economic diplomacy increasingly emphasizes the importance of ties with a number of Asian states. The danger of such a strategy is that it could bring about precisely the outcome these states are hedging against.

The United States remains a central actor in the Asia-Pacific region. Not only does its market remain important for the East Asian economies, despite rapidly increasing intra-Asian trade, but U.S. foreign direct investment, technology, and capital remain important for many regional economies, especially as a counterweight to Japan's economic influence. U.S. companies remain important actors in the aerospace, energy, and telecommunications sectors of many East Asian countries. The United States is also more willing to exercise political leadership within the region than are Japan and China, on behalf of its milieu goals. At the same time, however, U.S. influence in the region is declining, as the relative importance of the U.S. market, capital, and even security guarantee declines. For this reason, the United States' military engagement in the Western Pacific and its alliances with Japan and South Korea remain the key to regional stability.

Because of that military presence, Japan has achieved many of the objectives of its former co-prosperity scheme in East Asia, without the attendant negative consequences. Japan's role as a source of manufactured components used by Asian industries, foreign direct investment, loans, and foreign aid is unrivaled in East Asia. Japan is also increasingly willing to use its economic power to support its regional goals, some of which do not always coincide with U.S. interests. Although the United States encouraged such a Japanese role during the Cold War, it has become more wary of Japanese regional economic dominance in the post–Cold War era. This is in part because Japanese economic dominance in the fastest-growing economies in the world would strengthen the competitive strength of Japanese companies and provide them with an additional sanctuary shielded from competition with Western companies.

Japan's potential influence remains limited by domestic and regional constraints on what type of security roles it may undertake and by its continued failure to articulate its own milieu goals. Debate over whether Japan should remain a global civilian power or instead become a "normal" power is not likely to be resolved in the near term. Ozawa Ichiro, an important modern Japanese politician, attracted strong attention in Japan and overseas for his 1993 book, *Blueprint for a New Japan,* and subsequent speeches calling for Japan to adopt a more assertive foreign policy, befitting a "normal" power.[33] Even should Japan eventually seek to become a normal power, it is likely to seek to accomplish such an objective gradually, in order to allay regional suspicions over Japanese objectives.

Over the long run, Japanese and U.S. regional influence will likely be challenged by China. Indeed, how to deal with the almost inevitable rise of Chinese power constitutes the most important long-term problem for stability in the Asia-Pacific region.[34] On the one hand, Chinese economic growth can be harnessed as an engine for economic growth, with all nations within the region benefiting from absolute gains from trade. On the other hand, China remains a non-status-quo power that could challenge the existing order in the Asia-Pacific region. China's rapid economic expansion, combined with its rapid increases in military spending since 1990, has already not only alarmed Southeast Asian states and some in Japan, but even encouraged Russia to renounce its "no-first-use" nuclear policy. Even if Chinese economic growth stagnates, due to political turmoil, problems in privatizing state-run enterprises, or labor and environmental difficulties associated with rising urbanization, the future foreign and military policy of China, East Asia's largest military power, will remain critical to Asia-Pacific stability.

The key to whether a threatening or a friendly China emerges will be whether the United States and Japan can facilitate China's integration within the international community, especially within regional institutions and the Asia-Pacific economy, so that a secure and stable China develops that is committed to maintaining and strengthening the international order.

Rounding Out the Community: Smaller Powers

Despite the overarching importance of the triangular relationship, the role of middle and smaller powers will likely become more influential in shaping the post–Cold War architecture of the region. During the Cold War, the survival of domestic regimes often depended upon maintenance of close economic and military ties with a patron super-power. In turn, global superpower competition increased the strategic importance of these smaller powers and hence their ability to attract overseas development assistance, despite their economic insignifi-cance. Following the end of superpower competition, these states di-minished in strategic importance. At the same time, however, the region's continuing economic dynamism and growing share of world economic output raised the stakes of competition between three centers of economic power—the European Union, Japan, and the United States. Such economic competition increased the leverage of the smaller regional powers vis-à-vis the major powers. In the future, the leverage of these smaller powers will likely be further advanced by their potential alignment in an emerging tripolar Pacific.

As a result of such economic dynamism and a relatively benign security environment, Asian leaders such as Lee Kuan Yew and Mahathir bin Mohamad are increasingly assertive on issues ranging from "Asian" values to security and trade issues. Such subregional self-confidence may not necessarily prove to be a destructive force in terms of community building. Instead, whether rising nationalism proves a centrifugal or a centripetal factor will depend on whether it is constructively harnessed so that smaller states assume increased re-sponsibilities for maintaining regional order on a subregional (e.g., the Association of Southeast Asian Nations [ASEAN]) and a transregional basis (e.g., Asia-Pacific Economic Cooperation [APEC] and the ASEAN Regional Forum [ARF]).

The development of multilateral regional forums in the Asia-Pacific region has also benefited smaller powers by allowing them to mitigate against the impact of asymmetries in power with major powers that would otherwise occur in bilateral negotiations. For example, when human rights are discussed in a regional forum, Southeast Asian states may align with China. When multilateral regionalism also includes "indivisibility, generalized organizing principles, and diffuse reciproc-ity,"[35] it may benefit smaller powers by allowing them to lessen dis-criminatory treatment that would otherwise occur in negotiations between unequals.

Foremost among those smaller powers that will help shape the emerging architecture of the Asia-Pacific region are the ASEAN states and Korea and Taiwan. Other Pacific-rim actors, such as Australia, Canada, Chile, Mexico, and New Zealand, will likely have a more limited impact on developments in the community. This does not mean, however, that Australia and others cannot continue to exercise a disproportionate diplomatic influence (in comparison with their resources) through regional initiatives.

ASEAN

Southeast Asian states have played an increasingly influential role in shaping regional developments through their membership in the Association of Southeast Asian Nations. ASEAN was formed in 1967 in order to facilitate economic and cultural cooperation among its members. Its initial membership included Indonesia, Malaysia, Philippines, Singapore, and Thailand. With increasing economic complementarity, the Preferential Trading Arrangement (PTA) was implemented in 1977. Under this arrangement, internal (intra-ASEAN) tariffs were reduced on selected items, but individual ASEAN members continued to set external tariffs. Economic cooperation remained limited, in part due to a lack of complementarity between the ASEAN economies. At a summit meeting in Manila in 1987, ASEAN agreed to further promote trade liberalization.[36] This agreement, however, did not attempt to construct a free trade area or customs union.

Although ostensibly an economic organization, ASEAN was from the beginning a latent security community.[37] The most important initial function of ASEAN was to reduce tensions between its members. It promoted a dialogue between states which held conflicting territorial claims, had engaged recently in armed confrontation, or had formerly been united. ASEAN also promoted cross-border cooperation aimed at halting domestic insurgencies. Following Vietnam's occupation of Cambodia, ASEAN sought to isolate it diplomatically. Such diplomatic pressure eventually contributed to Vietnam's withdrawal in 1989.

ASEAN's annual Post-Ministerial Conference (PMC) was arguably the only multilateral institution in the Asia-Pacific region that proved effective in promoting regional cooperation on economic, political, and security issues during the Cold War.[38] The PMC consists of a series of discussions between the ASEAN foreign ministers and each dialogue partner and then a joint meeting of all the foreign ministers. Its origins date to 1972, when economic matters were discussed with the European Community (EC) after the annual meeting of ASEAN foreign ministers. Subsequently, Australia, New Zealand, Canada, Japan, and the United States joined between 1974 and 1977, while South Korea became a dialogue partner soon afterward.

While the PMC was an important forum for discussions of foreign aid, trade, and investment, as well as for other economic conflicts between ASEAN members and their dialogue partners, political and security issues were also salient. By utilizing PMC channels, ASEAN was more able to realize its agenda. Although the PMC was not at times efficacious in terms of promoting the resolution of conflictual issues between ASEAN and its dialogue partners, it did promote understanding through exchanges of information and viewpoints that were valued by its participants.

Following the end of the Cold War, security and economic issues continued to dominate the PMC agenda, although human rights were also discussed. At the July 1993 PMC meeting, an agreement was reached not to resort to force to settle territorial conflicts in the South China Sea. The Southeast Asia Nuclear Weapons Free Zone was also discussed. The United States lobbied ASEAN to attend the first APEC summit in Seattle. The dialogue partners agreed to a compromise reached within ASEAN, that the East Asian Economic Caucus (EAEC) would exist as a group under the umbrella of APEC. This still kept alive the option of creating an exclusive East Asian economic organization if NAFTA proved to be discriminatory. Despite the significance of this compromise, the most important achievement was an agreement to establish a regional forum on security—the ASEAN Regional Forum.

ASEAN has therefore been important in promoting a subregional identity and establishing a consensus on critical issues, through a process of continual dialogue among its members. By establishing a common position, ASEAN expands the bargaining leverage of its members in regional and global forums. Vietnam's accession to ASEAN in 1995 has further increased the organization's leverage against the major powers, especially vis-à-vis China. While this statement is an exaggeration, one scholar has even asserted that "international relations in Asia today, to a large extent, consist of a set of mirrors reflecting the Association of Southeast Asian Nations . . . the result is the 'ASEAN-ization' of Asian regional cooperation."[39]

Given differences in culture, economic development, and political systems among its members, however, ASEAN's capacity to exercise regional leadership remains limited, especially on political and security matters lying outside Southeast Asia. On a number of issues, ASEAN members "agree to disagree" and pursue divergent policies. For example, preceding the second APEC summit in 1994, Indonesia and Malaysia disagreed over the establishment of an open trading system in the Asia-Pacific region.

South Korea

With the largest economy of the four newly industrializing economies, South Korea will likely perform an important role in community building. Korea has a high savings rate, a highly educated workforce, a capable bureaucracy, and large-scale and diversified industrial groups (*chaebol*) that are capable of accumulating large amounts of capital and investing it for productivity gains. Despite striking similarities to Japan's strategy of industrial development, Korea's small size (approximately 40 million people) means its economic future is much more tied to maintenance of an open trading system. South Korea could therefore play a leadership role in strengthening both multilateral and regional efforts aimed at liberalizing trade. Such leadership would require successful liberalization of the Korean economy, however, including deregulation and a shedding of Korea's "hermit kingdom" mentality.

Korea's leadership potential remains limited, however. It is handicapped by its underdeveloped, indigenous technology base; its status as a late developer in an era of increased wariness among advanced economies over technology transfer; its small domestic market; and its rising import dependence on Japanese inputs in those industrial sectors viewed as a key to Korea's strategy of moving up the technology ladder. Korean exports are increasingly uncompetitive in advanced countries, increasingly crowded out by cheaper Chinese and Southeast Asian products at the low end of the technology spectrum and by better-quality Japanese and U.S. products made at transplant factories in Southeast Asia. Although new markets are developing in China and elsewhere, successful indigenous research and development efforts remain central to Korea's long-term economic outlook.

Even if peaceful reunification could be accomplished without severe economic costs and destabilizing social dislocations, Korea would be unlikely to emerge as a fourth center of power in the region. From a security standpoint, Korea would remain handicapped by its geographic position between China, Japan, and Russia. Korea's influence would therefore likely stem from how it aligned itself within the emerging tripolar Pacific. Korea's dramatic path of democratization between 1987 and 1993, however—including unfettered political competition, expanded individual and labor rights, and increased freedom of the press—may give it an important heuristic role as a showcase for economic development and democratization among developing countries. Korea may debunk the myth of a vast, unbridgeable chasm existing between "Asian-style" democracy (or at least its Korean variant) and "Western-style" democracy that would otherwise make the construction of an Asia-Pacific Community problematic.[40]

Taiwan

Taiwan will also play an increasingly influential role in the region, both as a trading state with immense foreign-currency reserves and as a major source of foreign direct investment in China and Southeast Asia. Taiwanese firms, as well as other ethnic Chinese firms, are performing a critical role in emerging transnational development zones, especially the Guangdong–Hong Kong–Taiwan and Fujian-Taiwan growth regions. Taiwan's recent path of democratization, standing in sharp contrast to political developments in China since 1989, has increased its stature in the West.

Taiwan's political influence, however, will continue to be limited as long as other regional actors seek to maintain cordial relations with China. Moreover, despite increasing investment in developing indigenous technologies, Taiwan remains dependent on imported technology and especially manufactured components and machinery from Japan. Alliances between Taiwan's small but dynamic family-run enterprises and technologically rich U.S. companies remain one potential avenue for decreasing Taiwan's dependence on Japan. The key to Taiwan's long-run economic development, however, is the stable and peaceful evolution of mainland China's economy and political system.

Institution Building in the Community

Security Institutions

Apart from remnants of a patchwork of bilateral and multilateral alliances the United States constructed during the Cold War, the level of institutionalization in the realm of collective security is relatively low in the Asia-Pacific region. There are no Asian equivalents to the European Union (EU) and the North Atlantic Treaty Organization (NATO). This is a legacy of the early Cold War. Construction of a NATO-type alliance proved impossible in the Asia-Pacific region, due to lingering suspicions among regional actors concerning Japan, initial U.S. reluctance to undertake commitments that would require it to defend a former enemy, and Japanese misgivings over membership in a multilateral alliance system.

After declining U.S. hegemony made it increasingly difficult for the United States to provide collective goods unilaterally in the region, U.S. policy turned to an emphasis on burden sharing in order to address outstanding economic and security problems in the Pacific. Nevertheless, despite the increasing capabilities of U.S. allies, the United States continued to provide most of the collective security goods. The U.S. approach to Asia-Pacific security at the dawn of the post–Cold War era was portrayed in a speech by Secretary of State Baker in 1991:

> To visualize the structure of U.S. engagement in the Pacific, imagine a fan spread wide, with its base in North America and radiating westward. Its central support is the alliance, and partnership between the United States and Japan. To the north, one spoke represents our alliance with the Republic of Korea. To the south, another line extends to our ASEAN colleagues. Further south, a spoke reaches to Australia.[41]

Also known as a "hub-and-spokes" approach, this policy emphasized a bilateral approach to regional security, or maintenance of multiple and separate spokes in the region, even if Baker did acknowledge the emergence of multilateral approaches to regional problems. Despite greater emphasis on multilateral institutions by the Clinton administration, emphasis on bilateral security ties continues to define U.S. policy toward the Asia-Pacific region. While such alliance ties remain critical to regional stability, given the weakness of multilateral approaches to security, the nature of these alliance relationships is increasingly anachronistic and will become a persistent source of tension in U.S. relations with its Pacific allies until these relationships are redefined.

ASEAN Regional Forum

The most important institutional development in the realm of security in the Asia-Pacific region after the Cold War is the ARF. The creation of an Asian foreign ministers conference to discuss regional security issues was proposed by Mikhail Gorbachev in a 1986 speech at Vladivostok. Although this proposal reflected new Soviet thinking on security, it was viewed skeptically by Japan and the United States as a Soviet stratagem designed to weaken the U.S. hub-and-spokes security structure in the Pacific. Similar proposals by Australia and Canada for a conference on security and cooperation in Asia were rejected by Japan and the United States, which pointed to supposed differences between Asian and European security, but in effect sought to maintain bilateralism as the basis for addressing regional problems.

The implementation of ARF, a regional security institution, was made possible by the end of the Cold War in Asia.[42] In particular, the Soviet withdrawal from Cam Ranh Bay, Vietnam's withdrawal from Cambodia, and the eventual breakup of the Soviet Union were important, in that they greatly reduced geopolitical rivalry between Russia, China, and the United States. The end of superpower competition in turn led to rising Asian concern over the United States' long-term commitment to the region and the consequences of a power vacuum should the United States disengage. In particular, Japan and ASEAN were concerned about future relations with China, which was no longer a potential ally against the Soviet Union or Vietnam and which, if unchecked, could threaten regional security. Such concerns were magnified by the revelation of U.S. plans to withdraw more than 10 percent of U.S. troops from East Asia and by the U.S. withdrawal from its Philippine bases. Furthermore, there was a perceived need on the part of Asia-Pacific states, including the United States, to engage China in security discussions.

The diplomatic origins of ARF can be traced to a PMC speech in Kuala Lumpur by Japanese Foreign Minister Taro Nakayama in 1991.[43] In the aftermath of the Gulf War and international criticism of Japan's role,[44] Nakayama announced that Japan was willing to participate in political discussions aimed at enhancing mutual security in the region and proposed using the PMC for such a dialogue. Initially, both U.S. and ASEAN responses were noncommittal, due to the Bush administration's reservations over entering into new multilateral security discussions, but at the 1992 PMC in Manila, ASEAN expressed support for the proposal. Execution of the proposal was assured when the Clinton administration decided to support a policy that supplemented (not replaced) U.S. security bilateralism with multilateral consultations and dialogue, including those which could even evolve into new multilateral security institutions. Following a 1993 PMC decision to implement ARF, the first security dialogue took place in July 1994.

The creation of ARF potentially represents a significant milestone in the development of an Asia-Pacific community. It may serve to mitigate some of the important regional security problems noted earlier, by promoting confidence-building measures, such as increased transparency in arms spending and arms transfers in the region, and by reducing the dangers of miscalculation through exchanges of view on military doctrine and security concerns. ARF encourages Japan to play a more active role in regional security by engaging it in multilateral discussions on key security matters. It also expands the scope of U.S. engagement in the Pacific. Most important, ARF deepens China's enmeshment within international regimes. If such fraternization encourages China to accept regional and international norms (especially if ARF ever develops principles of mutual respect for the independence, sovereignty, and territorial integrity of states and renunciation of the first use of force to settle international conflicts), then ARF will serve an important stabilizing role.

Despite its potential, ARF will likely prove inefficacious in terms of dealing with a number of key security problems. One problem arises from its membership composition. In addition to ASEAN and its dialogue partners, ARF membership includes China, Laos, Papua, New Guinea, Russia, and Vietnam. It does not, however, include India, North Korea, and Taiwan. ARF is therefore ill equipped to deal with core security problems such as the future of the Korean peninsula, Taiwan straits, the expansion of India's power projection capabilities in the Indian Ocean, and Indo-Chinese geostrategic rivalry. On the other hand, given its large membership, spanning the Asia-Pacific region, ARF is too unwieldy to deal with such serious security problems, especially those in regions outside Southeast Asia.

Although establishment of a regional security forum remains a significant step toward fostering a regional security dialogue, the creation of other multilateral security institutions more limited in geographic scope is especially needed. In particular, establishment of a Northeast Asia security consultative mechanism—composed of China, Japan, both Koreas, Russia, and the United States—remains an urgent task, necessary in order to deal with such problems as growing Chinese military capabilities, lack of transparency in China and North Korea, Korean reunification, maritime and nuclear arms safety, and territorial disputes. Also needed is a security dialogue dealing with the Taiwan problem, composed of China, Japan, Taiwan, and the United States, although China would likely resist internationalization of a "domestic" issue.

Economic Regionalism

The most visible institutional trend after the Cold War in the Asia-Pacific region is the emergence of regionalism and subregionalism. In the economic sphere, regionalism was encouraged by the decreasing economic importance of the United States as the economic "hub" of the Asia-Pacific region and the growing clout of Japan. As a counter to U.S. unilateralism (e.g., Super 301), bilateralism (e.g., the U.S. Structural Impediments Initiative), and NAFTA, Asian states began to consider exclusive subregionalism: a regional trade arrangement within ASEAN (the ASEAN Free Trade Area [AFTA]) and even the creation of an East Asian economic group. Middle powers, such as Australia, New Zealand, South Korea, and Taiwan, which were dependent upon an open trading system, favored the formation of nondiscriminatory regional arrangements. Japan, which benefited from informal bilateralism in its regional dealings but remained dependent on the North American market and a U.S. security guarantee, favored the creation of a shallow regional economic organization, partly in order to lessen pressure from the United States. As a compromise, APEC was created.

In response to a perceived need on the part of other Asia-Pacific nations for expanding regional dialogue on economic cooperation and security, as well as the increasing irrelevance of the United States as not only an economic but a political "hub" in the region, the Clinton administration embraced a policy of supplementing U.S. bilateralism with strengthening regional forms of cooperation. In a July 1993 speech in Tokyo, President Clinton identified "a more open regional and global economy" as one of three building blocks for the New Pacific Community.[45] In order to foster such a goal, U.S. policy adopted a multifaceted strategy that mixed bilateral, regional, and global approaches. In theory, as Douglas Irwin has written, these approaches are not necessarily incompatible with building an open trading system:

> Multilateral cooperation on trade policy is not necessary either for the
> liberalization of trade policy or for the prevention of illiberal trade

policies. . . . Similarly, bilateral trade policies cannot be uniquely praised or condemned. . . . Recent trade blocs exhibit the ability to expand membership rather than remain exclusive. If this expansion can be accomplished without harming efforts to strengthen the multilateral GATT approach, then the liberal postwar open trading system will be far from finished.[46]

NAFTA

Negotiation of the North American Free Trade Agreement (NAFTA) created the world's largest free trade area. In 1988 Canada and the United States concluded the Canada-U.S. Free Trade Agreement (CUSFTA). Although traditionally a strong proponent of a multilateral trading system, Canada became increasingly concerned that the General Agreement on Tariffs and Trade (GATT) regime would no longer adequately protect its economic interests with its largest trading partner. Mexico, which had recently undertaken a number of difficult economic reforms that directed its economy away from an industrial strategy of import substitution, requested in 1990 a similar agreement in order to assure its access to the U.S. market. This in turn led to negotiations which Canada joined in 1991, and which eventually resulted in the creation of NAFTA.

Under NAFTA, tariffs or quantitative barriers on most goods and many services are to be eliminated in ten years. NAFTA, however, sets no common external trade schedule for tariffs. Perhaps NAFTA's most innovative aspect is its creation of investigatory and dispute-resolution mechanisms for dealing with oversight of domestic policies involving environmental and labor issues. Although domestic opposition in the United States may preclude further extension of the scope of membership of NAFTA, membership may be extended to other countries, especially those in the Western Hemisphere. Chile is presently the most likely candidate to join.

AFTA

Prospects for an ASEAN economic community greatly improved after a sharp appreciation of the yen (*endaka*) provided the impetus for large-scale, Japanese foreign direct investment in Southeast Asia during the second half of the 1980s. As Japan increasingly moved its manufacturing industries to lower-cost sites in Southeast Asia, it transferred its export-led growth strategy to these countries. It is somewhat of an exaggeration, however, to characterize the pattern of trade that emerged as "a large-scale division of labor run from Japan on nationality-conscious lines."[47] Although the pattern of trade between Japan and ASEAN has tended to be vertical, East Asian reliance on Japanese components and machinery has been balanced in part by rising Japanese imports of Asian manufactured products and burgeoning foreign direct investment by companies from other Asian countries, such as Hong Kong, Korea, Singapore, and Taiwan.[48]

Behind the creation of AFTA was a desire to harness the potential high returns arising from economic liberalization within an integrative scheme that was not subject to the constraints of a larger trading group and that would also improve ASEAN's bargaining position within other economic institutions. Negotiation of AFTA took place during an impasse at the Uruguay Round of negotiations and within an environment of increasing trends toward regionalism elsewhere in the global economy. As a result, ASEAN reached an agreement to create a free trade area in manufactured products over a period of fifteen years at the Singapore summit in January 1992.[49] The establishment of a common effective preferential tariff meant that member states committed to reduce tariffs on intra-ASEAN trade in manufactures and agricultural products to a range of 0 to 5 percent. Subsequently, ASEAN agreed to advance the implementation of AFTA to 2003 and reached an agreement to increase the number of products on which tariffs would be reduced by January 1, 1995.

Although AFTA represents a significant step toward subregional community building, its impact may be limited by ASEAN's "6-minus-x" understanding that ASEAN signatories may freely withdraw from any part of the agreement without invalidating it, as well as provisions allowing for emergency measures designed to protect domestic industries from imports and to assist them in making adjustments. The agreement is also much less comprehensive than NAFTA: Nonprocessed agricultural products and services are exempt from the agreement, while there is no attempt to harmonize domestic regulations dealing with environmental and labor issues. The agreement also does not provide an adequate mechanism for dealing with nontariff barriers that are serious impediments to trade.

Another problem besetting AFTA is its lack of a centralized enforcement mechanism and formal dispute settlement procedures for settling grievances between ASEAN members. This reflects a general preference for informal rules and nonbinding decision-making processes (e.g., dialogue) over a legalistic approach that relies on formal rules and conflict management through judicial intervention. Instead of establishing legalistic commitments from the outset, ASEAN has preferred an "evolutionary approach" that initially establishes general principles and then is content "to let things evolve, work out and grow gradually, to rely on the market process to set the pace for economic integration and with the lowest degree of government intervention or direction."[50] For example, under AFTA, there is an ASEAN content requirement of 40 percent in order to be eligible for preferential tariffs. However, AFTA is vague on how to measure local content, and there are no established means for enforcing local content rules. Whether ASEAN can develop an alternative, nonlegalistic approach that is credible to the private sector as it attempts to upgrade its level of economic cooperation to a more integrative level is questionable.[51] Economic integration under AFTA will likely prove a gradual and conditional process.

Like its NAFTA counterpart, whether AFTA should be seen as a building block or a stumbling block in construction of an Asia-Pacific community remains unclear. It represents in part a hedging strategy by ASEAN—a defensive mechanism designed to respond to developments elsewhere in the global economy. Whether AFTA represents an attempt by a group of states sharing common interests to deepen integration at a pace faster than the GATT process, or represents movement toward the creation of a "fortress Asia" remains unclear.

An answer to this puzzle will in large part depend on whether Japan seeks to counterbalance North American and European regionalism with Asian regionalism. Japan's current global economic interests dictate against the creation of a protectionist Asian trading bloc. At the same time, however, Japan is also hedging against the potential for discriminatory regionalism by increasing the weight of Asia in its trade and investment portfolio. Unless a dramatic reversal in Japan's trade and investment patterns occurs, however, Japan is unlikely to jeopardize its economic ties with North America and Europe, in favor of exclusive regionalism. Instead, Japan is more likely to encourage nondiscriminatory, open subregionalism in which its firms would capture the largest gains from liberalization.

APEC

As the only institution that encompasses all the major economies of the region, the Asia-Pacific Economic Cooperation can be seen as a barometer of changes in the nature of the Asia-Pacific Community. APEC was inaugurated in November 1989 in Canberra, in response to Australian Prime Minister Bob Hawke's call for a regional ministerial-level gathering on economic cooperation. From the beginning, there was no consensus on the pace and scope of cooperation, reflecting the wide diversity of interests in the region. For example, the Bush administration was skeptical of Pacific multilateralism, while ASEAN felt threatened by the creation of a rival institution. As a result, APEC became an informal process for policy coordination and dialogue that worked through consensus and avoided contentious agendas. Even the absence of an institutional appellation in its title reflected its fragility.

APEC's basic guiding principles were agreed upon at its first meeting: (1) to sustain growth and development in the region in order to improve living standards and the growth of the world economy; (2) to encourage open dialogue and consensus; (3) to pursue a mode of cooperation based on informal exchanges of view and not negotiations; and (4) to strengthen an open multilateral trading system and not to encourage the formation of a trading bloc.[52] As a result, APEC functioned as an informal consultative mechanism and forum aimed at promoting dialogue among its members.

At the second APEC meeting in 1990, hosted by Singapore, working groups were established in order to explore potential avenues for cooperation. At the third APEC meeting hosted by South Korea in 1991, China, Hong Kong, and Taiwan became members, expanding the original membership composed of the ASEAN-6: Australia, Canada, Japan, New Zealand, South Korea, and the United States. At the fourth meeting, in 1992, hosted by Bangkok, over the objections of some countries, a small secretariat was established in Singapore with a budget of $2 million, reflecting APEC's increasing institutionalization. The Eminent Persons Group (EPG), composed of nongovernmental elites from the region, was formed in order to assess medium-term trends in trade and to make policy recommendations for expanding and liberalizing trade.

At the fifth APEC meeting, held in Seattle in 1993, APEC's institutional status was upgraded when Clinton invited state leaders to attend a summit designed to discuss the future pace and agenda of APEC. APEC membership expanded to include Mexico and Papua, New Guinea and its institutionalization further deepened with the establishment of the Committee on Trade and Investment, but U.S. interest in using APEC as a forum for promoting trade liberalization was opposed by ASEAN, especially Malaysia's Mahathir bin Mohamad, who opposed APEC's increasing institutionalization and did not attend the summit. Japan and China were also increasingly concerned that APEC and the New Pacific Community would become a vehicle for realizing U.S. trade preferences.

Before the second summit, which was hosted by Indonesia in 1994, the EPG issued a report recommending that APEC members undertake measures designed to create open regionalism. In addressing its "global versus regional" dilemma, the report recommended that in order to avoid exploitation by outside countries, open regionalism should be predicated upon the willingness of nonmembers that wished to secure the benefits of regional liberalization to engage in reciprocal measures. The EPG report outlined a specific program for accomplishing regionwide free trade in all goods and services by 2020, with implementation by 2000. According to the Bogor Declaration, APEC leaders all agreed to a modified timetable, committing all members to free trade by the year 2020 and the developed nations by 2010. Although the APEC leaders endorsed the statement unanimously at the summit, the path to free trade in the region will be slow in view of certain dissent expressed by some APEC members about whether the statement was binding and what exactly free trade would mean.

The results of the 1995 APEC summit meeting in Osaka represented a "reality check" for the vague commitments embodied in the Bogor vision. An approach that would seek to achieve free trade in the Asia-Pacific by turning APEC into a forum for the negotiation of a Pacific free trade arrangement was rejected by most Asian states. Instead, the Osaka Action Agenda stated that APEC members would achieve free and open trade and investment by encouraging in concert voluntary liberalization in the region; by supporting and stimulating further momentum toward global liberalization; and by taking collective actions to advance trade liberalization objectives.[53] The Action Agenda emphasized "flexibility" as one of several general principles for trade liberalization. In addition to trade liberalization, the Osaka Action Agenda also signified a return to emphasis on two other pillars of

APEC—trade facilitation, and economic and technical cooperation. These two pillars will be equally critical for the eventual realization of a Pacific community.

The results of the Osaka summit confirmed that realization of a vision of free and open trade and investment in the Pacific will be an long and arduous task. Unilateral commitments to reductions in trade and investment impediments are likely to be difficult in the present domestic environment in the United States, as long as public opinion insists on "reciprocity." Moreover, Japan remains both unwilling to undertake and incapable of undertaking a leadership role. Whether the principle of unilateral trade liberalization and facilitation in concert with other APEC members will result in effective "peer pressure" inside states by tilting the balance of power in favor of those domestic groups supporting trade liberalization remains uncertain.

Table 1.4 shows the present membership of the organizations reviewed in this section. In addition to definite members, the table indicates with a question mark cases where membership is very possible.

Toward an Asia-Pacific Community?

Defining the Asia-Pacific Community is an elusive matter. There is no shared meaning of the concept across the region. Should an Asia-Pacific community be seen as an embryonic institution with norms, rules, and principles, or should it be seen instead as a loose familial relationship, as favored by many Asian states? Despite a recent outpouring of regional attempts to foster institutionalized cooperation, such as APEC and ARF, Miles Kahler's trenchant criticism of the conceptual murkiness of earlier, failed attempts at regional institution building remains true at present. He noted that such endeavors lacked specificity in three areas: "boundaries, alternatives, and modalities."[54]

How does one define the geographic boundaries of the Asia-Pacific region? Should Argentina, Brazil, India, Pakistan, and Russia be part of this community? Building a community is a time-consuming matter that requires painstaking efforts, as European integration efforts have shown. The task is even more daunting in the Asia-Pacific region than in Europe. The Asia-Pacific region is marked by much more diversity than Europe, in terms of culture, economic systems, geography, military capabilities, political systems, size of economies, and stages of economic development. Given the heterogeneity of the region, it would

Table 1.4

Membership in Regional Organizations in the Asia-Pacific Region

	APEC	ARF	ASEAN	EAEC	NAFTA
Australia	•	•			
Brunei	•	•	•	•	
Canada	•	•			•
Chile	•				?
China	•	•		•	
European Union		•			
Hong Kong	•			•	
Indonesia	•	•	•	•	
Japan	•	•		•	
Korea	•	•		•	
Laos		•			
Malaysia	•	•	•	•	
Mexico	•				•
New Zealand	•	•			
Papua, New Guinea	•	•		•	
Philippines	•	•	•	•	
Russia		•			
Singapore	•	•	•	•	
Taiwan	•			•	
Thailand	•	•	•	•	
United States	•	•			•
Vietnam		•	?	?	

be difficult to define membership criteria on the basis of level of economic development or level of democratization, as the European Community did.

For Asia-Pacific nations there are a plethora of alternative identities and institutional affiliations to a Pacific one. Subregionalism and extraregionalism remain powerful forces that threaten the development of a meaningful trans-Pacific identity. Within North America an "Atlantic identity" is a much more powerful orientation than a Pacific identity. Both Canada and the United States remain tied to NATO, and the eventual creation of an Atlantic free trade area is possible. Similarly, a free trade area in the Western Hemisphere could someday lead to an "Americas identity." Within Asia there is a growing "pan-Asian" identity, resulting from growing intra-Asian economic linkages, increased communications and travel among Asians, economic success based on an "Asian model," and perceived excessive individualism and social decay in the United States. Growing emphasis on the wisdom of Asian values is common to diverse figures such as Ishihara Shintaro, Lee Kuan Yew, and Mahathir bin Mohamad. For most Asian countries, Japan and not the United States is the economic model they wish to emulate.

Nevertheless, U.S. popular culture remains attractive to Asia's growing urban middle class, while many of Asia's elite were educated in the United States. Trans-Pacific economic ties remain vital to most Asian countries. Moreover, rising immigration from Asia, growing interest in Asian cultures and languages, and Asia's increasing importance for the North American and Australian economies are changing the orientation of these economies. On both sides of the rim, therefore, a nascent but weak Pacific identity is forming. Such an identity, however, is never likely to be an exclusive orientation for most countries.

The final conceptual shortcoming of an Asia-Pacific community concerns its lack of specificity in defining the modalities that will be used to resolve economic, military, political, and social conflicts in the region. Most East Asian states generally prefer an evolutionary approach to community building that relies on dialogue and consultation, with agendas limited to noncontentious matters and decisions arrived at slowly through consensus building. On the other hand, Australia, Canada, and the United States have often favored formal institutions with dispute-resolution mechanisms and enforcement procedures. Although the heterogeneity of the region requires an evolutionary approach to community building, it is also true that simple dialogue cannot address most of the critical economic and security problems in the region.

As a result, until a more institutionalized Asia-Pacific community becomes a reality, serious attempts at addressing regional problems will necessarily rely on bilateralism and subregionalism. At the same time, foreign direct investment, trade, travel, and the development and spread of communications technology are resulting in the emergence of a nascent Pacific community. The potential for these technologies and other opportunities for collaboration in education, the environment, and security may provide an informal structure for a community that is already coalescing around common economic interests. The coming decade will be crucial in determining whether the countries that will define and create the New Pacific Community can overcome the forces that will push them into conflict, and capitalize on the natural and human forces that lead them to a common vision of their destiny.

Notes

1. See Peter Rime and Claude Comtois, "Transforming East Asia's Strategic Architecture: Transport and Communications Platforms, Corridors & Organization," paper presented at Northeast Asia Program Workshop, Australia National University, 11–13 December 1995; Paul Smith, "Asia's Economic Transformation and Its Impact on Intraregional Labor Migration," Council on Foreign Relations, Asia Project Working Paper, 1995.

2. For a general discussion of how economic interdependence can alter the calculus for war, see Carl Kaysen, "Is War Obsolete? A Review Essay," in Sean Lynn-Jones and Steven Miller, eds., *The Cold War and After: Prospects for Peace* (Cambridge, MA: The MIT Press, 1993), especially pp. 92–96. Edward Mansfield has claimed to find an inverse relationship between the incidence of war and levels of trade. See his *Power, Trade and War* (Princeton, NJ: Princeton University Press, 1994), chapter 4.

3. See Kishore Mahbubani, "The Pacific Way," *Foreign Affairs*, Vol. 74, No. 1 (January–February 1995), pp. 100–11.

4. Patrick Morgan, "Multilateralism and Security: Prospects in Europe," in John Ruggie, ed., *Multilateralism Matters* (New York: Columbia University Press, 1993), p. 336.

5. Robert Keohane, "The Demand for International Regimes," in Steven Krasner, *International Regimes* (Ithaca, NY: Cornell University Press, 1983), pp. 141–71.

6. See Robert Manning and Paula Stern, "The Myth of the Pacific Community," *Foreign Affairs*, Vol. 73, No. 6, November–December 1994.

7. Richard Betts, "Wealth, Power, and Instability: East Asia and the United States, after the Cold War," *International Security*, Vol. 18, No. 3 (Winter 1993–94), pp. 34–77; Barry Buzan and Gerald Segal, "Rethinking East Asian Security," *Survival*, Vol. 36, No. 2 (Summer 1994), pp. 3–21; Aaron Friedberg, "Ripe for Rivalry: Prospects for Peace in a Multipolar Asia," *International Security*, Vol. 18, No. 3 (Winter 1993–94), pp. 5–33.

8. This essay was commissioned as a joint research paper by the Center for Asia-Pacific Studies (CAPS) in Los Angeles. Each author bears independent responsibility for the contents of each section he wrote. (See the division of labor described in the main text.)

9. Calculations from statistics reported in World Bank, *World Development Report 1993*, pp. 242–43. "The Americas" include Haiti, Nicaragua, Honduras, Bolivia, Guatemala, the Dominican Republic, Ecuador, Peru, El Salvador, Colombia, Paraguay, Jamaica, Costa Rica, Panama, Chile, Venezuela, Argentina, Uruguay, Brazil, Mexico, Trinidad and Tobago, Puerto Rico, Canada, and the United States. "East Asia and the Pacific" includes China, Indonesia, Philippines, Papua, New Guinea, Thailand, Malaysia, Korea, New Zealand, Hong Kong, Singapore, Australia, Taiwan, and Japan. Certain countries were omitted because data were not available, or because they are not tracked by the World Bank.

10. World Bank, *World Development Report 1993*, pp. 240–41.

11. Paul Krugman, "The Myth of Asia's Miracle," *Foreign Affairs*, Vol. 73, No. 6 (November–December 1994), pp. 62–78.

12. Calculations from International Monetary Fund, *Direction of Trade Statistics*, various years.

13. Minoru Makihara, "Asia in the Pacific Rim: Toward the 21st Century," speech at the ISIS Malaysia Conference, December 9, 1994.

14. Linda G. Martin, "Population Aging Policies in East Asia and the United States," *Science,* Vol. 251 (1991), pp. 527–31.

15. World Bank, *World Development Report 1993.*

16. United Nations data cited in Tom Post, "Quality Not Quantity," *Newsweek* (November 28, 1994), p. 37.

17. Linda G. Martin, "The Graying of Japan," *Population Bulletin,* Vol. 44, No. 2 (July 1989).

18. Gordon Fairclugh et al., "Failing Grade," *Far Eastern Economic Review* (September 29, 1994), p. 63.

19. Douglas P. Murray, "America's Interests in China's Environment," *The Pacific Review,* Vol. 7, No. 2 (1994), pp. 215–22.

20. Patrick E. Tyler, "A Tide of Pollution Threatens China's Prosperity," *New York Times* (September 25, 1994), p. 3 (section 1).

21. Calculations from Internet newsgroups available at RAND, October 1995. Monthly traffic figures estimated based on two weeks.

22. See Richard Rosecrance, *Rise of the Trading State* (New York: Basic Books, 1986). Another school of thought argues that the increasingly destructive potential of conventional weapons and the "nuclear revolution" have also altered the general calculus for war.

23. Hadi Soesastro, "Implications of the Post–Cold War Political-Security Environment for the Pacific Economy," in C. Fred Bergsten and Marcus Noland, eds., *Pacific Dynamism and the International Economic System* (Washington, D.C.: Institute for International Economies, 1993), p. 369.

24. Shigeo Hiramatsu, "China's Naval Advance: Objectives and Capabilities," *Japan Review of International Affairs,* Vol. 8, No. 2 (Spring 1994), pp. 122–28.

25. See Andrew Mack and Desmond Ball, "The Military Build-up in Asia Pacific," *The Pacific Review,* Vol. 5, No. 3 (1992), pp. 197–208; Desmond Ball, "Arms and Affluence: Military Acquisitions in the Asia-Pacific Region," *International Security,* Vol. 18, No. 3 (Winter 1993–94), pp. 78–112.

26. *SIPRI Yearbook, 1992: World Armaments and Disarmament* (Stockholm: Oxford University Press), pp. 246–63; *SIPRI Yearbook, 1994,* p. 557.

27. Recent debate on the issue is found in David Baldwin, ed., *Neorealism and Neoliberalism: The Contemporary Debate* (New York: Columbia University Press, 1993).

28. Michael Mastanduno, "Do Relative Gains Matter?" *International Security,* Vol. 16, No. 1 (Winter 1991), pp. 73–113.

29. Courtney Purrington, "Governing an Alliance: The Political Economy of the Japan-U.S. Security Relationship," Ph.D. thesis presented to the Department of Government, Harvard University, Cambridge, MA, December 1993.

30. For example, extrapolating from a World Bank estimate, based on the purchasing power of the *renminbi,* China's GNP was roughly 2.37 trillion dollars in 1992. See *World Development Report, 1994.* The figure was obtained by multiplying China's 1992 per capita GNP of $1,910 (using 1992 dollars) by a 1992 population of 1.162 billion and then adjusting the corresponding figure for 1995 dollars.

31. The U.S. regional presence includes over 100,000 military personnel de-

ployed in Guam, Japan, and South Korea and five carrier battle groups based in Hawaii and the West Coast; additional troops are ready for rapid deployment to the region if needed.

32. Economic friction between the United States and its two largest Asian trading partners (and two largest sources of its trade deficit) could further hamper the development of the New Pacific Community. Sino-American economic friction will likely be very difficult to manage, since the two countries are not allies and do not have similar political systems.

33. Ozawa, Ichiro, *Nihon Kaizo Keikaku* [Blueprint for a New Japan] (Tokyo: Kodansha International, 1994).

34. This argument is also made by Thomas McNaugher, "U.S. Military Forces in East Asia," in Gerald Curtis, ed., *The United States, Japan, and Asia* (New York: Norton, 1994), p. 194.

35. Steven Weber, "Shaping the Postwar Balance of Power: Multilateralism in NATO," in John Ruggie, ed., *Multilateralism Matters: The Theory and Praxis of an Institutional Form* (New York: Columbia University Press, 1993), p. 273.

36. Hadi Soesastro, "Prospects for Regional Trade Structures," in Robert Scalapino et al., *Pacific-Asian Policies and Regional Interdependence* (Berkeley: Institute of East Asian Studies, University of California, 1988), p. 312.

37. Amitav Acharya, "The Association of Southeast Asian Nations: 'Security Community' or 'Defense Community,' " *Pacific Affairs,* Vol. 64, No. 2 (Summer 1991), pp. 159–78; Thanat Khoman, "ASEAN: Conception and Evolution," in K.S. Sandhu et al., *The ASEAN Reader* (Singapore: Institute of Southeast Asian Studies, 1992), pp. xvii–xxii.

38. This is the conclusion of Yuen Foon Khong, "ASEAN's Post-Ministerial Conference and Regional Forum: A Convergence of Post–Cold War Security Strategies," in T. Inoguchi, P. Gourevitch, and C. Purrington, eds., *U.S.-Japan Relations and International Institutions after the Cold War* (San Diego: University of California Graduate School of International Relations and Pacific Studies, 1995).

39. Michael Haas, *The Asian Way to Peace: A Story of Regional Cooperation* (New York: Praeger, 1989), p. 282.

40. See remarks by President Bill Clinton, "Fundamentals of Security for a New Pacific Community," *U.S. Department of State Dispatch,* Vol. 4, No. 28 (July 12, 1993), p. 511.

41. James Baker, "The U.S. and Japan: Global Partners in a Pacific Community," address before the Japan Institute for International Affairs, November 11, 1991. See also James Baker, "America in Asia," *Foreign Affairs,* Vol. 70, No. 5 (Winter 1991–92), p. 4.

42. The importance of the end of the Cold War for the emergence of ARF is argued by Yuen Foon Khong (1994).

43. Yoshihide Soeya, "Japan's Security Policy towards Southeast Asia," in Chandran Jeshrum, ed., *China, India, Japan, and the Security of Southeast Asia* (Singapore: Institute of Southeast Asian Studies, 1993), p. 110. Several strategic studies institutes in Southeast Asia (ASEAN ISIS) first proposed the idea.

44. See Courtney Purrington, "Tokyo's Policy Responses during the Gulf War and the Impact of the 'Iraqi Shock' on Japan," *Pacific Affairs,* Vol. 65, No. 2 (Summer 1992), pp. 10–21.

45. President Bill Clinton, "Building a New Pacific Community," *U.S. Department of State Dispatch,* Vol. 4, No. 28 (July 12, 1993), p. 488.

46. Douglas Irwin, "Multilateral and Bilateral Trade Policies," in Jaime de Melo and Arvind Panagairiya, eds., *New Dimensions in Regional Integration* (New York: Cambridge University Press, 1993).

47. James Fallows, *Looking at the Sun: The Rise of the New East Asian Economic and Political System* (New York: Pantheon, 1994), p. 274.

48. The share of manufactured goods in Japan's imports from ASEAN increased from 6.1 percent in 1980 to 9.2 percent in 1985, and to 27.3 percent in 1990. See Charles Morrison, "Southeast Asia and U.S.-Japan Relations," in Gerald Curtis, ed., *The United States, Japan, and Asia* (New York, Norton, 1994), p. 151.

49. An excellent examination of AFTA is found in John Ravenhill, "Economic Cooperation in Southeast Asia," *Asian Survey,* Vol. 35, No. 9 (September 1995), pp. 850–66.

50. Cornelis Luhulima, "Indonesia's Initiative in APEC," paper presented at International Conference on APEC and a New Pacific Community: Issues and Prospects, Seoul, Korea, October 13–14, 1994, pp. 10–11.

51. ASEAN Roundtable: 25 Years of ASEAN, AFTA: The Way Ahead, Singapore, 3–5 September 1992 Summary Record," ASEAN *Economic Bulletin,* Vol. 9, No. 2 (November 1992), p. 258.

52. The history given here is based on Jae-Seong Lee, "The Agenda for the Second APEC Summit," paper presented at the International Conference on APEC and a New Pacific Community: Issues and Prospects, October 13–14, 1994, pp. 3–5.

53. "APEC Economic Leaders' Declaration for Action," Asia-Pacific Economic Cooperation Economic Leaders' Meeting, Osaka, Japan, November 19, 1995.

54. Miles Kahler, "Organizing the Pacific," in Scalapino et al., *Pacific-Asian Economic Policies and Regional Interdependence,* p. 338.

2

Peaceful Cooperation between Asian Countries and the United States in the New Pacific Community of the 1990s

Robert G. Sutter

Introduction: Challenges for U.S. Policy

The United States faces a series of challenges as it endeavors to preserve and enhance American influence and interests in East Asia in the 1990s. As a power with an important stake in the status quo and in peaceful evolutionary change conducive to human progress in East Asia, the United States is in the lead among forces arguing for greater peaceful cooperation among countries throughout the Pacific rim.

Heading the list of forces posing challenges to American influence and interests is the economic dynamism of East Asia. If present trends continue, by the year 2010 the world's four largest economies will be of roughly similar size: Japan, China, the European Union (EU), and the United States. The Association of Southeast Asian Nations (ASEAN), which probably will include the Indochina peninsula, will be the fifth. Thus, three of the top five large economic groupings will be in East and Southeast Asia.

Although the U.S. economy is expected to grow and the U.S. military may upgrade its capabilities in the region and worldwide, the preeminence of the United States may be moving incrementally toward relative decline from now on. The reasons are not hard to find:

1. Economic growth rates in the Asian region, especially that of China, are higher than the U.S. growth rate.

2. Economic relations within the Asian region are growing more rapidly than those across the Pacific. For instance, Japanese exports to Asia surpassed Japanese exports to the United States in 1993 and continue to grow more rapidly.
3. The share of foreign investment in the Asian region that emanates from the United States is declining.
4. Communications networks within Asia are growing faster than similar networks between Asia and elsewhere.
5. American military commitments have been stable recently, but could decline; military modernization and capabilities are advancing rapidly in China and Southeast Asia.

By the year 2010, the U.S. gross national product (GNP), on a purchasing-power parity basis, will be roughly one-third the size of the East Asian GNP.

Backed by this continued economic growth and emerging military power, East Asian governments have become more assertive politically. They have been less willing than in the past to accept the guidance of U.S. leadership in world politics. Indeed, the peoples and governments of Asia are already adjusting their expectations and behavior to accord with what they see as future trends. In August 1994, of fifty Asian leaders polled by Asahi, fourteen thought that in the years ahead China would increase its role in the region, eleven thought Japan would, and only eight thought the United States would. In Asahi's poll of the Japanese public, reported on August 23, 1994, 44 percent thought that from now on China would be the most influential country in Asia, 30 percent said the United States, and 16 percent said Japan.

The Clinton administration appears to be aware of these trends and their possibly serious implications for the United States. The president has personally taken the lead in articulating strong American interest in being part of the New Pacific Community. For a time in 1993, the president seemed to be devoting so much of his limited foreign policy involvement to East Asia that proponents of U.S. relations with Western Europe and other traditional areas of U.S. interest were reportedly uneasy over the "tilt" in the administration's policy toward Asia. President Bill Clinton traveled widely to East Asia in 1993 and held a number of top-level meetings with Asian leaders, culminating in the Asian Pacific Economic Cooperation (APEC) leaders' meeting he hosted in Seattle in November 1993. Throughout it all, the president stressed to sometimes skeptical American audiences that the future of America's economic well-being rested heavily on closer interaction with the dynamic economies of Asia. He also made a strong case that the United States could deal with the peoples and leaders in the region in cooperative political and military ways in order to preserve and enhance U.S. interests in these areas as well.

Subsequently, the Clinton administration was subjected to a variety of criticisms from East Asian countries and from within the United States over its handling of U.S. interests in East Asia. Critics of the Clinton administration's policies toward China, Japan, and other East Asian countries contended that the United States was exerting much less influence and was becoming marginal in determining developments in this economically vibrant and strategically important area. Perhaps the most graphic sign that the United States appeared to be in trouble came in reports in May 1994 that Assistant Secretary of State Winston Lord had written a memo, which was being passed around Washington, citing a "malaise" that was affecting U.S. policy in the region. Commentators pointed to the fact that the United States currently had ongoing disputes with most East Asian governments. This was said to complicate U.S. ability to exert influence to pursue U.S. interests in the region, and to run the risk of alienating the United States from the countries there. Such an outcome was at odds with President Clinton's intent to closely link the future of the American economy with this most vibrantly developing part of the world.[1]

At the core of the problem were U.S. disputes with the two most important countries in the region, Japan and China. Other governments in Asia harbored resentments about their own individual disagreements with Washington, but they registered notable concern over frictions between the United States and China, and between the United States and Japan. At bottom, serious friction in either relationship runs the risk of prompting an uncertain realignment of power in East Asia that could have major implications for the stability and prosperity of the entire region.

Whether or not U.S. leaders come up with effective measures to deal with this challenging situation will depend on trends and inclinations both in the United States and among Asian countries. At present, the United States is still the most powerful country in the region. Therefore, it has the greatest degree of leeway in deciding which policy courses to take. These decisions will be influenced by the circumstances governing current interests of the United States, but they will also be affected by forces in American decision making that have deep historical roots in the American experience with East Asia.

The Evolution of U.S. Policy in Asia and the Pacific

Looked at broadly, current U.S. policy represents the culmination of a long-standing U.S. pursuit of three sets of objectives in policy toward Asia and the Pacific. First, the United States remains concerned about maintaining a balance of power in Asia that will be favorable to American interests. This implies that U.S. policy is determined to oppose efforts at domination of the region by a power or group of powers hostile to the United States. Second, the United States wishes to advance its economic interests in the region through involvement in economic development and through expanded U.S. trade and investment. A third major goal centers on U.S. culture and values. It has involved efforts to foster democracy, human rights, and other culturally progressive trends in Asia, along with other parts of the world. The priority given each of these goals has changed over time. U.S. leaders have varied in their ability to set priorities and organize U.S. objectives as part of a well-integrated national approach to Asia.

The roots of American foreign policy in Asia go deep into history and the formative experiences of the eighteenth and nineteenth centuries.[2] In those earlier centuries, the United States endeavored to be seen as a nation interested in peaceful and friendly dealings with the world. This entailed primarily commercial and cultural affairs. American–East Asian relations were, like U.S. relations with other parts of the world, characterized by informal activities such as trade, tourism, and missionary endeavors. Military and related diplomatic considerations played only a minor role and were almost always subordinate to commerce and shipping. Economic activities, in turn, were secondary to cultural relations. American trade with Asia never amounted to more than a small percentage of the U.S. total, whereas thousands of Americans went to Asia as missionaries and in other capacities, to take American civilization to Asia. The U.S. initiatives in this regard were timely, in that Japan, China, and Korea were in the midst of the process of modernization—a process that benefited from the presence of American educators, scientists, engineers, travelers, and missionaries who would offer Asian elites and others needed advice and information. Thus, in the first phase of their encounter, which ended with the nineteenth century, America and Asia met at three levels—strategic, economic, and cultural—but the cultural dimension was clearly the most significant.[3]

The situation changed markedly as the United States fought a war in the Philippines, started a naval expansion program, and acquired Pacific possessions. The United States developed as a major power in the Pacific and, by extension, in Asia as well. Simultaneously, American trade and investment in Asia grew. The United States exported industrial products and invested capital in railways and mines in East Asia as well as elsewhere. The period between the Spanish-American War and World War I was a time of transformation in U.S. policy. By 1914, the United States had one of the largest navies in the world, with naval bases in the Caribbean and the Pacific; the Panama canal had just been opened. The world's leading industrial producer, the United States had become a major exporter of manufactured goods, especially to Asia and Latin America.

The American experience in Asia now became as much military and economic as cultural. Thousands of American soldiers and sailors experienced warfare in the Philippines. Many thousands served during the Boxer uprising in China at the turn of the century. Hundreds of marines were left behind in China to safeguard Peking's access to the sea. The American military began considering the possibility of war with Japan which, too, was developing as a military power in the Asia-Pacific region. The United States did not contemplate a war with Japan in the immediate future, but it became concerned with maintaining some sort of balance of power in the region, a task which it could not leave to the other powers alone. Economically, too, there was strong competition between American and Japanese cotton textiles imported into Manchuria. The United States affirmed its interest in the economic open door as official policy, in part in order to prevent Japan from establishing its dominance over the China market. Concurrently, economic ties between the United States and Japan grew. Japan shipped 30 percent of its exports to America. Japan obtained hundreds of millions of dollars in U.S. loans as it fought a war against Russia and managed its expanding empire on the Asian continent.[4]

The cultural dimension of U.S. policy also remained strong. The Progressive movement reinforced the American sense of mission. The reformist impulse found an outlet in Asia, particularly in China, which was trying to transform itself into a modern state. Many reformers in China were open to the Progressive emphasis on education; they were coming to the view that educational reform must precede other changes. In their efforts to chart a new political order for China following the collapse of the Manchu dynasty, some Chinese reformers also eagerly turned to the U.S. Constitution for a model. Japanese reformers, on their part, drew inspiration from American capitalism, and Japanese radicals drew it from American socialism. Thus, the sense of cultural connections grew. What was missing was a sense of order among the various aspects of American-Asian relations. Balance-of-power politics, trade, and reform movements all went on together, but without a clear sense of priority or interrelationships.

More coherence for U.S. foreign policy was provided by President Woodrow Wilson. He set out a comprehensive definition of international affairs in which military, economic, and cultural aspects were integrated, so as to establish a more progressive world order. International peace would be maintained by a system of collective security, economic interdependence, and cultural change, so as to promote democracy and human rights everywhere. To carry out such a foreign policy, the United States would play a military role in cooperation with other nations. Economically, the United States would make its resources available, to open up the markets of the whole world, to help other countries through loans, investment, and technology transfer, and to collaborate with other advanced nations for the development of dependent areas. Culturally, Wilson attempted to use U.S. universalistic values and reformist ideals to transform world conditions. Of course, Wilson's conception was not just an agenda of selfless ideals. It meshed international and national affairs in ways that promoted U.S. national interests.

For East Asia, Wilson's approach called for an end to the naval race with Japan and to the latter's attempted domination of China, and sought a new security arrangement on the basis of cooperation with Japan, Britain, and other powers. Economically, the policy challenged Japan's and other nations' monopolistic enclaves in China and called for outside powers to accept anew the doctrine of the open door. Culturally, America promoted democratization in Asia as well as elsewhere, and supported reformist movements in China and Japan.

For a time, the Wilsonian agenda put an end to the wartime antagonism between the United States and Japan. There was a sort of collective security in the Pacific on the basis of naval disarmament agreements and other accords, such as those at the Washington Conference of 1921–1922; American goods, capital, and technology flowed into China and Japan. Japan shifted its China policy away from military to economic interests. Culturally, the decade saw the Americanization of Japan and China through the spread of American movies, consumer goods, and, even more important, political, economic and social ideas.

In contrast, the 1930s saw the coming to power of leaders in Japan who were oriented toward military strength. Military expenditures grew much faster than the economy. To justify such increases, the military undertook aggressive acts in China and prepared for war against the Soviet Union, the United States, and Britain. In order to pay for the expenditures, Japan sought to establish control over the resources and markets of the Asian continent and the European colonies in Southeast Asia.

Japan undertook these ultimately destructive policies as part of a misguided effort to establish an autarkic region, an area of economic self-sufficiency in Asia which would, it was thought, enrich the country as well as contribute to financing the military force. This search for autarky was in turn related to the Great Depression and the world economic crisis that undermined the Wilsonian system of global interdependence. Rather than relying on close economic relations with the United States and an open door in China, the Japanese decided to reduce their dependence on the West and to monopolize the markets and resources of Asia. Culturally, the Japanese never quite gave up their fascination with, and even dependence on, America's material and popular culture, but Japanese leaders during the 1930s were determined to reduce the influence of the ideals of democracy, individualism, and human rights. To counter these influences, Japanese leaders focused on the absence of racial equality that could be seen in the practice of U.S. policy at home and abroad. The Japanese military in the 1930s repeatedly asserted that their determination to get Westerners out of their region was Asia's answer to American (and Western) racial injustice.

Initially, Americans seemed to respond to the challenge of Japan, and the threat posed by Nazi Germany and others to the Wilsonian world order, by reversion to a traditional isolationist posture. Over time, however, President Franklin D. Roosevelt formulated what some refer to as a "new Wilsonianism" to bring the world out of the turmoil and chaos of the 1930s.[5] Roosevelt's vision shared with the original Wilsonianism a commitment to an integrated world order, militarily, economically, and culturally. Militarily, the United States would be more willing than earlier to augment its armed forces and to be involved in different parts of the world to maintain balance of power. It also would cooperate more closely with a few other powers to police world order. This was still selective security, but with a greater readiness to use force. Economically, the past stress on the open door and interdependence remained, but the government, not just the private sector, would be ready to help other countries to undertake economic change. At the same time, worldwide bodies such as the International Monetary Fund (IMF) and the World Bank would be established to monitor and, to some extent, to control trade and monetary transactions among nations to ensure a more open international economic system. Culturally, Roosevelt's "four-freedoms" speech of January 1941 contained principles that were Wilsonian—such as human rights and self-determination—but it also mentioned such new values as social justice and racial equality, values of particular importance to Asians.

Roosevelt's vision defined a new phase of American-Asian relations. After defeating Japan, the United States and its allies (including China and other Asian countries and peoples resisting Japanese aggression) would reestablish regional order on the basis of this definition. As codified at the Cairo, Yalta, and Potsdam conferences as well as through various other meetings, the new regional arrangement would be based on close cooperation among victorious nations, in particular America, China, Britain, and the Soviet Union. Japan would be disarmed and democratized. Korea would be unified and would eventually become independent, while the European colonies in Southeast Asia would be ultimately granted independence and in the meantime placed under a trusteeship scheme under the aegis of the United Nations. Economic liaisons would be fostered throughout the Asia-Pacific region.

The complications of the postwar situation in Asia and the start of the Cold War severely undermined this scheme. Principles of economic interdependence, human rights, and democratization remained, but these were now subordinated to an overall strategic conception in which military confrontation between the United States and the Soviet Union became the overriding framework of American policy. Asia became part of a global anti-Soviet coalition. American troops and bases were maintained in Japan, Korea, the Philippines, and eventually Taiwan and elsewhere. Japan was encouraged to rearm; defense alliances were established with these countries, and with Australia and New Zealand. The communist People's Republic of China (PRC) was ostracized—denied recognition and trade.

The military-strategic considerations of the Cold War provided the key to Asian international affairs and American-East Asian relations for at least two decades, throughout the 1950s and the 1960s. Accounting for more than half of the world's income and industrial production at the end of the war, billions of dollars and tens of thousands of lives were put forth by the United States to uphold the arrangement. The United States fought two wars for the same purpose. It is clear to most observers that the origins and consequences of the Korean and the Vietnam wars were part of the same picture, the primacy of strategic considerations in America's approach to Asia. What is subject to more debate is the notion that had the vision of Franklin Roosevelt retained a stronger influence in postwar American policy, there might have been a greater readiness to come to grips with the profound social and cultural changes taking place in China, Korea, Vietnam, and elsewhere, and to deal with them in an integrated fashion, not simply in the framework of the global balance of power.

One consequence of America's Cold War strategy in Asia was Japanese economic growth. American officials thought an economically healthy Japan would be the best guarantee against its falling under Soviet or Chinese influence. Washington helped Japan's reentry into the international economic arena through membership in such organizations as the General Agreement on Tariffs and Trade (GATT) and the IMF. The United States even tolerated trade between Japan and the PRC which, if small in comparison with Japanese trade with the United States or Southeast Asia, steadily grew in importance for China because of its increasing alienation from the Soviet Union. In retrospect, it seems remarkable that America was supportive of Japanese economic interests; Japan appeared to give little in return. In part, this was because the 1950s and the 1960s were periods of high growth, and until at least the late 1960s, the United States could afford to engage in a costly war in Southeast Asia and to remain calm even as Japan and the European nations expanded their trade and industrial production and began to challenge American economic supremacy.

The U.S.-PRC rapprochement, the U.S.-Soviet détente in nuclear arms, and the oil shocks of the 1970s shook the foundation of the Cold War system in Asia. The United States incorporated mainland China into the Asian security system and turned to the Asian countries to contribute much more to their own defense. U.S. leaders expected Japan as well as the European countries to do more to help stabilize international economic conditions. As the world entered a period of zero or minus growth combined with double-digit inflation, the United States could no longer function as the dominant promoter of international economic transactions. Instead, it became much more concerned with safeguarding its own more narrow interests. Significant gaps developed between the security and economic aspects of U.S. relations with its allies, especially Japan. As trade disputes grew, voices began to be heard within the United States criticizing Japan for taking advantage of American protection to get a free ride on its defense, and asking whether Japan should contribute more to regional security. The Japanese leaders, however, were rather adamant about not devoting more than 1 percent of the GNP to defense; the 1976 "general guidelines for defense policy," the first formal enunciation on security matters by a Japanese cabinet, reiterated the nation's commitment to a small-scale military force for purely defensive purposes. In this context, some American officials began considering China as a more reliable potential ally.

U.S. Policy after Vietnam

Following the collapse of U.S.-backed regimes in South Vietnam and Cambodia in 1975, U.S. policy in Asia was in considerable disarray. Indeed, authority was challenged from several quarters in the United States. The Watergate scandal and the ensuing resignation of President Richard Nixon in 1974, followed by Hanoi's takeover of South Vietnam the following year, left American credibility badly damaged and its policies (especially toward Asia) uncertain in the eyes of both friends and adversaries. There was particular concern in the U.S. government, just after the fall of Saigon, that North Korea might think the time was opportune to strike militarily against South Korea.[6]

Within the United States there was a rising concern over issues of morality regarding both the ends and the means of foreign policy. America had become involved in a policy of détente; the idea that there were good as well as bad communists confused many people.

Higher standards were demanded and additional constraints imposed upon the presidency.

The War Powers Resolution imposed new restraints on the president's freedom to use military force. Congress passed laws requiring countries that received U.S. economic or military assistance to meet certain minimum if vague human rights standards domestically, and later the administration was required to publish an annual report on human rights conditions in all countries. Congress enacted numerous "legislative vetoes," requiring the president to provide it with notice of proposed arms deliveries and allowing it to veto such actions.

President Jimmy Carter came to office holding many of the beliefs of the critics of the Vietnam War and of the Nixon-Kissinger emphasis on political realism and balance-of-power policies. The president seemed determined to shift the emphasis of U.S. policy from power toward morality, and to give less attention to seeking specific short-term advantages over the Soviet Union. He achieved several genuine accomplishments: the Panama Canal treaty, the Camp David accords, and the establishment of full diplomatic relations with China.

Yet the Carter administration was ultimately overwhelmed by a combination of events over which it had little control, combined with its own divisions and vacillation. Among the key events were the Iranian revolution and the ensuing hostage crisis, the second oil shock, and growing Soviet strategic military power. The Soviets became more assertive in several parts of the world. Notably, Moscow intervened militarily in Afghanistan at the end of 1979 to shore up the communist regime, which had seized power in a coup in 1978 but was threatened by internal conflicts and the growing strength of anticommunist tribesmen. The different approaches of Secretary of State Cyrus Vance and National Security Adviser Zbigniew Brzezinksi in dealing with the Soviets were never clearly resolved by Carter until Soviet aggressiveness and Vance's resignation in the wake of a failed hostage rescue attempt in 1980 made the issue moot. Carter's public vacillation on such issues as the neutron bomb and his startling statement that he had learned more about the USSR as a result of its invasion of Afghanistan than he had ever known previously convinced many Americans he was naive, inept, and indecisive. Despite his emphasis in the late 1970s on rebuilding U.S. military power, there was a widespread American (and foreign) view that the U.S. position vis-à-vis the Soviet Union was deteriorating.

Carter initially benefited from the lack of serious challenges faced by the United States after the fall of South Vietnam. Nonetheless, his administration from the outset faced a problem in Asia because of his 1975 public statement that the United States should withdraw its ground troops from South Korea over the next several years. Carter had been critical of the Republic of Korea (ROK) for its suppression of human rights, and the "Koreagate" scandal involving alleged Korean gifts of money to U.S. congressmen in an attempt to secure continued U.S. support of South Korea's military security had generated widespread criticism of Seoul. While President Carter insisted that U.S. Air Force units would remain in Korea and the U.S.-ROK Security Treaty would still be valid, South Koreans of all political persuasions were fearful that withdrawing U.S. troops would remove a key factor deterring North Korean aggression. The Japanese government as well as most friendly Asian nations were also worried about what they saw as a further American retreat from Asia and as another example of American unilateralism on an issue of vital interest to many Asian countries. (The administration's efforts to normalize diplomatic relations with Vietnam, while ultimately unsuccessful, increased the concern of congressional critics over Carter's initial approach to Asian issues.) Even China, though it publicly called for the removal of U.S. troops from Korea, was widely reported to have told U.S. officials that it understood the need for its presence.

Two factors led President Carter to reverse his position and agree early in 1979 to keep U.S. ground troops in South Korea. First, there were few domestic political pressures pushing him to follow through on his promise. Second, opponents of the move pressed for a major intelligence study of the North Korean military forces, which in 1978 concluded that North Korean forces were much larger, better equipped, and more offensively oriented than previously thought, providing the justification Carter needed to shift his position.

The Carter administration devoted considerable effort to completion of the formal structure of U.S.-Chinese reconciliation, begun during the Nixon administration, by establishing full diplomatic relations with the PRC. The problem facing the administration was how to recognize the PRC and break diplomatic relations with the Republic of China (ROC) on Taiwan—which Beijing insisted upon—without either undermining that island's possibility of determining its own future or creating a political backlash within the United States. On December

15, 1978, the U.S. and PRC governments announced their agreement to establish full diplomatic relations on January 1, 1979. The announcement indicated a measure of flexibility on the part of Beijing. The U.S.-ROC security treaty would end, but only a year after the United States notified the ROC of its intent to terminate the treaty, following the procedure specified in the treaty. Second, Beijing insisted that U.S. arms sales to Taiwan were unacceptable, while the United States said they would continue. The two countries established diplomatic relations despite disagreement on this key issue.

The agreement was supported by U.S. allies in Asia, although with varying degrees of enthusiasm. While the agreement won broad support within the United States, particular aspects were subjected to considerable criticism by certain groups. Congressmen were upset over the administration's failure to consult with Congress before shifting recognition from the ROC to the PRC, as called for in a nonbinding amendment to the International Security Assistance Act of 1978. The administration had known it would have to absorb such attacks, but had felt that widespread consultation would have resulted in leaks that could have upset the delicate negotiations with Beijing. More serious were the charges raised by moderates, some liberals, conservatives, and many Democrats, as well as most Republicans, that the communique issued by Washington and Beijing and the draft law on relations with Taiwan submitted by the administration were much too vague, and that U.S. concern about Taiwan's security and its right to purchase arms needed to be written into law.

President Carter's Asian policy played a significant role in the 1980 presidential campaign. Ronald Reagan attacked Carter's emphasis on human rights, which he argued was applied more strongly against U.S. allies than was appropriate. He castigated Carter's admission that the Soviet invasion of Afghanistan had taught him much about Soviet behavior as an indication of Carter's naiveté. Reagan also attacked Carter's policy toward Taiwan, saying that we should reestablish "official" relations with Taiwan as a loyal and dependable ally.

After the 1980 election, continued rancor between President Ronald Reagan's hard-line foreign policy stance and the Congress, which was divided between a Democratic House and a Republican Senate, appeared likely. In fact, there emerged a growing spirit of bipartisanship in U.S. Asian policy during the 1980s. In part this had to do with the fact that the Reagan administration's actions were seldom as strong as its rhetoric might have suggested. Democrats also came to see a need for a stronger U.S. defense and foreign policy in the face of continued Soviet expansion, and the administration and Democratic leaders were willing to consult and compromise on key issues.

Shortly after he took office, President Reagan invited South Korean President Chun Doo Hwan to the United States and gave him strong public backing. There was apparently at least an implicit agreement that President Chun would release opposition leader Kim Dae Jung and allow him to leave the country, which he did. President Reagan could thus point to an early success for quiet diplomacy, and Seoul felt it had a firm friend in the White House.

The administration also formulated its strategy and tactics toward Japan in a calm manner. Instead of publicly criticizing Japan for not spending enough on defense in relation to GNP, the administration focused on the appropriate roles and missions Japanese forces should undertake in conjunction with U.S. forces. Tokyo in 1981 accepted the primary responsibility for it own air defense, and agreed to develop the capability to help defend sea-lanes extending 1,000 miles east and south. Japan's steady though small increases in defense spending were regarded by the U.S. administration with satisfaction. Congressional criticism continued but had no major effect on U.S. policy.

President Reagan also found ways to compromise his past strong backing toward the Taiwan while standing firm in the face of escalating PRC demands for a cutback in U.S. arms sales to Taiwan and other issues. The success of the U.S. military buildup and the rise of a closely cooperative U.S.-Japanese security relationship under the leadership of Japanese Prime Minister Nakasone had the effect of reducing China's strategic importance to the United States. The administration was able to establish a consensus among U.S. policy makers by the mid-1980s that lowered the importance of the PRC in the U.S. policy calculus and precluded the United States from feeling compelled to make additional sacrifices regarding Taiwan for the sake of ensuring close relations with the PRC.

The stability of the balance of power in Asia in the 1980s was underscored by the more moderate Soviet foreign policy in the region following the coming to power of Mikhail Gorbachev in 1985. At a minimum, Moscow seemed interested in the latter 1980s in easing tensions around its periphery, thereby gaining at least a temporary "breathing space" in which to revive the ailing Soviet economy. At the same time, Gorbachev highlighted political and economic initiatives designed to increase Soviet influence abroad. Gorbachev had more difficulty in expanding Soviet influence in Asia than in Europe, and he appeared to view an opening to China as a key link in efforts to improve Soviet influence in the region. Soviet leaders followed through on their repeated pledges to ease military tensions with China by addressing substantive Chinese security concerns. Beijing had summarized these concerns as the so-called three obstacles to improved Sino-Soviet relations posed by Soviet military occupation of Afghanistan, Soviet military presence along China's northern border, and Soviet support for Vietnam's military occupation of Cambodia.

The more stable security situation for U.S. interests in Asia in the 1980s offset the rise in U.S. economic disputes, especially with Japan. Economically, the 1980s were truly phenomenal for Asian countries. Starting the decade with barely 10 percent of the world's output, by the late 1980s the Asian nations—including Japan, China, the newly industrialized countries (NICs), and the ASEAN countries—accounted for close to 20 percent. Their combined export trade expanded rapidly, increasing from 15 percent of the world's total to 25 percent by 1988, and they recorded huge surpluses vis-à-vis the United States ($27 billion in 1981, $105 billion in 1987). American trade with these countries surpassed that with the Europeans. The Asian economies grew more rapidly than those of other parts of the world, and their funds began to enter the United States to finance part of its deficits. America and Asia, in other words, were economically more interdependent than ever.

This economic interdependence, however, was seen by many as exacerbating a perceived decline in U.S. relative power in the world—a source of concern to many Americans. America's ability to counter Soviet power and promote economic growth and political stability abroad was based heavily both upon U.S. economic strength and upon the willingness of the United States to make economic "sacrifices" to achieve military and political goals. A large if fluctuating military budget, a substantial foreign aid program, and a willingness to allow the exports of other countries steadily greater access to the U.S. market were regarded as prices that could be paid without undue sacrifice by most Americans. U.S. economic predominance eroded somewhat in the 1970s, and in the 1980s America's economic position was seen by some to be so seriously weakened that its long-term ability to sustain its role in the world was cast into doubt.

These adverse economic trends occurred for many reasons. Economic progress abroad, especially in East Asia, intensified competitive pressures to a level America had not experienced since before World War II, when foreign trade had a much smaller impact on the U.S. economy. But many of the causes were at home, in the United States. Educational standards had declined, as had product quality, and businesspeople gave increasing priority to short-term profits and financial mergers. Investment levels were inadequate for a more competitive international environment, and America's already low levels of savings declined, especially as a result of the rising federal budget deficits. The dollar rose, and with it the U.S. trade deficit, greatly increasing the pressures for protectionism.

The danger of protectionism grew for two main reasons. The first was economic. In 1971, the United States had its first trade deficit since World War II. Trade deficits increased in size through most of the 1970s and the early 1980s, and averaged roughly $25 billion annually in 1979–1981. But a surplus in services meant that the United States had a current account surplus and was earning and paying its way in the world, except briefly in 1977 and 1978.

From 1980 there was a dramatic rise in the trade account deficit, which in 1986 amounted to $153 billion. This was due mainly to a sharp rise in imports from $245 billion in 1981 to $370 billion in 1986, while exports declined from $234 billion in 1981 to $217 billion in 1986. The deficit in the trade balance with Asia increased from $21.8 billion in 1981 to $95.7 billion in 1987. The total deficit for 1987 rose further, to $159 billion, despite the fall in the dollar, with exports rising to $253 billion but imports continuing to increase to $412 billion. These trade deficits made the United States a debtor nation for the first time since World War I. It soon became the world's largest debtor nation.

Second, the Reagan administration was not following policies designed to ease trade tension with Asia. There were several factors behind the sharp rise of the U.S. trade deficit. The Latin American debt crisis, which forced many U.S. trading partners to curtail their imports, and slower growth in Europe—especially in 1983 and early 1984—played a part. Yet the greatest single cause was the high dollar, which increased in value by over 50 percent between 1980 and early 1985 in relation to the currencies of the ten largest industrial countries. This was caused mainly by rising federal budget deficits (especially serious when personal savings were falling), which forced the United States to hold real interest rates higher than would otherwise have been necessary in order to attract capital from abroad. Administration leaders long denied that there was a problem with the high dollar, which they saw as a sign of strength. The administration's foreign trade and monetary policies were simply to leave things to the market.

By mid-1985, key figures in the administration were convinced that, unless it changed its hands-off policy regarding the trade deficit, Congress would be swept along on a tide of protectionism and would pass legislation along those lines. Thus in September 1985 the administration dramatically reversed its position of noninterference in the foreign exchange markets and worked out an agreement with the finance ministers and central bankers of the other four key industrial powers (Japan, Germany, Britain, and France) in the Group of Five to intervene in order to bring down the value of the dollar. It also undertook a number of specific initiatives to protect U.S. industries or to open foreign markets. But by that time the surge toward protectionism was steadily gathering strength, a trend that continued in 1986 and 1987 since the declining dollar initially increased rather than reduced the trade deficit. Moreover, some important trade partners, such as South Korea and, initially, Taiwan, resisted letting their currencies appreciate much relative to the dollar, and many corporations in Japan and Europe chose to hold price increases to a minimum in order to maintain market share even at the cost of greatly reduced profits.

Omnibus trade legislation passed both houses of Congress in 1987, although with many quite different provisions. Both bills had a mixture of trade-enhancing provisions (authority for a new round of multilateral trade negotiations, worker retraining provisions, and so on) and a variety of protectionist features. The dramatic upheavals in world financial markets in October 1987 induced some caution about any "protectionist" legislation.

The compromise bill approved by the House-Senate conference eliminated most of the strongest protectionist features in each bill but was vetoed by President Reagan because of a nontrade provision involving plant-closing notification to workers. A bill was passed in late 1988 without this provision and became law, and its broad support suggested that the movement toward a more protectionist trade policy was unlikely to disappear from the political scene.

The decline in U.S. economic power relative to Japan and other up-and-coming world economic actors lay at the heart of the growing argument of those who saw the United States entering a period of decline. If Asia-Pacific geopolitics appeared more stable, economic vitality appeared to be the main source of political legitimacy in the 1990s. It is not necessary to agree with those who see the decline in U.S. power to note that U.S. influence in the Asia-Pacific region in the 1990s was relatively stable but considerably less than it was before the 1970s. One must be careful, however, not to allow the change in U.S. military-economic influence to translate into a view of U.S. cultural influence. In this arena, there seemed to have been no decline in U.S. influence. Indeed, the democratization movements in China, South Korea, the Philippines, Burma, and elsewhere were all inspired at least in some part by the American example. The 1989 student uprising in Beijing would not have been as massive or, at least initially, as successful without the knowledge that Americans were watching the event on television. Revolutionary innovations in information and communications technology, many of them products of American engineering, were weaving countries of the world closer together into a global network, and the sense of instantaneous communication was nowhere more pronounced than in the hitherto closed societies of Asia. Even in a more open society like Japan, there were forces tending further to Americanize people's lifestyles. The two governments' attempt to discuss structural impediments in Japan that obstructed a freer flow of American goods and capital into the country were clearly an effort to alter Japanese cultural habits.

At the same time that American influence was transforming Asian societies, American society, too, was coming under increasing Asian influence. U.S. legislation on immigration passed in the mid-1960s, combined with various measures to resettle refugees, brought about an influx of Asians to the United States. Eventually, Asians came to account for 2.4 percent of the total population. In California the ratio was much higher, and there was an expectation that before long Asians might constitute one-third of the state's inhabitants. Immigrants from Vietnam, Thailand, Korea, Singapore, Taiwan, mainland China, and elsewhere were now much more visible in American society than earlier, and the American people became accustomed to Asian food, clothing, and religious practices. There were also hundreds of thousands of temporary visitors from Asia as tourists and students. In 1988, close to 3 million Japanese tourists came to America, and over 200,000 additional Japanese citizens resided in the United States, studying and working. The numbers of Korean and Chinese students seem to have been even larger than the number of Japanese students, and it was particularly significant that at the time of the Tiananmen crackdown in June 1989, as many as 40,000 Chinese students were scattered all over the United States.

Post–Cold War Developments

The thaw in the Cold War that began in the latter part of the Reagan administration and continued into the Bush administration had a major impact on the American approach to world affairs and to policy toward East Asia in particular. With the final collapse of the Soviet Union, the clear strategic emphasis in American policy toward the region was gone. It was replaced by a much less well defined policy approach that included, with varying degrees of emphasis, the salient economic and political as well as strategic American concerns that had evolved in East Asia over the previous century.

The Clinton administration inherited this situation and endeavored to capitalize on perceived advantageous trends while avoiding major pitfalls in developing policy toward the region. The results are widely seen as mixed, at best. The administration is widely criticized over perceived shortcomings in its policies.

An important question for U.S. policy at this juncture is: how serious are these perceived shortcomings?

- For the U.S. media, they clearly appear to be very serious indeed.
- For many U.S. foreign policy experts also, they appear to be very serious, especially judging by the large number of critical articles by prominent experts being printed in professional journals and on op ed pages.
- For the American people and their representatives in Congress, the reaction to Clinton's policy has been more mixed, with public opinion polls showing—at least until recently—about half of the American people approving of his handling of foreign policy.
- For leaders in East Asia, there are a few public complaints and more private grumbling, but there also appears to be an awareness that Clinton's policies are meeting their fundamental security and economic needs in the post–Cold War environment.

In order to better understand and to make judgments regarding U.S. policy in East Asia under the Clinton administration, a useful path of analysis is to first review underlying trends both in East Asia and the United States in the post–Cold War environment, and then to assess how well or poorly the president's policies work in that context.

East Asian Trends—Economic, Security, Political

Economic

Since the mid-1980s, East Asia has been the area of greatest economic opportunity in the world. It has seen remarkable growth by Japan, the newly industrialized countries (NICs) (e.g., South Korea), new NICs (e.g., Thailand), and now China and Vietnam.

A key role has been played by Japan and the NICs. Through investment, technology sharing, and so forth, these countries serve as dynamic centers of "clusters of growth" resulting from cascading outside, or foreign, investment. Examples include Hong Kong and Taiwan involvement in coastal China, Singapore involvement in Indonesia, and Thailand involvement in Indochina.

East Asian assets include capital, know-how, competitive advantage, complementary economies, good access to raw materials, and good access to markets. At bottom, East Asian leaders remain generally confident about their economic policies. An important worry is protectionism and emerging trading blocs in their major markets in the West, particularly in the United States. Protectionism is seen as coming generally from poor or stagnant economic conditions in the West. At the same time, the United States is seen in the post–Cold War environment to have less of a political-military incentive than in the past to tolerate large trade imbalances with Asian countries in the interests of maintaining a strong united front against Soviet power.

Security

An ironic situation has developed. On one hand, the security environment has markedly improved for Asian countries because:

1. The collapse of the USSR has seen East-West rivalry and Sino-Soviet rivalry replaced by U.S.-Russian and Chinese-Russian cooperation.

2. The U.S. strategic withdrawal from the Philippines was handled smoothly, with little disruption to the region.
3. Regional hot spots appear to have subsided (e.g., Cambodia, Afghanistan, Taiwan Strait); North Korea is an exception.
4. Political legitimacy in East Asia is seen to rest more on performance in economic development and nation building and less on military power and expansion. North Korea is an exception that proves this rule.

On the other hand, Asian countries reflect considerable anxiety about one another and there is a general arms buildup under way in the region. South Korea worries about Japan, Japan worries about China, China worries about Japan, and the ASEAN countries worry about each other as well as about China and Japan. Why is there this continued anxiety? Probable causes include:

1. Asian countries did not cause and control the recent security changes affecting their region; things could change again, for the worse.
2. The pullback of the USSR and other outside powers gives a higher profile to intraregional issues and disputes that were present in the past but were relatively less important than the ongoing big power bloc competition of the Cold War.
3. The collapse of communist/anticommunist ideology has prompted many Asian leaders to fall back on nationalism; territorial claims are the grist for this mill.
4. In many respects, East Asian leaders did not have to deal with each other outside of power blocs in the past, and many of the past dealings they did have (such as Japan's rule in Korea and the Sino-Japanese war) left a legacy of distrust. Now they have to deal with one another as equals and are finding it hard to build elements of trust.
5. Few Asian countries have adequate intelligence operations. Thus their leaders tend to think in worst-case terms when a neighbor issues a statement about territorial claims or begins the process of improving military power projection.

At bottom, Asian leaders' ongoing nervousness about the security situation explains why they uniformly want the U.S. military presence to remain as it is in Asia. The U.S. presence is seen as an effective counterweight to possible expansionist ambitions of the stronger against the weaker. The United States is trusted more than others in the region.

Political

The new definition of political legitimacy in East Asia rests heavily on economic development and nation building. The record of most East Asian governments is good in this area, and this gives them confidence for the future. On the other hand, their development requires increasing openness to the outside world, including the West. Economic prosperity has brought about rising consumption patterns, educational levels, and social changes, which lead to a series of new demands for power sharing and accountability in the government.

The democratic governments of Asia have institutions and processes to handle these pressures, albeit not always gracefully. Several of the authoritarian rulers of East Asia see these pressures as a threat to be resisted. Unfortunately for them, the challenges don't just focus on one or two policy areas; they cover a broad range of demands for change, including environmental issues (e.g., excessive logging, trading in endangered species), trade practices (e.g., intellectual property rights, market access), health (e.g., AIDS prevention), antidrug issues, antiterrorism issues, and refugee issues. Of course, the issues that get the most publicity are those related to human rights and democracy.

The Clinton administration has strongly identified with policies in these areas that are seen as challenges by some authoritarian rulers and other interest groups in Asia.

U.S. Trends

Like East Asia, the United States is also undergoing many changes in the post–Cold War environment. These changes are caused by the following factors, among others:

1. the end of the Cold War and of the USSR,
2. the protracted American economic difficulties during the late 1980s and early 1990s,
3. the generational change of U.S. leaders.

This has led to shifts in American policy, including:

4. There is a focus on domestic issues (economic recovery, government spending deficit, and health care).
5. Defense and security issues may no longer be paramount in U.S. foreign policy.
6. The ability of the president, the executive branch, and/or foreign policy elites to control foreign policy has been reduced.

For example, during the Cold War, presidents could argue that the danger of miscalculation in East–West relations was so great—leading ultimately to mutual destruction—that individuals in Congress and elsewhere who represented special interests needed to subordinate those interests for the overall national good, as defined by the president. Today, representatives of many diverse interests are no longer cowed by such arguments. As a result, effective policy requires a much more time-consuming and often messy process of consensus building among a much wider circle of actors than would have been considered effective during the Cold War. The following factors have an effect:

1. American people and their leaders have greater self-confidence in their ideology and values and want these reflected in American policy.
2. American people and their leaders want to adjust the costs and benefits of U.S. foreign involvement in ways that will reduce the costs and/or increase the benefits for the United States.

Unfortunately, there is strong disagreement about how this should be done:

1. One view sees the United States as having important interests in the international situation but judges that U.S. power to preserve these interests is less than in the past. Thus, it urges U.S. leaders to accommodate pragmatically to and work cooperatively with other important power centers in the world. In Asia, this would involve cooperative relations with both Japan and China. (Bush administration leaders followed this line of reasoning to some degree.)
2. A second view sees the international situation as disadvantageous

for the United States and believes that U.S. power and influence are in decline. Those holding this view judge that a major pull-back is needed in order to end draining foreign involvement and build up American strength at home. (Ross Perot reflects this view in several respects.)

3. A third view sees the United States as having important interests in the world but disagrees that U.S. power is less than before. In this view, the collapse of the USSR has left a power vacuum which other powers are unable to fill. China, Russia, and India are preoccupied with domestic development. Both Japan and Germany have great economic strength and great economic prob-lems but likely cannot wield economic power more forcefully because of historical reasons and current suspicions. Only the United States has the combination of economic and military power, and the political will and cultural attractiveness to lead in the world. According to this view, the United States is "bound to lead" and should use its power to assert its policy agenda (collec-tive security; economic development; democratization; and envi-ronmental, refugee, and other issues) in world affairs. National Intelligence Council Director Joseph Nye argues along these lines in his book, *Bound to Lead*.[7]

Clinton's Approach and Record

Looking past the media criticism and specialists' attacks on Clinton's foreign policy, a case can be made that the United States is meeting basic needs of East Asian countries, and is doing so in a way that is sustainable despite the breakdown of the Cold War foreign policy consensus in the United States.

In general, the administration's approach is transactional rather than transformational—seeking consensus rather than leading dramatically toward a new vision of American foreign policy. As noted above, this process is inherently messy, time-consuming, and undramatic, but the policies that result may reflect accurately the interests of a broad cross section of America and therefore should be more likely than not to reflect the "national interests" of the United States.

It is important to note here that our review of U.S. policy in the first half of the twentieth century showed that apart from the period of World War II and the Cold War, when U.S. leaders could point to a commonly perceived threat, transformational foreign policy has not done well. Even some of the best minds of the U.S. presidency (e.g., Woodrow Wilson and Franklin D. Roosevelt) found that their well-integrated visions of American interests and policies in world affairs fell flat soon after they were formulated, either because they were unsustainable domestically or because international events arose which made them irrelevant or unattractive.

The Clinton administration, while it has focused on domestic issues and on seeking consensus in foreign affairs, has not been without broad direction in its foreign policy, and at times has successfully asserted itself to preserve that direction. At its core, Clinton's foreign policy direction appears to be rooted in his concern with U.S. economic well-being. In this regard, the president and his administration have taken several important steps to foster an international environment conducive to American economic well-being, as they see it. Notable examples are the administration's successful defense of the North American Free Trade Agreement (NAFTA), the U.S.-initiated meeting of Asian leaders in Seattle, and the conclusion of the Uruguay Round of the GATT talks.

From the perspective of the underlying concerns of Asian leaders, it is hard to deny that U.S. trends under Clinton have helped some of their basic concerns in the post–Cold War world:

- Economic factors: The growing health of the U.S. economy means that the economic impetus behind protectionist forces in the United States will likely weaken. Clinton's tough stance on trade disputes (notably with Japan) and his firm commitment to economic openness, as seen in the NAFTA and GATT episodes, serve on the one hand to give protectionist forces fewer grounds for criticizing U.S. government policy while demonstrating the determination of the Clinton government to an open world trading system.
- Security factors: Despite continued military cutbacks in other areas, there has been little sign of significant change in the 90,000 to 100,000 U.S. forces deployed in East Asia. Through the more open and flexible approach taken by the Clinton administration as compared to previous U.S. administrations, to regional security dialogues and other discussions, the United States has positioned itself to take the lead in reducing the high level of anxiety over

security issues that has developed in East Asia in the post–Cold War setting. The continued strong U.S. security presence in East Asia owes a lot to continued strong U.S. concern with North Korea. Although there was some concern in East Asia in the past that the Clinton administration would undertake some ill-considered or precipitous action in the face of North Korea's intransigence, the United States has now settled in to a longer-term strategy for dealing with the problem—a strategy that enjoys broad support in the region.

- Political factors: This area remains the focal point of Asian concern with Clinton administration policy, but even here a case can be made that the administration has been endeavoring to channel American concerns that U.S. values be reflected in foreign policy in ways that effectively promote change and do not unduly jeopardize American security, economic, or other interests. Most notably, the record shows that the administration has managed to balance strongly held American concerns about prisoners of war (POWs) and service personnel missing in action (MIAs) with other foreign policy interests in ways that now allow U.S. economic interaction with Vietnam; it has narrowed past linkage of China's trade status with issues of U.S. values; and it has endeavored to balance U.S. concerns over human rights conditions in East Timor with broad American security and economic interests in the country.

Given the above line of analysis, one may need to focus elsewhere to discover the central weaknesses and shortcomings in Clinton's policy toward Asia. In general, these flaws seem to be centered on the style and perceived competence of American policy makers and the coherence of American policy. By contrast, as noted above, a lot of what the United States is doing in areas of economic development, security policy, and even political values can be seen as serving broad interests in Asia and reflecting a pragmatic effort to seek a working consensus among a wide range of often competing interests in the United States.

In particular, some individuals or groups who make a strong case for American values and interests in interaction with Asian counterparts may be seen as adopting a "superior" position that makes mutually respectful give-and-take and compromise more difficult. This position, which applies to issues ranging from human rights to market access to environmental concerns, may alienate Asian officials and play into the hands of chauvinists in countries that warn about American "hegemonic" designs.

Perceived shortcomings in the competence and coherence of American policy stem in part from the practice of U.S. officials of seeking consensus among a broad array of U.S. decision makers for particular foreign policies. This leads to sometimes contradictory impulses being reflected in the same policy, and subjects the policy to a variety of U.S. domestic forces capable of shifting the policies in one direction or another depending on circumstances.

Some experts argue that the perceived lack of coherence in American policy toward Asia may not be adequately addressed unless the president or his designee is more closely involved in regional affairs. As it stands now, there are a variety of sometimes contending actors within the administration, reflecting the sometimes conflicting interests of Americans in relations with Asia; no one but the president seems to have the authority to sort out the issues and set priorities. Absent the president's involvement, which is most of the time, or a more structured or channeled decision-making process, the spectacle of bureaucratic maneuvering on policy issues is on display for all to see at home and abroad. It does not instill confidence in the administration's ability to carry out effective foreign policy.

Finally, it must be noted that the sense of drift and vacillation widely seen in U.S. foreign policy almost certainly will have an effect on U.S. policy in Asia. Thus, for example, while Asian leaders are reassured by the continued U.S. military presence in the region, they may come to doubt the willingness of U.S. leaders to use those forces effectively. They may also come to believe that tough language or threats coming from some administration leaders may be offset by the more moderate approach favored by others in the administration. As a result, assertions of U.S. firmness on a particular issue may not be taken seriously.

Prospects

Whatever one thinks about the success or failure of recent Clinton administration policy in East Asia, the future of cooperation in the region will be determined in considerable measure by the interaction of the three main powers in the region: the United States, Japan, and China. Indeed, this way of thinking is what lies behind the concern over U.S. policy today. As noted earlier, the core of the problem seems to involve disputes with Japan and China. Other governments in Asia harbor resentments of their own against the United States, but they register notable concerns about frictions between the United States and China, and between the United States and Japan. At bottom, serious friction in either relationship runs the risk of prompting an uncertain realignment of power in East Asia that could have major implications for the stability and prosperity of the entire region.

To place this concern in an appropriate context, what follows is a brief assessment of the problems in U.S. relations with Japan and China, a discussion of the extent of U.S. influence with both powers over the next few years, and a brief recounting of U.S. policy options.

The Setting: A New Triangular Relationship in Post–Cold War Asia

During the Cold War, East Asian politics were dominated by the East-West conflict. The wars in Korea and Vietnam underlined this trend. Sino-U.S. reconciliation created a "great power triangle" of the United States, the USSR, and the People's Republic of China (PRC) that dictated political alignments in the region in the 1970s and during much of the 1980s. Japan played an increasingly important international role, especially in economic matters, but did so largely as a partner of the United States.

The demise of the USSR and the end of the Cold War were among conditions that reduced, at least for a time, Russia's role in East Asia. By contrast, the growing economic, political, and military power of China and Japan reflect their important roles in determining the East Asian order. As the state with clearly superior military power projection and as the economy providing the most important market for East Asian exporters, the United States continues to play a leading role in regional affairs.

An optimistic scenario for the post–Cold War period held that the three powers (Japan, China, and the United States) would work closely and cooperatively to foster their mutual interests in Asian stability and prosperity. The powers would see such stability and prosperity as a kind of strategic goal that would allow them to set policy priorities clearly and to cooperate smoothly. Most other Asian countries would view such great power cooperation as in their best interests.

In fact, however, developments have turned out differently, leading to the more complex triangular relationship we see today.

In part, this outcome is caused by the strong domestic focus of each government: China's leaders remain focused on fostering internal economic development while retaining political stability at a time of major leadership change. Japan faces a difficult, confused, and fluid political situation at the time of the most serious economic recession since the start of the Korean War. The United States voted out a president with strong foreign policy credentials in favor of a state governor who promised to shift America's focus toward greater government concern for domestic affairs. In sum, the inward focus of each government appears to have reduced its inclination to take the lead in fostering greater East Asian cooperation and development.

In part, the current outcome also reflects the competing and/or conflicting domestic imperatives of the three powers. U.S. policy makers are free from the past need to accommodate the interests of allies and associates for the broader strategic goal of checking Soviet power in the Cold War. As a result, American leaders have formulated new policies reflecting U.S. domestic pressures for change and adjustments in the perceived costs and benefits of U.S. relations abroad. In the case of Japan, U.S. officials have adopted a harder line against unfair Japanese trade practices that have a deleterious effect on the health of the U.S. economy. In the case of China, U.S. officials have been prompted to press harder for changes in Chinese human rights and political practices that have been seen in a notably negative light by a wide spectrum of Americans since the 1989 Tiananmen crackdown.

Unfortunately for U.S. policy, these initiatives have run up against similarly strong countervailing forces inside Japan and China. The changes in Japanese politics have made political leaders weaker, less willing to confront entrenched bureaucrats and special interests, and therefore less able to make concessions sought by the United States. The poor economic conditions in Japan underline Japanese unwillingness to shift policies in ways that might cost Japan more than in the past. Chinese leaders' determination to resist U.S. pressure for political change is said to have been strengthened both by the close call Beijing's communists experienced in spring 1989 and by the "lessons"

Chinese leaders have drawn from the collapse of other communist and authoritarian regimes since that time.

The result has been protracted and highly publicized tensions in U.S. relations with both Japan and China. As noted above, this situation has alarmed other countries in Asia. In the view of some American and other critics (as noted in the next few paragraphs), the outcome has demonstrated the ineffectiveness of U.S. policy and has run the risk of isolating and "marginalizing" the United States in the region.

Ineffective U.S. Policy

After spending over a year confronting China and Japan on human rights and trade issues, respectively, the Clinton administration has been compelled to back off. Evidence includes President Clinton's compromise decision extending China's most favored nation (MFN) status, and recent U.S.-Japan talks leading to compromise on so-called framework negotiations with Japan. The reasons for the U.S. shift center on a growing awareness by American leaders of the ever closer dependence of the American economy on relations with both Japan and China.

Reduced U.S. Influence in Asia

Contrary to the difficulties they face in relations with the United States, Japan and China have worked hard through leaders' meetings and through growing economic, political, and even security exchanges to consolidate their leg of the triangular relationship in post–Cold War Asia. Japan has markedly boosted its economic stake in China, as the largest Chinese trading partner. Japan has long been the largest source of bilateral aid for China, but 1992 and 1993 saw a large boost in direct Japanese investment motivated by perceived economic opportunity in the China market. The structure of the Japanese economy appears likely to result in continued large current account surpluses for several more years, and some analysts predict that Japanese investors will focus such funds on the rapidly developing markets in Asia, especially China.

To nurture and preserve these growing economic interests in China, Japan is seen in some analyses—including Winston Lord's memo—as moving a distance from Washington on issues sensitive to China. Thus, Prime Minister Morihiro Hosokawa was said to have pulled his punches on human rights issues during a recent visit to China—a contrast to Japan's close collaboration with U.S. policy over China in the period after the Tiananmen incident. Japanese leaders have also lobbied hard to persuade U.S. officials to change policy on human rights by de-linking Chinese human rights practices and MFN trade status.

Chinese leaders have welcomed Japan's initiatives. Beijing has a long history of trying to improve its own position in the triangular relationship by utilizing Japanese-American competition and differences. China benefits economically by having both capitalist powers bidding for greater access to the Chinese market. Politically, Beijing probably hopes U.S.-Japan differences will prevent the creation of a U.S.-led international united front pressing Chinese leaders for greater political change and liberalization.

Sources of Continued U.S. Influence

It is easy to exaggerate the above line of analysis to a point where the United States appears isolated and "marginalized" in East Asia. In fact, the recent U.S. problems with China and Japan have not as yet fundamentally altered the advantageous U.S. position in the triangular U.S.-Japan-PRC relationship in post–Cold War Asia. This can be seen by reviewing the difficulties Japan and China have with one another and how those difficulties reinforce other factors, inclining each nation to seek closer relations with the United States.

In the view of some knowledgeable analysts, the elements keeping China and Japan separate from one another and each reliant on the United States are strong enough to suggest that there is no meaningful triangular relationship among the three powers. In this perspective, Japan will move closer to China and China to Japan only under conditions in which the United States remains closely involved in Asian affairs and in particular sustains a close military relationship with Japan. Thus, if the United States becomes seriously estranged from Japan, Tokyo will be less—not more—inclined to seek improved ties with China, and China will be more—not less—suspicious of Japan.

Japan

Japanese leaders are of two minds about China. They are attracted to the economic opportunities there, but they have deep-seated fears about this close and increasingly powerful neighbor, as follows:

1. China is a military threat of growing concern, especially as it funnels new economic wealth into the improvement of military capabilities.
2. China is an economic threat. The country could be capable of using its massive market, its cheap labor, and other factors to dominate markets and commercial endeavors important to Japan.
3. China would be a threat to stability if it were to become politically disorderly and disunited, prompting potentially massive refugee flows and other developments that would severely complicate Asian security and prosperity.

Japanese leaders also worry about American-Chinese cooperation at Japan's expense. In particular:

4. Japanese reportedly feel unique and culturally isolated and insecure vis-à-vis Americans and others, whereas they perceive Americans as inclined toward and attracted to the Chinese from historical and cultural points of view.
5. More practically, Japanese sometimes worry that American frustration with Japan's closed economic system and China's vibrant growth could prompt the United States to tilt toward China economically, in terms of U.S. policy. This pattern is said to resemble the Nixon-Kissinger frustration with Japan strategically and the American tilt toward China in the 1970s.

Japan continues to depend heavily on Japan's ever closer economic interdependence with the U.S. market and Japan's continued dependence on the United States for security guarantees in an East Asian environment full of potential dangers to Japanese peace and prosperity.

China

China wants to avoid overdependence on Japan. It needs the United States for balance against what otherwise could be a quasi-dependent economic relationship similar to the relationships Japan maintains with South Korea and Taiwan. The latter two countries have been unable to press Japan to change economic policies contrary to their interests because enterprises in Taiwan and South Korea have become so heavily dependent on technology, spare parts, and other economic connections with Japan.

China is concerned with Japan's military power. PRC planners are aware that Japanese power projection capabilities and potential are far ahead of China. Beijing does not want reduced American influence until it is more certain that China's military would be able to deal with possible contingencies.

It is likely that China does not want U.S.-China friction to reach a point where Japan is forced to choose between the two. Under such circumstances, past practice and current realities seem to show that Japan would side with the United States against China.

U.S. Options

Assessment of the new triangular relationship in Asia seems to show that the United States retains the most advantageous and influential position. Prospects for fundamental change in this equation or the "marginalization" of the United States are poor, even if the United States continues to have difficult relationships with Tokyo, Beijing, and other Asian capitals.

A question for U.S. policy is how best to pursue U.S. security, economic, and political interests in this regional environment. One option argues for continued American assertiveness, using Japanese and Chinese interest in good relations with the United States and other sources of influence to compel both countries to adjust policies in ways favored by the United States. This approach may antagonize and concern many in Asia, and could destabilize the region, at least over the short term. The longer-term prospects could be for greater triangular cooperation and regional stability, provided Tokyo and Beijing accommodated the American demands. Alternatively, the longer-term result could be confrontation among the three great powers and serious regional instability.

Another option favors a more accommodating American stance. The United States would pull back some of its more contentious initiatives in the broader interest of promoting stability and prosperity in Asia, which would be beneficial to a wide circle, including the United States. This approach would likely be difficult to support internally in the United States, as domestic constituencies might register dissatisfaction in the voting booth or elsewhere. There is no guarantee that Asian peace and stability would foster the kinds of political, military, and economic policies in the region that are in the longer-term interest of the United States.

Regardless of which option or variation is chosen, U.S. Asian specialists frequently urge U.S. leaders to carefully assess the broader "strategic" trends affecting developments in Asia and to use those trends effectively to come up with U.S. policies for meeting longer-term American interests. As it stands now, these specialists sometimes see U.S. policy as buffeted by issues of the moment and unable to differentiate or set priorities to establish foreign policy courses suitable for U.S. concerns into the twenty-first century.

Notes

1. See Susumu Awanohara, "About Face," *Far Eastern Economic Review*, May 19, 1994, for review of the debate and of Winston Lord's memo.

2. Among the interesting interpretive works on this subject are: Akira Iriye, *Across the Pacific: An Inner History of American-East Asian Relations*, Harcourt, Brace and World, New York, 1967; James C. Thomson, Jr., et al., *Sentimental Imperialists: The American Experience in East Asia*, Harper and Row, New York, 1981; Earnest R. May and James Thompson (eds.), *American-East Asian Relations, A Survey*, Harvard University Press, Cambridge, Mass., 1972; Tyler Dennett, *Americans in East Asia: A Critical Study in United States Policy in the Far East in the 19th Century*, Barnes and Noble, New York, 1963; Akira Iriye, *The Cold War in Asia: A Historical Introduction*, Prentice Hall, Englewood Cliffs, N.J., 1974; Tang Tsou, *America's Failure in China*, University of Chicago Press, 1963; Warren Cohen (ed.), *New Frontiers in American-East Asian Relations*, Columbia University Press, New York, 1983.

3. This analysis is based heavily on an analysis presented by Akira Iriye at the Woodrow Wilson Center for Scholars, Washington, D.C., September 26, 1990.

4. Whitney Griswold, *The Far Eastern Policy of the United States*, Harcourt, Brace, New York, 1938, provides a useful overview of this period.

5. Based on Akira Iriye's review, September 26, 1990, op. cit.

6. This summary is based particularly on the thoughtful assessment of William Barnds, "Trends in U.S. Politics and Their Implications for America's Asian Policy;" in Robert Scalapino et al. (eds.), *Asia and the Major Powers: Domestic Politics and Foreign Policy*, University of California, Berkeley, California, 1988.

7. For background on these different views, see *Foreign Policy Debate in America*, by Charlotte Pearce and Robert Sutter, Library of Congress, Congressional Research Service, Washington, D.C., CRS Report 91–833 (November 27, 1991).

3

The United States and the Two Koreas: An Uncertain Triangle

Rinn-Sup Shinn

In mid-1994, the United States, South Korea, and communist North Korea became embroiled in a mounting crisis over the North's suspected nuclear arms program. The crisis is defused, for now, under the October 1994 U.S.–North Korean Agreed Framework signed in Geneva. Nonetheless, uncertainty persists partly because of North Korea's poor history of adhering to agreements and because of an inter-Korean impasse, not to mention conflicting interpretation of the Geneva nuclear accord. The United States continues to maintain its 36,000 troops in the South to help the latter safeguard its stability and security.

In the months and years ahead, if not already, the U.S. policy toward the two Koreas seems certain to be buffeted by changing parameters of peace and security on the Korean peninsula. That is because Washington is obliged to go beyond its traditional South Korea–centered policy to cope with a new challenge: balancing the need to secure Pyongyang's cooperation for denuclearization of the peninsula and the need to maintain the U.S. security commitment to South Korea, without getting on North Korean nerves. The outcome of this delicate challenge will hinge significantly on how the Korean triangle—Washington, Pyongyang, and Seoul—will deal with the three major interrelated issues: the Ko-

Views expressed in this paper are personal and should not be construed as those of the Congressional Research Service of the Library of Congress, or of any other U.S. government agency.

rean armistice of 1953; the implementation of the Geneva Nuclear Accord; and North Korean–South Korean dialogue.

In the near term, tripartite cooperation might not readily materialize because of the conflicting inter-Korean approaches to reconciliation, peace, and security. Pyongyang's "my way or no way" approach to both Seoul and Washington foreshadows an uncertain future for the Korean triangle. Evidently, North Korea, or the Democratic People's Republic of Korea (DPRK), has little incentive to deal with South Korea, for now at least, as it may have judged that the Geneva deal provides all the leverage it needs to eventually gain the upper hand over the South, or the Republic of Korea (ROK). The United States and South Korea are faced with a beleaguered North Korea, which is determined to leverage the Geneva accord as a vehicle for tilting the balance of forces in its favor. Depending on how the Geneva accord plays out, several years down the road, the Korean triangle could become embroiled again in the same old dispute over Pyongyang's refusal to allow "special inspections" requested by the International Atomic Energy Agency (IAEA). Potentially, the dispute could have implications for the future of U.S. military presence in the South, for South Korea's capacity to deal with the North, and for U.S.–South Korean relations.

This paper presents an analysis of how the triangular relationship has evolved over such issues as Washington's North Korea policy, the Korean War armistice, North Korea's nuclear arms program, and inter-Korean dialogue. The unifying thread through all these issues is North Korea's two long-term aims: one designed to seek U.S. military withdrawal from South Korea; and the other to gain the high ground in inter-Korean relations—and eventually to unify Korea on its terms following the U.S. withdrawal.

Evolution of the Triangular Relationship

Background

Situated at the strategic geopolitical intersection of East Asia, Korea has for centuries suffered a historical "tied-in fate" at the hands of neighboring powers. At the turn of this century, Japan, China, and czarist Russia vied for hegemony over Korea, with Japan emerging triumphant in wars with both, in 1894–95 and in 1904–05. Korea was annexed by Japan in 1910 but regained its freedom in 1945, only to be met by yet another cruel fate as a divided nation. In 1950, aided by Josef Stalin, North Korea's Kim Il Sung invaded the South, calculating that the United States would not try to rescue South Korea. The effect of the Korean War (North Korea calls it "The Fatherland Liberation War") was to turn the divided halves of Korea into frontline states in the Cold War, which pitted North Korea and China (with the Soviet Union concealing its active support role) against South Korea, the United States, and 15 other allies responding to the United Nations Security Council call for collective action against the North. The conflict ended in armistice, in July 1953, signed by the military commanders of North Korea, the Chinese "people's volunteers," and the United Nations Command (UNC) established under the UN Security Council resolution of July 7, 1950. Technically, neither the United States nor South Korea is a signatory of the armistice, but both continue to adhere to it through a military armistice commission.[1] No peace agreement has replaced the armistice, and thus a condition of belligerency continues to this day.

In the postwar decades, two kinds of Cold Wars affected the dynamics of conflict on the divided peninsula: one between the communist bloc and the West; and the other between Pyongyang and Seoul. The former ended with the collapse of the Soviet Union, but the latter has not ended, despite Pyongyang's protestation to the contrary. Mutual distrust and antipathy, a bitter legacy of the Korean War, still beset inter-Korean relations. Since 1972, North and South Koreans have met intermittently at the border village of Panmunjom and alternately in Pyongyang and Seoul, but to no avail. The landmark inter-Korean agreement on "reconciliation, nonaggression, exchange and cooperation" signed at the end of 1991 has since remained on the shelf (see "North-South Dialogue," below).

Shift in U.S. Approach to Pyongyang

U.S. policy toward North Korea since 1953 has been a function largely of its close bilateral relations with the South. Since the late 1980s, however, this has been redefined by force of events. Underlying the shift were the shared concerns of both Washington and Seoul that North Korea should be prevented from disrupting the 1988 Summer Olympics hosted by Seoul, from developing a nuclear weapons program, and from disrupting South Korean political stability.

Before the Seoul Olympics (September 17 through October 2,

1988), Washington signaled to the North its intention to open limited contact with it soon, conditioned on Pyongyang's good behavior during the Summer Games. This came against the backdrop of Pyongyang-sponsored terrorism in November 1987, when a South Korean passenger plane was exploded over the Indian Ocean by bombs planted by North Korean agents. Apparently, Pyongyang's motive was to lend credence to its assertion that Seoul was not a safe place to go for Olympians from other countries. After the Olympics, the United States announced a package of steps to deal with the North. The initiative was in support also of a July 1988 South Korean overture to Pyongyang aimed at drawing it out of isolation, encouraging cross-border exchanges of people and goods, and cooperating in international forums. The package was intended to authorize U.S. diplomats to hold discussions with North Koreans in neutral settings; to facilitate nongovernmental exchanges for family and academic and cultural purposes; and to permit trade in goods meeting basic humanitarian needs.

The October 1988 initiatives led to the first low-level contacts in Beijing two months later. This development had the full support of Seoul, which had agreed with Washington that an isolated and "cornered" North Korea increased the risks of instability on the peninsula. In contacts through May 1993, U.S. diplomats informed North Koreans of a need for Pyongyang to:

- Undertake serious dialogue with South Korea about steps leading to reduction of tensions, confidence building, and reconciliation.
- Sign and comply with an IAEA safeguards agreement, as mandated under the Nuclear Non-Proliferation Treaty (NPT).
- Regularize a process for returning all 8,100 Korean War remains of American servicemen missing in action (MIAs).
- Stop disinformation and incendiary rhetoric against the United States.
- Renounce state-sponsored terrorism.
- Demonstrate greater respect for human rights.
- Stop exporting ballistic missiles and related military technology.

Pyongyang's Strategic Goal: No U.S. Troops in South Korea

Beginning in March 1974, North Korea has eagerly sought to engage Washington in a bid to undermine the U.S. rationale for maintaining its troops in the South. After its 1974 overture for direct talks went unanswered, the North changed its stance in 1984, appealing to the United States (but not to South Korea) for a tripartite meeting including the South. To do this, the North had to reverse itself on its 1979 decision not to accept a proposal, then being advanced by the United States and South Korea, for a three-way conference. The 1984 proposal was also ignored because, if Pyongyang had its way, Seoul would have had only a marginal role. Besides, Seoul was not amused by Pyongyang's "effrontery," coming as it did in the wake of Pyongyang's terrorist bombing against a South Korean presidential entourage in October 1983, then on a state visit to Rangoon, Burma.

U.S. military presence in South Korea has been a thorn in the side of Kim Il Sung and his anointed successor Kim Jong Il. To the late "great leader," it was a painful and costly reminder of his failed venture to take the South. As an antidote to the U.S. military presence in the South, the North has had to undertake a costly arms buildup at the expense of its economy. The U.S. presence has meant a decidedly unfavorable correlation of forces against the North—a source of insecurity as well as the barrier to unification. Kim Il Sung died in July 1994, unable to finish the last chapter of the Korean War he was still fighting. The unfinished task of forcing U.S. troops out of the South, or more aptly the daunting political task of securing "a level playing field," has been passed on to the fifty-three-year-old "supreme leader" Kim Jong Il.

The Korean Armistice

In its tactical effort to engage the United States, North Korea has since 1974 emphasized the need to replace the 1953 armistice with a peace agreement with the United States. It has argued that peace and security on the peninsula were matters to be resolved between North Korean and U.S. military authorities, without South Korean interference. The overture was amended in April 1994, when Pyongyang proposed that, in addition to a peace agreement, the two sides should establish "a new peace guarantee system."[2] The 1994 overture contains the following elements:

- The United States has systematically violated the armistice by bringing into the South sophisticated weapons, including 1,000 nuclear warheads, and thereby has turned the armistice accord into "an empty sheet of paper."

- The North and the United States—"the actual parties to the armistice . . . as the two warring opponents"—must conclude a peace agreement and establish "a new peace-guarantee system" to end "the hostile relations" between the two sides.[3]
- South Korea is not qualified to discuss the armistice since it did not sign the 1953 accord.
- In any case, South Korea has no authority to address the armistice, since the actual power of command and control over the South Korean military is in the hands of U.S. military authorities.

According to Pyongyang's latest position, "nonhostile relations and rapprochement" between the North and the United States will be possible if the two sides agree to establish "a new peace guarantee system." Indications are that the North will not let up on the armistice issue, according to clues in the *Minju Choson* (the DPRK's official daily organ). The authoritative daily argued as follows about why the United States should embrace Pyongyang's overture:

- The North's proposal is consistent with the 1994 U.S.-DPRK Agreed Framework signed in Geneva.
- "The U.S. must clearly know that [absent a new peace system] the hostile relations between the two countries cannot be improved nor can genuine reconciliation be achieved."
- "The United States must respond without delay to our proposal for establishing a new peace mechanism, if its promise at talks and meetings with the DPRK is not a lie."[4]

Pyongyang's intention to turn the armistice into a new round of bids to chip away at U.S. military presence in the South was evident in July–August 1994. At that time, it sought to include the armistice as an issue to be addressed at DPRK-U.S. talks in Geneva. Although rebuffed, Pyongyang seems certain to try again and again (see "Prospects," below).[5]

In anticipation of Pyongyang's full-court press on the armistice, Seoul is exploring several options. One option reportedly calls for the conversion of the armistice into "a regional security regime" to be based on a North-South peace agreement through the good offices of the United States and China. The latter two will then "endorse and sign" the agreement themselves.[6] A tripartite approach is another idea tossed around in Seoul; it involves a simultaneous, paired approach to peace agreements between the two Koreas, on one hand, and between the North and the United States, on the other.[7]

The United States refuses to be drawn into separate negotiations with Pyongyang, mindful that the armistice and related issues of peace and security on the peninsula are matters for the Korean governments themselves to resolve. The United States remains prepared, however, to talk with both Korean sides, if so desired by them and presuming, of course, that the North and South Korean sides are full and equal participants in such talks.

The armistice is a volatile issue, as South Koreans seem to suspect that Washington will make a separate deal with Pyongyang. They believe that the Clinton administration—too eager for a nuclear deal—ceded the upper hand to the North without adequate regard for South Korea's security interest. According to Seoul, U.S. negotiators were outsmarted by North Koreans in the 1993–94 standoff, and this situation could repeat itself over the armistice. South Koreans generally share the view that the armistice could become a litmus test of their "special relationship" with Washington. Their concerns are that:

- With South Korea being the first victim of North Korean aggression, the North should be held answerable to its war crime and should agree to replace the armistice with a North-South peace pact.
- Any DPRK-U.S. talks about the armistice, without South Korean participation, would add insult to injury.
- The Clinton administration yields as readily to North Korean pressure as the South Korean government yields to U.S. pressure.[8]
- South Korea, "for a change," should "stand up" to both Washington and Pyongyang if its credibility is to be regained—and if its capacity to deal with North Korea one-on-one, on equal terms, is to be maintained.

North Korea's Nuclear Program

Pyongyang's nuclear ambitions seem to have derived from two major factors: its sense of insecurity dating back to the late 1950s against the backdrop of growing uncertainty about Pyongyang's geopolitical environment;[9] and its strategic aim to rid South Korea of U.S. military presence. Adding to these factors was a new urgency spawned by adverse changes in Pyongyang's external economic and security environment since the fall of the Berlin Wall in 1989. The North responded by accelerating the development of its nuclear arms option as a means of compensating for growing sources of regime vulnerability and of creating leverage for the attainment of economic, political, and security benefits from the United States.

Background

In the mid-1960s Pyongyang first obtained limited assistance from the Soviet Union for what was intended as a peaceful nuclear energy program. Pressed by Moscow, the North in 1985 signed the NPT, apparently as a condition of receiving further Soviet assistance, but failed to follow up by signing a safeguards agreement with the IAEA, as obligated under the NPT. Pyongyang's nuclear intentions became a source of growing international concern.

U.S. interest in a nuclear-free Korea had begun even before the North Korean case. In the 1970s, for example, the United States had leaned heavily on South Korea to forgo its suspected nuclear arms program.[10] It was not until 1989–90 that the United States became suspicious about Pyongyang's nuclear program in the face of its refusal to accede to the NPT safeguards regime; Pyongyang also aroused international concerns in February 1990, when it hinted at a possible withdrawal from the NPT in a Vienna-based IAEA meeting. In 1991, faced with persistent North Korean charges that the United States had stored some 1,000 nuclear warheads in South Korea, the Bush administration reportedly withdrew U.S. nuclear arms from South Korea. In November 1991, South Korean President Roh Tae Woo unilaterally declared that there were no nuclear arms in the South. At that time, he also declared that his government would "not manufacture, possess, store, deploy or use nuclear weapons"—this in the midst of contentious North-South negotiations about the terms of reconciliation and denuclearization. These negotiations produced, on December 31, 1991, the historic Joint Declaration on the Denuclearization of the Korean Peninsula, whereby North Korea and South Korea agreed not to "test, manufacture, produce, receive, possess, store, deploy or use nuclear weapons." They even agreed not to "possess nuclear reprocessing and uranium enrichment facilities."

In January 1992, Pyongyang was rewarded with an unprecedented U.S.–North Korean high-level meeting, in New York, between Undersecretary of State Arnold Kanter and Kim Yong Sun, a senior North Korean party official in charge of international affairs. From the standpoint of the North, the meeting represented a long-coveted breakthrough in its decades-long quest for a symbolically significant contact with Washington. Perhaps the meeting could have also helped to validate Pyongyang's judgment that the DPRK could force Washington "to sit up and listen" by linking the nuclear issue with Washington's top priority agenda for nuclear nonproliferation. At the high-level meeting, Kanter's apparent intent was to convey to President Kim Il Sung an "unfiltered" version of U.S. concern over the North's nuclear program as well as U.S. interest in the resumption of North-South dialogue and in Pyongyang's acceptance of South Korea's proposed challenge inspections. For his part, Kim Yong Sun's intent apparently was to express Pyongyang's willingness to comply with the IAEA's safeguards regime and to plead for a bilateral solution of the nuclear dispute; in addition, he reportedly stressed Pyongyang's interest in establishing "a permanent contact" with Washington and its intention not to press for U.S. withdrawal from the South, at least in the near term. Tactically, his intent was not to let the troop issue detract from Pyongyang's hard-earned, more strategically pivotal effort to engage the United States in nuclear negotiations.

At the end of January 1992, after the Kanter-Kim meeting, Pyongyang finally signed a safeguards agreement after six years of stonewalling. Thereafter and through February 1993, it allowed the IAEA to inspect Pyongyang's declared nuclear facilities on six occasions. Cooperation was not forthcoming, however, in talks with Seoul aimed at implementing the North-South denuclearization accord as the North raised a new argument that the nuclear issue should be resolved in talks only with the United States.

By late 1992, IAEA inspectors had reasonable grounds to suspect that the North had probably separated more weapons-grade plutonium than it had declared to the IAEA. Their request for "special inspections" of two nuclear waste sites at Yongbyon, which could reveal the history of reprocessing from 1989, was rejected. In March 1993, the North announced its withdrawal from the NPT, contending that the IAEA had violated its mandate for "impartiality" by relying on intelligence provided by "a third country" (the United States). It alleged that the request for such "intrusive" inspections was part of a U.S. plot to "stifle," or crush, North Korea.

Unable to impose its will on a defiant North Korea—short of a war—the Clinton administration decided to negotiate. In June 1993, the North agreed to "suspend" its withdrawal from the NPT. More negotiations followed in July 1993, but the crisis mounted after May 1994, as Pyongyang removed 8,000 fuel rods laden with some 30 kilograms of plutonium from its 5-megawatt graphite reactor. Faced with possible UN economic sanctions, the North threatened to take appropriate "self-defense" countermeasures, claiming that it would regard the sanctions as "an act of war." The crisis was defused thanks to former President Jimmy Carter's visit to Pyongyang for talks with Kim Il Sung. A new round of negotiations opened in Geneva on July 8, but was cut short by Kim's sudden death. A North–South Korean summit, planned for late July and also made possible by Carter, was put off indefinitely.

Resumed on August 5, the Geneva talks resulted in an "agreed statement" of August 12—an outline of guidelines that both sides said should be part of a final resolution of the dispute. After more hard bargaining in Geneva from September 23, these elements became the basis for the U.S.-DPRK Agreed Framework, which was signed on October 21, 1994.[11] The Geneva accord thus has a confidential annex.

U.S.-DPRK Agreed Framework

The Agreed Framework establishes a long-term, interlocked process by which Pyongyang would eventually abandon its nuclear program—in return for an attractive package of incentives. Implemented as designed, the accord could serve as an important step toward resolving all or nearly all aspects of the nuclear dispute and toward advancing the broader interests of U.S. allies in Northeast Asia and other Pacific rim states, with stakes in regional stability and prosperity.

From the U.S. perspective, the nuclear issue divides into three dimensions—past, present, and future—the latter two defined as "clearly more pressing priorities" to be addressed "in the near term." Admittedly, U.S. negotiators "would have preferred" to deal with the "past" first, since that was the main source of angst in Seoul as well as the focus of the IAEA request for "special inspections," but they opted to defer the past to a later stage, their assumption being that information that can reveal Pyongyang's "past activities" at the suspected waste sites at Yongbyon "is not perishable" as a scientific fact.[12]

North Koreans approached the nuclear issue from a different perspective—hence establishing a potential ground for a conflicting interpretation of the Geneva accord. For, in addition to obtaining diplomatic and economic benefits from Washington, their apparent strategy is to capitalize on the accord in a bid to fulfill Kim Il Sung's post–Korean War agenda for "peace and security" on the peninsula—an agenda for replacing the armistice with a DPRK-U.S. peace treaty and for developing bilateral relations with Washington.

In agreeing to the Geneva document, both sides accepted the fact that they had no mutual trust and that, therefore, making the accord work would hinge on reciprocal and verifiable actions in good faith. Failure by one side to comply with a required step would cause the other to withhold cooperation. There are no ironclad assurances that the Geneva agreement will be implemented as envisaged. In fact, difficulties can be anticipated because of the ambiguous language of the accord, to say nothing of Pyongyang's penchant for reinterpreting agreements to suit its interest as circumstances unfold. The Geneva accord is designed to be implemented in the following stages:

Phase I (1994–2000)

The main emphasis during the first stage is on the present and the future.[13]

- With regard to the present, North Korea will freeze, under IAEA monitoring, a 5-megawatt operational reactor, a reprocessing facility that North Koreans call the radiochemical laboratory, and 8,000 spent fuel rods removed in May 1994 from the 5-megawatt reactor. (The 5-megawatt reactor will remain shut down and the spent fuel rods will not be reprocessed, nor will plutonium be separated.)
- With regard to the future, the North will freeze both 50-megawatt and 200-megawatt reactors that would have been completed in the next few years.[14]

In return for Pyongyang's agreeing to freeze and eventually dismantle its nuclear program, the United States will, in accordance with

President Clinton's October 20, 1994, letter to DPRK Supreme Leader Kim Jong Il, perform the following actions:

- The United States will undertake to make arrangements for the provision to the DPRK of a light-water reactor (LWR) project with a total generating capacity of approximately 2,000 megawatts (electrical) by a target date of 2003.
- Pending completion of the first LWR unit, the United States will make arrangements to offset the energy foregone due to the freeze of the DPRK's graphite-moderated reactors and related facilities, with the first shipment of U.S.-funded 50,000 metric tons of heavy fuel oil to be delivered by January 21, 1995. (The burden of future shipments—100,000 tons in 1995 and 500,000 tons annually until the first LWR unit is completed—is to be borne by an international consortium, or the Korean Peninsula Energy Development Organization [KEDO]).
- The United States will organize and lead an international consortium to finance the LWR project, in which the United States, South Korea, and Japan are to play "a leading role," with South Korea additionally playing "a central role" in financing and construction.[15]
- The United States, "representing the consortium, will make best efforts to secure the conclusion of a supply contract with the DPRK within six months [by April 21] of this Document for the provision of the LWR project."

(See "The Current Status of the Geneva Nuclear Deal," below). In addition:

- Both sides will, within three months, "reduce barriers to trade and investment, including restrictions on telecommunications services and financial transactions."
- Each side will open a liaison office in the other's capital following resolution of consular and other technical matters through expert level discussions.
- Both sides will, as progress is made on issues of mutual concern, "upgrade bilateral relations to the Ambassadorial level."

Phase II (2000–2003)

The second phase is arguably the most critical juncture for the Geneva accord. If North Korea does decide to level the playing field on the

Korean peninsula by leveraging its "nuclear card," it could press the issue during Phase II by refusing IAEA-requested "special inspections" (see "North Korea's Grand Strategy," below).

The Geneva Agreed Framework reads: "When a significant portion of the LWR project is completed, but before delivery of key nuclear components, the DPRK will come into full compliance with its safeguards agreement with the IAEA . . . *including taking all steps that may be deemed necessary by the IAEA* [emphasis added], following consultations with the Agency with regard to verifying the accuracy and completeness of the DPRK's initial report on all nuclear material in the DPRK." The Clinton administration explains "all steps that may be deemed necessary by the IAEA" as including the disputed "special inspections"; however, Pyongyang remains adamant that such inspections not only are "unfair" and "invalid" but also constitute an intrusive plot to undermine the security of the North.

However, when and if Pyongyang fully complies with the IAEA safeguards regime,

- The KEDO will reciprocate by delivering key nuclear components for the first LWR.
- North Korea will ship 8,000 spent fuel rods out of the country by around 2003 to a third country yet to be designated through DPRK-U.S. talks.
- The process of dismantling all reactors and related facilities will begin around 2003, when the first LWR is anticipated to become operational.

Phase III (2003–2005)

With the second LWR unit operational by 2005, the dismantling of the nuclear facilities would be complete. Optimistically, relations among Pyongyang, Seoul, and Washington could have substantially improved but then this might not be the case (see "North Korea's Grand Strategy," below).

Other Relevant Points

Under the Geneva deal:

- North Korea agreed to remain a party to the NPT and hence its formal intention to comply with the NPT safeguards regime.
- In the event of unforeseen difficulties "beyond the control of the

DPRK" in implementing the Geneva accord, President Clinton confirmed, in a letter to Kim Jong Il, his intention to "use the full powers" of his office to "provide"—"to the extent necessary . . . subject to the approval of the U.S. Congress"—the LWR project or "interim energy alternatives" from the United States.

- As part of its pledge to work with the North "for peace and security on a nuclear-free Korean Peninsula," the United States will provide "formal assurances" not to threaten to use or use nuclear weapons against the DPRK.[16]
- North Korea agreed also "to engage in North-South dialogue, as this Agreed Framework will help create an atmosphere that promotes such dialogue."

The last point, however, is problematic, as the two sides differ on whether the dialogue should proceed in tandem with the implementation of the Geneva accord, as the United States and South Korea maintain, or whether the North-South dialogue and the Geneva pact are "separate matters," as Pyongyang argues (see "North-South Dialogue," below).

The accord has had mixed receptions. It was warmly received by many as a smart deal that an impoverished Pyongyang could ill afford to renege on.[17] Foreign reactions, particularly Chinese, Japanese, and Russian, were generally favorable, regarding it as a promising step toward regional peace and stability in Asia. South Korea reacted similarly, even though it seemed to have serious concerns over the "past" aspect of the accord.

Skeptics in Congress, among independent experts and foreign diplomats, and in the media tended to view the accord as having high financial costs that could not be met, as "one-sided" in favor of Pyongyang, and as a bad precedent that could encourage other "outlaw" countries to use "nuclear blackmail" for financial and political gain. Even as they regarded the Geneva nuclear deal as far from being what it should be, however, critics seemed to be generally resigned to the notion that the accord, if implemented with some "fixing," could help ease an ominous nuclear threat on the Korean peninsula.[18]

The Current Status of the Geneva Nuclear Deal

In late November 1994, North Korea announced that it had frozen its nuclear reactor program and went on to reaffirm its pledge to implement the Geneva accord. In January 1995, it also announced the lifting of "restrictions on the import of U.S. commodities and the ban on the entry of U.S. trading ships into North Korean ports." For its part, the United States delivered 50,000 tons of heavy fuel oil to the North aboard two non-American tankers; and President Clinton signed an executive order lifting a few of the barriers to U.S. trade with the North, but leaving untouched "about 99 percent" of the legal restrictions in place since the Korean War. The remaining barriers could be eventually lifted, depending on how North Korea deals with issues of concern to Washington such as North-South dialogue, human rights, and exports of missiles to the Middle East.[19]

These promising steps were not matched, however, by similar progress on the light-water reactor issue, as North Koreans balked at the idea of receiving "South Korean standard-model" LWRs.[20] North Korea threatened to walk away from the Geneva deal—and to resume its nuclear activities rather than being "forced" to accept South Korean reactors of unknown quality. Pyongyang asserted that:

- South Korean LWRs cannot provide "a technological guarantee for safety," as they have not been manufactured yet for test or for export; hence the United States cannot force an unproven "ghost" model on the North.
- South Korea has a "sinister" plot to use the LWR issue in a bid to "drive a wedge between the DPRK and the USA, refurbish [its] poor image and get the upper hand in North-South confrontation."
- U.S. support of the "South Korean puppets who have nothing to do with the implementation" of the Geneva accord not only violates the spirit of the accord but also amounts to a challenge to Pyongyang's "magnanimity and good will."
- "Regrettably," the United States is double-dealing, expressing "understanding" at the negotiating table, and doing "an irrelevant business behind the scene."[21]

Pyongyang bristles at U.S. and South Korean suggestions that its "principled stand" is actually a brinkmanship move designed to extract more concessions. However, in the period leading up to the Geneva agreement in October 1994, North Korean diplomats are said to have "made quite clear that they would accept South Korean reactors." According to U.S. Ambassador Gallucci, "this issue was raised, discussed and, I would argue, disposed of in our negotiations."[22] On the other hand, North Korean ambassador to the United Nations Pak Gil Yon is quoted as having "vigorously denied" that North Korea had ever agreed to South Korean reactors. In an interview, Pak reportedly made "very clear" what Pyongyang's position had been on the issue: "Selection of the South Korean-type of reactor is a violation of the Geneva agreed framework."

North Korea's anti-Seoul stance was also mirrored in its refusal to deal with, let alone recognize, "any organization the objective of which is to provide the South Korean model." This was an allusion to the KEDO that was formally launched on March 9, 1995, in New York, under an executive board consisting of three "original members"—the United States, South Korea, and Japan. The charter setting up KEDO specified that this consortium would finance and supply two LWRs of "the Korean standard nuclear plant model," provide for the supply of interim energy alternatives, and also provide for the implementation of "any other measures deemed necessary to accomplish the foregoing or otherwise to carry out the objectives of the Agreed Framework."

Under the Agreed Framework, an LWR supply contract was to have been concluded between KEDO and North Korea by the target date of April 21, 1995, but nothing came of it due to Pyongyang's objection to the South Korean model. The dispute was finally resolved through U.S.-DPRK negotiations held in the Malaysian capital of Kuala Lumpur, May 19 to June 12, 1995. Under the compromise Joint Statement announced on June 13, the negotiators skirted the touchy subject of the South Korean model by agreeing that the LWR model, to be selected by KEDO, would be an "advanced version of U.S.-origin design and technology currently under production." They also agreed that the United States would serve "as the principal point of contact" with North Korea, that KEDO delegations and teams would be headed by American citizens, that KEDO would select a prime contractor for the LWR project, that an American firm would serve as "program coordinator" to assist KEDO in supervising overall implementation of the project, and that the program coordinator would be selected by KEDO. North Korea pledged to conclude a supply agreement at the earliest possible date and to meet with KEDO as soon as possible to negotiate "the [unspecified] outstanding issues of the LWR supply agreement."

The possible crisis over the LWR issue has been defused, for now at least, under the compromise. North Korea gloated about the outcome of the Kuala Lumpur talks, claiming that it successfully exercised the right to choose the model it wanted. For its part, the Clinton administration assured Seoul that to all intents and purposes the reference model referred to in the Joint Statement was South Korea's "Ulchin reactors Nos. 3 and 4" and that South Korea would play "a central role" in the LWR project. Nevertheless, even as South Korea endorsed the Joint Statement, there was no public celebration in Seoul, given the South Korean perception of the certainty that North Korea would try to undercut Seoul's role by dealing exclusively with the U.S. side.[23]

North-South Dialogue

When to dialogue, what to discuss, and on whose terms has always been contentious, as dialogue itself has been at once a form and a substance of inter-Korean confrontation. By training and temperament, North and South Koreans are more accustomed to the rules of "playing safe" than to the uncertain ramifications of conciliation and compromise.[24]

South Korean Approach

South Koreans maintain that even under the new regime of Kim Jong Il, the North has not abandoned the late Kim Il Sung's agenda for undermining and eventually communizing the South. They are quick to recall numerous instances since the 1960s of Pyongyang's anti-South activities, including attempted assassinations, guerrilla infiltration, kidnappings, espionage, hostile propaganda, and terrorism. They are irked by Pyongyang's continued vilification of the South, despite its 1991 pledge not to do so, or to meddle in South Korean internal affairs. As if to confirm the veracity of Seoul's contention, Pyongyang continues to incite South Koreans to "overthrow" their "fascist" regimes[25]; to that end, the North continues to maintain a clandestine anti-South–anti-U.S. organization now called the "Korean National Democratic Front" but known until mid-1985 as the ostensibly South Korea–based "Revolution and Reunification Party" (actually located in the North).

While rejecting Pyongyang's repeated efforts to make Seoul nervous by broaching political and military issues, South Korea has proposed incremental "small steps" for family reunion; postal, telecommunication, and cultural exchanges; and trade and economic exchanges and cooperation. These steps are supposed to foster a neighborly relationship that would be conducive to peaceful coexistence and would lead to the resolution of thorny political and military issues in later stages.

North Korean Approach

North Korea is wary of South Korea's "small-step" approach, aimed at promoting cross-border humanitarian and economic contacts. It has scoffed at Seoul's approach as a "politically impure" and time-consuming scheme that would only prolong the "agony of division" and thereby serve America's "two-Koreas" policy. Therefore, it has sought to concentrate on military and political issues with a view to eventually denying South Korea the U.S. military presence that Pyongyang believed decidedly tipped the balance of power in Seoul's favor. In Pyongyang's judgment, a South Korea freed of American troops would be like a "house of cards" or a North Korea–friendly political environment. To that end, North Korea continues to urge South Koreans to press for the withdrawal of U.S. troops, to pressure their government to abrogate its national security law, and to allow South Koreans of all persuasions to freely participate in Pyongyang-sponsored mass rallies for unification. These demands are viewed in Seoul as a prescription for political destabilization, a familiar united front ploy since the 1960s designed to isolate South Korean authorities and brand them as "anti-unification and anti-Korean puppets" beholden to the United States.

Pyongyang's diametrically opposed agenda can be attributed to its fears that cross-border contacts with the South would expose the North to the potential hazards of infectious capitalist/democratic influences from the South. The fears are spawned by Pyongyang's jolting discovery in 1972 (when a North Korean delegation for the first time went to Seoul for a historic North-South dialogue) that South Korea was economically robust and prosperous, a far cry from Pyongyang's propaganda that had portrayed the South as "a living hell." Pyongyang's rude awakening coincided with then-emerging indications of what was to become a steady downturn of the North Korean economy. Most tellingly, Pyongyang turned suddenly silent about its post–Korean War overtures to the South for economic exchanges and cooperation. In August 1973, it broke off dialogue with Seoul; and its 1974 proposal to Washington for direct talks on security issues on the Korean peninsula turned out to be Kim Il Sung's major political statement about his intentions to end-run South Korea and eventually to destabilize it by driving a wedge between Washington and Seoul (see "North Korea's Grand Strategy," below).

Inter-Korean Nexus after Kim Il Sung

Long before Kim Il Sung's death in July 1994, absent in inter-Korean relations was a language of civility. The situation has become even more testy since his death. Optimistically, it could have been different had Kim Il Sung not died before he could have met with South Korea's Kim Young Sam in a truly historic inter-Korean summit slated for late July 1994. By sheer force of his personality, the North Korean leader could have moved the North toward a more neighborly agenda. That would have entailed a retreat from his self-serving creed that South Korea was his "internal affair" and that therefore he had a moral obligation to support South Koreans' antifascist and anti-American "revolutionary struggle."[26] Realistically, though, a more likely outcome would have been Kim Il Sung's attempt to sell his scheme of unification to South Korea and to urge South Koreans to become more "independent" in dealing with inter-Korean affairs, i.e., to rid the South of U.S. military presence.[27]

Will the successor regime of Kim Jong Il be able to make a break with the past and meet the South halfway? Its recent answer was ambivalent: "no" to any dialogue with the current Kim Young Sam administration; but, "yes" if his administration met the following three preconditions:

- "Traitor" Kim Young Sam must "apologize" for his "antinational crime" of not having allowed South Koreans to express condolences at Kim Il Sung's death. (Lately, Pyongyang seems to have toned down on this demand.)
- The "puppet" regime must revoke its National Security Law.[28]
- South Korea should repatriate to the North three "unconverted prisoners" of conscience from the Korean War who refuse to renounce communism and loyalty to the North Korean regime.[29]

From Seoul's perspective, the first two of these are volatile issues that, if mishandled, could be politically perilous for Kim Young Sam. In any case, if Pyongyang has its way, the dialogue would be confined to unification issues per se—and hence its contention that the Geneva accord and "North-South dialogue" are unrelated issues.[30] Of course, such contention flies in the face of Ambassador Robert Gallucci's testimony before the U.S. Senate that "steps towards improving North-South relations, as specified in the Agreed Framework, will be an important factor, both in resolving the nuclear issue and in serving these broader goals" (such as regional stability and prosperity).

Prospects

In 1984, the *New York Times* carried a story on the United States' current attitude toward North Korea, which included the following comments:

- There is no country in the world that is held in lower esteem by the Reagan administration than North Korea, State Department officials said today. . . . North Korea has a brutal, repressive government that continually schemes through a mixture of threats, terrorist actions and occasional conciliatory gestures to put an end to the pro-Western South Korean Government. . . . The United States has no diplomatic relations with North Korea and is not interested in having any, officials said.[31]

In a measure of how the times and political climate have changed, the United States and North Korea are currently moving toward establishing "liaison offices" in each other's capitals, as stipulated in the Geneva accord. The two countries have also started taking steps toward improving their political and economic relations. These signs augur well for the future of U.S.-DPRK relations per se, but not necessarily for U.S.-ROK relations, nor for Pyongyang-Seoul relations, which have been virtually frozen since the death of Kim Il Sung.

Since the Geneva accord, South Korea has announced measures aimed at promoting North-South economic cooperation. In early November 1994, for example, South Korean President Kim Young Sam made a significant overture toward the North by lifting the old ban on business investment in the North and by simplifying procedures for North-South trade, which, despite official restrictions, had been steadily rising from $1 million in 1983 to nearly $250 million in 1994.[32]

North Korea spurned the overture as an insidious attempt to mask the dark designs of the [South Korean] puppets for national division and total confrontation. The rebuff has not slowed the brisk pace of inter-Korean trade, nor has it affected Pyongyang's apparent desire to induce South Korean private investment into the Rajin-Sonbong free trade zone and other areas, without allowing any South Korean government involvement. Such private-sector-only investment would, of course, dampen the prospect for the intergovernmental-level negotiations that South Korea says would be necessary to address such technical issues as investment guarantee, taxation, exchange rates, and the safety of visiting South Korean businessmen.

North Korea's Grand Strategy

Pyongyang seems to concede, for now, that South Korea is way ahead in economic and military terms (assuming continued U.S. military presence in the South). This explains why the North wants to stiff-arm the South, aware that the South has the advantage over the North. Thus the North continues to pursue its post-1974 strategy, which is designed to undercut the South Korean power structure by dealing with Washington. In fact, if the DPRK foreign ministry statement of July 25, 1994, is any clue, Pyongyang seemed to unwittingly confirm the existence of a "Washington-first–Seoul-later" approach, which is expected to lead to what the foreign ministry called "a decisively favorable phase in North-South relations." Pyongyang envisions that such a commanding position will emerge from "a practical improvement" in the DPRK-U.S. relations.[33]

Pyongyang's "America-first" strategy seems likely to derive from the following assumptions:

- that the Geneva accord represents the convergence of U.S.-DPRK interests over the nuclear issue and that, therefore, implemented in good faith, the Geneva nuclear deal would foster confidence building and dissolve "hostile relations" between the North and the United States;
- that, as a result, the United States could be persuaded to eventually withdraw from South Korea; and

- that the withdrawal would lead to "a decisively favorable phase" in Pyongyang's campaign to gain the high ground over Seoul in a bid to stage-manage South Korean affairs without U.S. interference.

What the North might do in the "decisively favorable phase" raises a number of questions. On a pessimistic note, would Pyongyang try another crack at unification in the 1990s by "guns," to quote from Vice Marshal Choe Kwang's December 23, 1993, rhetorical bombast?[34] Would Pyongyang follow through on its March 1994 threat to turn Seoul into "a sea of flames"? Or would North Korea go for a low-risk civil strife that could make it difficult for Seoul and Washington to invoke their mutual defense treaty against the North?

Optimistically, the "favorable" phase could put the North in a position to press its case for Kim Il Sung's 1980 formula for unification under "a democratic confederation" of the two "regionally autonomous Korean governments." The confederation scheme may not be acceptable to Seoul in its present formulation, but it has a fighting chance if certain changes are made in its structure and platform.

Realistically, the "decisively favorable" turn of events may not materialize as long as Pyongyang refuses to deal with Seoul on neighborly terms—assuming, of course, that South Korean authorities would have a less condescending attitude toward and a healthier respect for North Korea's capacity for craftiness and opportunism. A North Korea bent on a "my way or no way" agenda seems certain to be frustrated in its quest for political, economic, and security dialogue with neighbors. Then North Korea might decide to turn the tables on South Korea, the United States, and the international community by denying the IAEA request for special inspections. Whereupon, confronted with KEDO's predictable refusal to provide the core components for LWRs, the North could revive the argument that the two nuclear waste sites are "military facilities" not subject to IAEA inspections, and could threaten to restart its nuclear activities if the core components are withheld. Pyongyang could also argue that continued U.S. military presence in the South was contrary to the U.S.-DPRK pledge in Geneva to "work together for peace and security on a nuclear-free Korean Peninsula."[35] Conceivably, depending on how the United States responds to Pyongyang's brinkmanship, which was honed to perfection during the 1993–94 standoff over the nuclear issue, the following scenarios can be anticipated:

- Pyongyang could announce its intention to withdraw from the NPT several years down the road, without repudiating the Agreed Framework.
- North Korea could try to leverage the "special inspections" issue to bargain for a peace treaty with Washington, a treaty with an annexed timetable for U.S. withdrawal from the South—possibly a few years after the completion of the LWR project.
- When and if Washington signs the treaty, South Korea—still without substantive breakthroughs in relations with the North— would probably have to brace for U.S. withdrawal from the South in exchange for Pyongyang's full compliance with IAEA special inspections.
- However, in the event that South Korea, the United States, Japan, and the IAEA chose not to make an issue of Pyongyang's refusal to allow special inspections, U.S. military presence in the South would probably continue.
- Either way, North Korea would have received two light-water reactors, heavy fuel oil, and other diplomatic and economic benefits for having shipped fuel rods out of the North and dismantled its nuclear facilities.
- However, South Korea, which would have provided a substantial portion of financing for the $4 billion-plus LWR project, would have to contribute more toward the maintenance of U.S. forces in the South, on top of its nagging concerns about Pyongyang's secrecy over its nuclear "past."

Whatever the outcome of triangular relations, North Koreans could arguably be as insecure in 2005 as in 1995. To be sure, there could be more trading and more controlled economic cooperation and exchanges with South Korean and other nations. By 2005, North Koreans could be perhaps even better off by tapping into Japanese money, goods, and technology, and yet could remain prisoners of a repressive and politically "closed" system. Worse yet, a North Korea suspected of hiding nuclear arms would remain an outcast—and that situation in and of itself would continue to be worrisome to its neighbors.

Implications for the Korean Triangle

The two Koreas have something in common to strive for: peace and security on their peninsula. But their motives being as mutually exclusive as their means of achieving peace and security, their chances for an early accommodation appear to be very slim. South Korea, victimized by Kim Il Sung's surprise invasion in 1950, sees peace and security essentially in terms of constant vigilance, a strong defense buildup, a robust market democracy, and continued U.S. military presence in the South. Essentially, it would like the status quo on the Korean peninsula to continue. For its part, North Korea sees the equation differently, as achieving peace and security will ultimately require the withdrawal of U.S. forces from the South; it sees the U.S. military presence as tilting the inter-Korean balance of power in favor of the South. North Korea would like nothing better than a South Korea freed of U.S. troops for a radical change in its security environment. What makes the inter-Korean situation so volatile is the uncertainty of North Korean intentions toward the South. Ironically, that uncertainty, more than anything else, seems responsible for continued U.S. military presence in the South.

It seems highly improbable that Pyongyang will ever sue for peace with Seoul, except on its own terms. An insecure Pyongyang is trying to leverage its nuclear card to secure the high ground over Seoul and Washington. Evidently, since the Agreed Framework of 1994, the North seems to have become emboldened to a point where it believes it could write its own rules for dealing with the South and the United States. A case in point is Pyongyang's strategic decision to deal with Washington on substantive issues affecting even South Korea. Pyongyang appears confident that its "take-it-or-leave-it" approach to the nuclear issue could force Washington to side with the North if only to save the Geneva nuclear deal and—more to the point, that South Korea could be sacrificed on the altar of the Clinton administration's NPT agenda. Left unchallenged, Pyongyang's self-conceit could pose, several years down the road, a major challenge to peace, denuclearization, and triangular cooperation on the peninsula.

South Korea's security dilemma seems likely to continue in the foreseeable future, given its relative lack of physical power resources. Without U.S. forces in the South, it is arguable whether Seoul could ever provide security for itself. Washington, therefore, is faced with two Koreas that, at least in the short run, need the United States in order to maintain themselves—North Korea by freezing its nuclear program and South Korea by playing a significant LWR role and by bearing a larger share of costs for U.S. troops in the South.[36] The

Korean triangle seems assured of at least ten years of "Cold Peace" through 2005, assuming that North Korea will not resort to a new round of a "crisis diplomacy" aimed at extracting more financial, economic, or political concessions.

It took Pyongyang twenty years to get to where it is today—in a position to deal with the United States over South Korea's head—and hence the likelihood is that Pyongyang will not walk away from the Geneva accord. Should Pyongyang decide to renege on the Geneva accord, could it get a better, new deal from Washington? It might do this by forcing the Clinton administration to revisit the summer of 1994; but then, it might not do it, if Republicans in Congress have their way. In any case, if a new deal is to be worked out, Pyongyang seems certain to face a more patient Washington—and this time, the chances are that South Korea might become more assertive in trying to protect its own financial and security stakes in the uncertain triangular quest for a denuclearized Korea.

Notes

1. In postarmistice statements on July 27, 1953, South Korean President Syngman Rhee declared, inter alia, "I have opposed the signing of the truce because of my conviction that it will prove to be the prelude to more war, not less; to more suffering and ruin; to further Communist advances by war and by subversion," but "we [do not] intend to obstruct its implementation."

2. The latest proposal broke the North's pledge under the historic December 1991 inter-Korean basic agreement that the Kim Il Sung regime would "endeavor together [with the South] to transform the present state of armistice into a solid state of peace" and "abide by the present Military Armistice Agreement until such a state of peace has been achieved."

3. Reference to "a new peace guarantee system" appears for the first time, without elaboration, in a DPRK foreign ministry proposal on April 28, 1994. According to a George Washington University study group visiting Pyongyang in January 1995, North Koreans explained this new system to mean "an interim arrangement that is something between the present armistice and a peace agreement."

4. "Establishment of New Peace Mechanism Is Urgent," *Minju Choson* [Pyongyang], January 23, 1995, as cited by Pyongyang's [North] *Korean Central News Agency* (hereinafter cited as *KCNA*), January 23, 1995. The allusion to a "[U.S.] promise at [sic] talks and meetings with the DPRK" is suggestive of possible discussions that could have taken place on the armistice since the summer of 1994. When questioned, a senior U.S. government official denied the existence of any "promise," while acknowledging that the North Korean side repeatedly pressed the issue.

5. In pleading for a new peace system, North Korea is certain to invoke the

part of the Geneva accord that reads, "Both sides will work together for peace and security on a nuclear-free Korean peninsula." This can be inferred from its threat to scrap the accord if the United States and South Korea renewed their joint Team Spirit military exercise in 1995; Pyongyang contended that such exercise amounted to "a rehearsal for nuclear attack" on North Korea. For the latest North Korean restatements, see the DPRK foreign ministry memorandum entitled "A Peace Guarantee System Must Be Established without Delay on the Korean Peninsula," *Minju Choson*, June 30, 1995; "There Is No Change in Our Stand," *KCNA* in English, August 4, 1995; and "Foreign Ministry Spokesman on S. Korea's 'Idea of Peace Mechanism'," *KCNA*, August 14, 1995.

6. *Dong-A Ilbo* [Seoul], January 8, 1995.

7. *Yonhap* News Agency [Seoul] in English, October 19, 1994. In July–August 1995, South Korea was mulling over an option for a four-way meeting of the two Koreas with the United States and China; see *Kyonghyang Sinmun* [Seoul], August 3, 1995. North Korea rejected Seoul's latest idea as "a trick to hinder the establishment of DPRK-proposed new peace mechanism" (*KCNA* in English, August 14, 1995).

8. Seoul is said to be exploring all options, including a more "independent stance toward the United States." See *Seoul Sinmun* [Seoul], January 9, 1995.

9. Pyongyang's insecurity is derived from several developments: the withdrawal of Chinese "people's volunteers" from the North by late 1958; a power grab by generals in Seoul in a May 1961 coup (two months later, Kim Il Sung hurried to Moscow and Beijing to sign mutual defense treaties); deterioration of Sino-Soviet relations in the early 1960s; and Soviet Premier Nikita Khrushchev's "retreat" in the October 1962 Cuban missile crisis (Pyongyang seemed to have viewed the retreat as portending a similar Soviet retreat in a future Korean crisis involving the United States, North Korea, and the Soviet Union). In December 1962, North Korea enunciated a new military doctrine aimed at turning the North into a self-reliant garrison state.

10. Apparently, the nuclear program in question was designed to deal with unsettling prospects over South Korean security, prompted by two major developments: reports out of Beijing in 1975 that Chinese officials had cautioned Kim Il Sung not to launch an attack on South Korea, at the time of Kim's sudden visit to Beijing only days before the fall of Saigon in April; and the uncertainty of having to fend for itself after Jimmy Carter's 1976 campaign pledge to pull U.S. troops out of South Korea.

11. For in-depth analyses of the nuclear issue, see Larry A. Niksch, *North Korea's Nuclear Weapons Program* (Washington: Library of Congress, Congressional Research Service, updated regularly), CRS Issue Brief 91141; and Richard P. Cronin (with the assistance of Violet Jie Moore), *North Korea: U.S. Policy and Negotiations to Halt Its Nuclear Weapons Program, An Annotated Chronology and Analysis* (Washington: Library of Congress, November 18, 1994), CRS Report 94–905 F.

12. Robert Gallucci, chief U.S. negotiator, in testimony before the Subcommittee on East Asian and Pacific Affairs, the Senate Committee on Foreign Relations, December 1, 1994.

13. The time frame—1994–2000, 2000–2003, 2003–2005—is adapted from Gary Mihollin's statement before the Subcommittee on East Asian and Pacific Affairs, the Senate Committee on Foreign Relations, December 1, 1994, p. 10.;

and "LWR Project and Special Inspections Due for Completion by 2003," *Hanguk Ilbo* [Seoul], October 21, 1994.

14. According to U.S. sources, the two reactors, once operational, would have been able to produce "hundreds of kilograms of plutonium by the end of this decade," enabling the North not only to build a substantial stockpile of nuclear weapons but also become a plutonium exporter.

15. References to "a leading role," "a central role," or "KEDO" are not expressly contained in the Geneva Agreed Framework; they are taken from Ambassador-at-Large Robert Gallucci's December 1, 1994, testimony before the Senate Subcommittee on East Asian and Pacific Affairs.

16. North Korea interprets this point more expansively than the United States; it can be argued that several years down the road the North would invoke this point in refusing to allow "special inspections" and in seeking U.S. withdrawal from the South.

17. For reports on supportive views, see George Perkovich, "The Korea Precedent," *Washington Post*, September 28, 1994, p. A23; Jim Mann, "U.S. Deal with N. Korea Averts Riskier Alternatives," *Los Angeles Times*, October 20, 1994, p. 1; Jessica Mathews, "A Sound Beginning with North Korea," *Washington Post*, October 21, 1994, p. A25; Michael Kramer, "A Tough, Smart Deal," *Time*, October 31, 1994, p. 34; Merrill Goozner, "U.S. Effort With N. Korea Worth the Risk," *Chicago Tribune*, October 23, 1994, pp. 1, 7; Peter D. Zimmerman, "Win-Win with North Korea," *Christian Science Monitor*, November 21, 1994, p. 18; and William J. Perry, "Korea: The Deal Is Working," *Washington Times*, January 24, 1995, p. A17.

18. For reports on critical views, see Robert S. Greenberger, "U.S. Will Sign Korean Nuclear Accord Amid Skepticism of Agreement's Value," *Wall Street Journal*, October 19, 1994, p. A4; "Nuke Ransom for Pyongyang: A Poor Cause for Euphoria," *Korea Herald* [Seoul], October 20, 1994, p. 6; "Clinton Blinks: North Korea Rewarded for Its Nuclear Intransigence," *Far Eastern Economic Review* [Hong Kong], November 3, 1994, p. 5; Albert Wohlstetter, " 'Breakthrough' in North Korea"? *Wall Street Journal*, November 4, 1994, p. 6; Caspar W. Weinberger, "The Appeasement of North Korea," *Forbes*, November 21, 1994, p. 35; Richard V. Allen and Daryl N. Plunk, "Salvaging the Inadequate North Korea Agreement," *Washington Times*, December 30, 1994, p. A17; and Paul D. Wolfowitz, "Lifeline to North Korea?" *Washington Post*, February 21, 1995, p. A15.

19. For initial steps taken by both sides, see U.S. Department of State, Office of the Spokesman, "Easing Sanctions against North Korea," January 20, 1995 (memorandum); the Korea Society–Washington Office, *The U.S.-Korea Review*, III, No. 1, January–February 1995, pp. 6–8; R. Jeffrey Smith, "Clinton Slightly Lowers Some Bars to U.S. Trade with North Korea," *Washington Post*, January 21, 1995, p. A11; James Sterngold, "North Korea Reports Fulfilling a Nuclear Vow," *New York Times*, November 21, 1994, p. A5; Kate Webb, "N.K. to Lift Curbs on U.S. Imports, Port Calls," *Korea Herald*, January 10, 1995, p. 1.

20. Pyongyang seems to be angling for more aid through a self-serving interpretation of the scope of the LWR project; a case in point was its new demand during U.S.–North Korean talks in Berlin, in early February 1995, for additional assistance worth up to $1 billion. See R. Jeffrey Smith, "N. Korea Seeks More

Aid under Nuclear Agreement," *Washington Post*, February 8, 1995, p. A24; and also "North Korean Demands Puzzle U.S. Negotiators," *Washington Post*, September 23, 1994, p. A32.

21. North Korean foreign ministry spokesman, "Even if DPRK-U.S. Agreed Framework Collapsed, We Would Have Nothing to Lose or Fear," *KCNA*, March 10, 1995; also, "Destiny of DPRK-U.S. Agreed Framework Depends on U.S. Attitude," *KCNA*, March 10, 1995.

22. Steven Greenhouse, "U.S. Presses North Korea to Accept Reactors Made by South," *New York Times*, March 10, 1995, p. A11.

23. Pyongyang seems determined to marginalize South Korea in an attempt to undercut the latter's potentially significant technological presence in the North through the LWR project; Pyongyang seems to worry that the South may bring destabilizing influences to bear on the North, which is economically drained and faces a major problem of "food insecurity." According to South Korean estimates, some 1,200 South Korean specialists may have to stay on to help North Koreans run LWRs, even after the project is completed. See *Yonhap* News Agency, October 19, 1994. Sooner or later, Pyongyang may demand that KEDO or Washington arrange for a payment of billions of dollars, as compensation for North Korea's research and development connected with its "graphite" nuclear reactors designed to generate electrical power. See R. Jeffrey Smith, "North Korean Demands Puzzle U.S. Negotiators," *Washington Post*, September 23, 1994, p. A32. If North Korea has its way, its request for compensation may eventually add up to tens of billions of dollars.

24. See Rinn-Sup Shinn, *North Korea: Policy Determinants, Alternative Outcomes, U.S. Policy Approaches* (Washington: Library of Congress, Congressional Research Service, June 24, 1993), CRS Report 93–612F; and Rinn-Sup Shinn and Robert Sutter, *South Korea under Kim Young Sam: Trends, Nuclear and Other Issues* (Washington: Library of Congress, Congressional Research Service, July 27, 1994), CRS Report 94–599F.

25. "Kim Young Sam Traitorous Group Must Be Overthrown at Once," *Nodong Sinmun* [Pyongyang], November 10, 1994, as cited by *KCNA*, November 10, 1994.

26. For Pyongyang's consistent argument, see "It is Our Legitimate Duty as the Same Nation to Support the South Korean People's Struggle," *Nodong Sinmun*, April 26, 1974.

27. As used by Pyongyang, the term "independence," or *chaju,* is a North Korean code word for South Korean "national liberation" from U.S. occupation of the South.

28. Some South Korean analysts argue that if the national security law is abrogated for "unavoidable reasons," South Korea may have to temper the pace of democratization in the face of a potential upswing in pro–North Korean left-wing activities.

29. In 1993, the Kim Young Sam administration repatriated one such "unconverted" prisoner, anticipating that Pyongyang would reciprocate by returning some of 429 South Koreans known to be still in North Korean detention. South Korean pleas on twenty-two occasions since 1980 for the repatriation of these prisoners remain unanswered, however. See *Korea Herald*, August 10, 1994.

30. For Pyongyang's typical argument, see "Implementing the DPRK-U.S.

Agreed Framework and North-South Dialogue Are Separate Matters," [North] Korean Central Broadcasting Network, February 8, 1995.

31. "U.S. Has Little Use for North Korea," *New York Times*, July 11, 1984, p. A10.

32. The nuclear deal opened the door for South Korean business groups to expand northward, enticed by the lure of cheap labor and new consumers. See "Let the Moneymaking Begin," *Newsweek*, October 31, 1994, p. 44.

33. *Pyongyang Times*, July 30, 1994, p. 8.

34. From a speech by Vice Marshal Choe Kwang, chief of the General Staff of the Korean People's Army and member of the Political Bureau of the Central Committee of the ruling Korean Workers (communist) Party, as cited by the Korean Central Broadcasting Network, December 23, 1993.

35. A DPRK foreign ministry spokesman's statement on August 20, 1994, sounds eerily prophetic about the certainty of "a special inspections crisis" looming several years down the road. It reads: "We will never allow the inspection of the military sites at the expense of our sovereignty in order to receive LWRs. . . . Another conflict cannot be avoided, if they [South Korean and Japanese authorities] continue trying to complicate matters, citing the 'special inspection' that we have never allowed and cannot allow in the future either, as a 'precondition' to the solution of the [nuclear] issue." See "We Do Not Recognize the Term 'Special Inspections,' " *Nodong Sinmun*, August 18, 1994; also " 'Special Inspections' Will Never Be Allowed," *Nodong Sinmun*, August 21, 1994; and *Pyongyang Times*, August 27, 1994, p. 8.

36. In this context, the U.S. role is variously referred to as "facilitator," "peacemaker," "honest broker," and "intermediary." Whatever its role, Washington is pivotally positioned to play "an important supporting role" in promoting inter-Korean reconciliation. For a conceptual framework for such a possibility, requiring "parallel, sequenced negotiations by the DPRK with both the United States and the ROK," see Scott Snyder, "Beyond the Geneva Agreement: A Framework for Achieving Reconciliation on the Korean Peninsula," *Asian Survey*, August 1995, pp. 699–710.

4

The Military Role of Asian Countries in the New Pacific Community of the 1990s

Edward A. Olsen and David Winterford

Asia's adjustment to the post–Cold War period is simultaneously tenuous and upbeat. The 1990s mark a decade that holds the potential for symbolizing a transition between the Cold War years in which American hegemony shaped the Asia-Pacific region, on the one hand, and a vision of the twenty-first century as the Pacific century, on the other hand. Clearly this prospect causes optimism in Asia, but it also generates considerable uneasiness as Asians contemplate a future in which they may not be assured of the kind of American leadership to which they have grown accustomed—sometimes reluctantly.

These mixed feelings in Asia are manifested in many aspects of regional affairs. This analysis will focus on one facet—the strategic context of Asia in the mid- to late 1990s, looking toward the twenty-first century. It is vital to note at the outset that Asian strategic affairs incorporate both the hard and the soft sides of strategy—military issues as well as geo-economic and assorted diplomatic matters. These issues will be examined here as a whole, but with special attention to their interrelationships.

The Cold War in Asia differed significantly from the Cold War in Europe. Because the differences influence the nature of the post–Cold War situation in Asia, they are worth assessing as the context for this analysis. For the most part, the U.S.-USSR Cold War had its roots in the ideological struggle between the two countries and the territorial impact those tensions had on Middle Europe and Eastern Europe.

Clearly, both Washington and Moscow had a Eurocentric focus throughout the Cold War. Nonetheless, the Cold War also shaped Asia's post–World War II milieu. The most direct manifestations were the spread of Marxist regimes and revolutionary movements to Asia. Events that traumatized the region—the Chinese revolution and the creation of two rival claimants to Chinese legitimacy; Korea's division at war's end, which yielded Asia's closest parallel to European confrontations through the Korean War; the postwar stalemate along the infamous Korean demilitarized zone (DMZ), which ranked with the Berlin Wall as a symbol of the Cold War; and the prolonged struggle in Indochina that devastated three nations—also inflicted lasting scars on American willingness to play an armed role in Asia. Less obvious but nonetheless real were the spread of U.S.-led containment arrangements that constructed a network of bilateral security ties and associated subregional pacts which partially supplemented the U.S. connections. Even less obvious were the ways much of Asia was drawn into the Cold War's web via the early Eurocentrism of U.S. policy. This Eurocentrism caused Washington to try to manipulate the decolonization process for the benefit of postwar European states that asserted a need for the economic reinforcement which the colonies could provide for Europe's revival.

Asia was definitely a party to the Cold War, but there was—with the exception of Korea—a spillover quality to the Asian theater of the Cold War. Just as it had during World War II, Asia took a back seat to Europe while the superpowers waged this peculiar form of "war." U.S. and Soviet policies usually were designed with Europe in mind and then applied generically to other areas—including Asia. Despite the derivative nature of these policies, Asia played an important supporting role in the Cold War; in addition, the two major "hot wars" within the Cold War (Korea and Vietnam) were Asian in origin and resolution, and the late Cold War economic dynamism of much of East Asia, which was a by-product of U.S. Cold War policies, contributed mightily to the Soviet Union's eventual collapse. The USSR simply could not bear the costs of competing militarily and economically against the United States and an array of strategic cohorts. Asia's "economic miracles" clearly composed a daunting proportion of the group that precipitated the Soviet Union's demise. In these terms, noncommunist Asia was on the winning side in the Cold War and shared in the victory.

When the Cold War ended in Europe, it was supposed to be over in

Asia too. In general it was, but the nagging remnant of the Cold War on the Korean peninsula and the persistence of three prominent communist regimes kept its overtones alive in the region well beyond its lifetime in the rest of the world. Of course, *the* Cold War—which is defined in U.S.-USSR terms—died with the Soviet Union, but a quasi–Cold War aura lingers in the region to haunt its efforts to move on to the post–Cold War era. In this context, the military role of significant Asian countries is undergoing a complex and uncertain transformation. The end of the global Cold War and the continuing and extraordinary economic dynamism of East and Southeast Asia are undermining decades-old security relationships, elevating new security relationships, and altering the calculus of peace and conflict in the region.

Powerful economies are being created throughout the region.[1] The four newly industrialized "tigers" (South Korea, Singapore, Taiwan, and Hong Kong) have averaged 6 percent annual growth for nearly 20 years; Japan has boomed and been transformed; China has been in "takeoff" mode since 1979; and most observers see Malaysia, Thailand, Indonesia, and perhaps Vietnam as the next "tigers."[2] The Asia-Pacific region "has become an engine of the global economy and a defining part of the post–Cold War international system."[3]

Economic factors are providing the driving force for regional optimism—and, perversely, also are providing a foundation for regional unease. While resurgent economies are producing regional economic interdependence,[4] rapid growth also facilitates sharply higher allocations to defense, raising troubling prospects of a rivalry for regional leadership and a regional arms race.[5] As the nations of East and Southeast Asia increasingly forge a coherent economic sphere, hitherto relatively contained subregional security issues have become of wider regional concern. This entire process is made more visible and more important by the disappearance of the need to contain the Soviet Union's influence in the region. Absent that central organizing principle, new dynamics revolving around an Asian balance of power have emerged as a surrogate theme.

The present analysis examines six key themes of the changing military role of Asian countries: (1) the impact of the end of the global Cold War on the Asia-Pacific strategic balance; (2) the impact of residual Cold War–like conditions in the region on post–Cold War strategic circumstances with particular attention paid to the Korean peninsula's version of the Cold War, its staying power, and its influence on other

Asian countries; (3) the contemporary threat perceptions of significant Asian military powers; (4) an assessment of the military balance of power among Asian states, and evaluation of domestic and international influences on that balance, and an estimate of likely trends in the dynamics of that balance; (5) prospects for strategic scenarios that might test the durability of the emerging balance of military power; and (6) an assessment of U.S. strategic options when confronted by the emerging military power balance and the likely consequences of those options for Asian states.

Post–Cold War Security Concerns

In the wake of the global Cold War, the strategic balance in the Asia-Pacific region experienced a profound shock due to the demise of the Soviet Union, the elimination of superpower competition, and a consequent reappraisal of the goals and missions of the United States. Three new regional developments are central to the unfolding post–Cold War security order. First, the most obvious yet most complex result of the end of the Cold War is the (re)emergence of more military actors in the region. The military prowess of Japan, China, India, and—prospectively—a unified Korea have altered the Cold War strategic balance. Second, old conflicts have resurfaced, involving competing territorial claims and subnational challenges to state integrity, and new conflicts have emerged—particularly conflicts over ownership of vital natural resources. Third, most regional actors now feel compelled to use their newfound wealth to enhance their defense capabilities in order to possess a means of dealing with possible regional contingencies and to reinforce their prestige commensurate with their prosperity. This has resulted in substantial defense buildups throughout the region, as many countries have been acquiring advanced air and maritime defense capabilities, including (for some) ballistic missiles or weapons of mass destruction. Each of these three developments will be examined briefly in turn.

Regional Military Leadership

One of the most enduring regional security concerns involves Japan's military capability and intentions. Under pressure from the United States to help in "burden sharing," Japan agreed to undertake maritime operations to a distance of 1,000 nautical miles, bringing it almost as far south as the Philippines. In global and regional terms, Japan has a large and very modern naval force, including nearly one hundred maritime combat aircraft, sixty-two principal surface combatants (including seven destroyers and fifty-five frigates), and seventeen submarines.[6] During 1993–94 the Maritime Self-Defense Force commissioned two more *Harushio*-class submarines (with two more being built), and two *Uzushio*-class have been retired. The first *Kongo*-class destroyer has been commissioned, armed with a Harpoon. Three more will be built. The last two (of six) *Abukuma*-class frigates have been commissioned.[7] Japan also is in the process of building several *Yukikaze*-class destroyers equipped with the *Aegis* system. Japan is modernizing its submarine fleet; is planning to acquire tanker aircraft to extend the range of its air coverage; and continues to debate the acquisition of "defensive" aircraft carriers.[8]

These illustrations of Japan's continuing defense modernization underline Tokyo's continuing security concerns. Although the Soviet Union has disappeared, Russian military might in the Far East is still seen by some Japanese defense analysts as formidable.[9] New threats are also seen emerging in the post–Cold War period. These include China's development of power projection capabilities, particularly in view of China's continuing rapid economic growth; North Korea's missile and nuclear programs; instability in Russia, China, and Korea; the risk of an influx of large numbers of refugees; and the potential blockading of vital sea lines of communication (SLOCs). Among these preoccupations with regional instability, the 1994 edition of the Defense Agency's annual White Paper gives priority to North Korea.[10] All these concerns serve to blunt the call for substantial cuts in Japanese defense spending and provide a new post–Cold War rationale for the Self-Defense Force. Japan's prudent national defense expectations were clearly displayed in a report prepared by an advisory panel appointed by Prime Minister Hosokawa. The title of the report is "The Modality of the Security and Defense Capability of Japan: The Outlook for the 21st Century," and it was delivered on August 12, 1994.[11]

While these considerations shape the contours of Japan's military posture, defense planners throughout the region, especially in China and South Korea, warily note each new calibration of Japanese military power. Indeed, South Korea's procurement acquisitions for a "360-degree defense" (that is, inclusive of threats from Japan) are now openly discussed in the international media.[12] Although Seoul's focus on Japan's potential armed threat stirred some controversy because these two countries are the United States' key allies in Asia and are not normally presumed to be potential adversaries, it actually is part of a broader phenomenon in South Korea. On the military side, the Republic of Korea (ROK) Ministry of National Defense (MND) highlighted what it calls "new military diplomacy" during Defense Minister Rhee Byong-tae's spring 1994 tour of Germany, Russia, and Japan, to draw a distinction between it and what MND sources referred at as its former "U.S.-only policy."[13] In turn, this approach is part of a broader diplomatic effort by Seoul to adapt to the post–Cold War era through economic and political diversification. This amounts to a South Korean version of Japan's long-standing comprehensive security doctrine that envisages a multifaceted form of security.[14] In keeping with that innovative approach, Seoul took the lead as an advocate of multilateral security venues in the form of a "mini-CSCE" for the Northeast Asian subregion based on the ASEAN Post-Ministerial Conference (PMC) security dialogue[15] and then elaborated on that idea by encouraging the development of a Northeast Asian security dialogue in the wake of the first meeting of the ASEAN Regional Forum (ARF).[16] In doing so, South Korea clearly acknowledged the shifting balance of power in Asia that compels Seoul to retain its American strategic safety net to bolster the ROK's defenses against North Korea's threat and to offset through skillful diplomacy the growing military power of Japan and China.

China's military modernization and its long-term plans for a blue-water navy have drawn more attention from regional and western analysts than Japan's continuing defense buildup.[17] The People's Liberation Navy commissioned the first *Luda*-class guided missile destroyer in 1971; it has been subsequently overhauled and fitted with ship-to-ship missiles, anti-submarine war (ASW) equipment, a satellite navigation system, and a helicopter deck. The navy has also completed the modernization of another *Luda* destroyer and now has at least four helicopter-equipped ships. In total, seventeen *Luda*-class ships have now been built. The first of a new class of larger destroyers, the *Luhu,* able to sail further and faster, has been commissioned. The development of frigates has similarly been relatively rapid. Of the 38 frigates in the fleet, the latest to enter service is the *Kaifeng* class of fully enclosed escorts.[18] This class is capable of operating in nuclear, biological, and chemical environments.

Another key priority is the strengthening of a major submarine force. Excluding about fifty nonoperational Romeo-class submarines, China has forty-six submarines, including one *Xia*-class strategic missile nuclear submarine (SSBN), five *Han*-class nuclear attack submarines (SSNs), one modified *Romeo* cruise missile conventional submarine (SSG), six improved *Ming* submarines, and thirty-three *Romeo* submarines. Reports now suggest that China has abandoned the construction of additional *Xia* SSBNs and, instead, is planning the development of a larger and more modern ballistic missile submarine. This new design was believed to be close to construction[19] although it has yet to materialize.[20] Meanwhile SSNs are slowly being launched at the rate of one every three years.[21] With the reduction in tensions between China and Russia,[22] most of China's new defense spending is being allocated to new weapons and upgrading of the navy and the air force. These decisions reflect China's new appreciation of its maritime interests and its new maritime strategy.[23] Beijing concluded a $1 billion agreement with Moscow for an initial acquisition of a squadron of twenty-four Su-27 advanced fighter aircraft[24]—an agreement which includes advanced weapons and logistical support.[25] Two more squadrons of Su-27s are on order, as well as two squadrons of Su-31 fighter interceptors. Reports indicate that the Su-27s are based in Shanghai and rotated through Hainan Island and will soon be able to provide air cover for the Chinese navy in the South China Sea, especially over the sensitive Spratly Islands region.[26] When fully deployed, China's Su-27s will decisively alter the military balance in Southeast Asia in favor of the People's Republic of China (PRC), as China will have an air capability encompassing all the region and indeed beyond to South Asia as well.[27]

Negotiations are also under way with Russia to purchase MiG-31 *Fox-Hound* interceptor fighters; agreements with Moscow are thought to include technology transfers allowing China to produce both Su-27 and MiG-31 interceptors.[28] The MiG-31s may eventually fit into a comprehensive air defense network China is reportedly seeking to purchase from Russia. Russian arms manufacturers are also believed to have offered Beijing the supersonic Tu-22M bomber, which would substantially increase China's power projection. The Tu-22M has a range of more than 4,000 kilometers, has air-refueling capabilities, and can carry heavy bomb and missile loads.[29] China has also expressed interest in acquiring *Kilo*-class submarines from Russia, as well as

Tu-26 *Backfire* bombers for long-range maritime strike operations. Their acquisition would greatly enhance China's capability to carry out military operations in East Asia, Southeast Asia, and South Asia.[30]

In the interim, extending the range of Chinese aircraft is a vital interest for the PRC's security. The navy must have maritime air power if it is to become an effective, three-dimensional force in East and Southeast Asia.[31] To support its naval operations China has placed top priority on air-to-air refueling capability. China is known to have acquired second-hand American mid-air-refueling technology from Iran.[32] China is also reported to have acquired air-to-air-refueling technology from Israel.[33] Using in-flight refueling will considerably lengthen the reach of China's fighter bombers. For example, in any operation in the Spratlys against Vietnam, the Philippines, or Malaysia during the next decade or so, China would have total air superiority.

All these developments have been analyzed with vigilance by defense planners from Taiwan to Thailand, with many regional actors believing it necessary to counter some of the new Chinese capabilities. Part of the regional unease stems from China's resistance to transparency, to making known the strategic purposes and potentials of its new capabilities.[34] Another concern is Beijing's continuing threats to invade Taiwan on the one hand, and its extensive claims to sovereignty and supremacy in the South China Sea on the other.[35] Finally, regional worries in East and Southeast Asia are spurred by fears of a potentially disastrous arms race between China and Japan in the early part of the twenty-first century, as each seeks to bolster its claim to regional leadership.[36] Underlying all these concerns is a long-term regional anxiety over China's traditional Sinocentric worldview and its potential impact on Beijing's ambitions to regain what Chinese often see as its proper place at the apex of a regional hierarchy. As if that were not sufficiently worrisome, Asians also are anxious about Japan's possible intention of establishing a Nipponcentric regional hierarchy, which seems all too reminiscent of Imperial Japan's grandiose schemes to create a "Greater East Asia Co-prosperity Sphere."

East and Southeast Asia also are becoming ever more aware of India as another potential emerging Asian power.[37] New Delhi's robust plans for military modernization have been scaled back in recent years, because India's economic crisis of the early 1990s quickly led to budgetary difficulties. Nevertheless, with its population rapidly nearing 1 billion and with major economic reforms being undertaken which expose the Indian economy to more vigorous competitive market forces, India is poised to join the ranks of Asia's fast-growing economies. It seems likely that the anticipated faster economic growth will permit the resumption of sustained higher defense spending, and indeed the process has already begun.[38] New Delhi remains committed to the acquisition of another aircraft carrier, and reports indicate that Russia has offered to sell India one of the Russian navy's three *Kiev*-class carriers. Moscow is also willing to sell India more *Kilo*-class submarines.[39] The Indian navy continues to press for more surface combatants and additional maritime aircraft.

New Delhi also continues to develop its naval and air facilities on the Andaman and Nicobar islands near the Malacca Straits. Perhaps coincidentally, China has extended its sphere of political, economic, and military influence to nearby Burma. Some regional analysts see a geopolitical rivalry for influence and dominance in post–Cold War Asia intensifying between India and China, with the first round of this contest most evident in Burma.[40] Indeed, significant and troubling Sino-Indian rivalry in the region seems certain, given China's access to naval and other facilities in Burma.[41] Chinese and Indian cross-regional interests clash in Burma, and a potential Sino-Indian naval rivalry in the area would have significant consequences not only for Southeast Asia's security[42] but for East Asia as well. The growing Chinese sphere of influence in Burma has prompted New Delhi to reassess its policy toward Rangoon and to utilize the new opportunities of the post–Cold War era to emphasize complementary interests between India and the United States,[43] between India and ASEAN,[44] and between India and Japan[45] in containing China's growing economic and military influence in the Asia-Pacific region. According to one observer, India's determination to develop a degree of regional dominance comparable to that of China "means that sometime early in the next century, New Delhi might slip into the role of the main counterweight to its giant neighbour."[46]

Amidst these Asian great power rivalries, the region also faces the prospect of a fledgling great power on the Korean peninsula after the two Koreas reunify. Ever since Korea's division at the end of World War II, Koreans in both halves of Korea have fervently wished for unification. Now that the superpower Cold War is over, North Korea has been made vulnerable by the loss of a major ally and by a weakened economy, and the controversial nuclear question is being resolved, it is increasingly possible that Korea will be reunified. The Korean people's fervent wishes may—at long last—come true. While this generally is welcomed, one should recall the saying, "Be careful about what you wish for, because it may come true." This is especially salient for the U.S.-ROK alliance.

The post–Cold War Korean situation is simultaneously a relic of the Cold War and a unique set of circumstances involving two states in one nation whose policies were shaped by the Cold War. Were Korea to reunite, both facets would end along with the end of Korea's Cold War. Whether Korea reunites through peaceful negotiations in parallel to the resolution of the contentious nuclear problem,[47] through the collapse of the beleaguered Democratic People's Republic of Korea (DPRK) economy, or through a gradual process of strategic attrition, the re-creation of one Korea is likely to be socially traumatic and economically costly. These factors are well known to Koreans in both halves of that nation, who worry about the significance of Germany's experiences. These geopolitical parallels are cause for some anxiety among Americans, too, because of the potential demands for support the Koreans may impose upon the United States either directly or as an intermediary in sanitizing Japan yen transfers to a united Korean government.[48]

Of equal concern are the possible serious consequences for the U.S.-ROK alliance and for the overall strategic posture of the United States in the Western Pacific. South Korea has been engaged in some contingency planning for that future environment through the efforts of President Kim Young Sam to develop a more multilateral approach toward regional security via—inter alia—the ASEAN Post-Ministerial Conference (PMC) Asian Regional Forum, the CSCA counterpart to the CSCE, and the MND's "new military diplomacy" cited previously

In a sense, these Korean moves are harmonious with the Clinton administration's partial shift toward greater security multilateralism based on a set of bilateral defense relationships the United States intends to retain in the region. The problem today is that American policy toward the Western Pacific region, and toward Korea, incorporates an essentially straight-line projection regarding a continued need for U.S. forces in Korea for the sake of Korean and regional stability. This approach clearly is logical for the short run in terms of reassuring South Korean allies and deterring potential North Korean adversaries. However, this approach is not well thought through with regard to the long-run circumstances that would surround a unified Korea.

As Americans, South Koreans, and Korea's neighbors in Asia look forward to a unified Korea after Korea's Cold War ends, there are several crucial questions that must be asked. Will Seoul expect the United States (and Japan) to help pay for unification? Are Americans (and Japanese) prepared for such expenses? What kind of political leadership will emerge from a united Korea? What will a united Korea's strategic interests be? Will it perceive any credible threats? If so, from whom? How will China, Russia, and Japan perceive a unified Korea in their midst? What will the indigenous East Asian balance of power look like after the Korean Cold War is terminated?

Regional Conflicts and the New Security Order

The termination of the global Cold War has significantly altered the strategic environment of the Asia-Pacific region. The Cold War American-devised system of bilateral security alliances in the Pacific region, coupled with the forward deployment of substantial American military personnel and materiel, was an effective response to Washington's assessment of the danger of Soviet expansionism. With the collapse of the Soviet Union, and the stunning reversal of fortunes for communism as a global ideology, the Cold War alignment of states has suddenly become considerably less cohesive and less predictable. For regional defense strategists a critical question must be "How relevant is a leftover Cold War era security structure for dealing with a struggle among Asian powers for regional hegemony in the post–Cold War years?"[49]

Perhaps one of the more surprising responses has been the reciprocal extension in East and Southeast Asia of the localized security horizon to encompass broader regional tensions.[50] Concerned over prospects for a substantial reduction in American commitment of military resources to the region—and therefore in any "buffer role" the United States might play in the region—and in view of the jockeying for regional leadership by Japan, China, and India, the ASEAN states have taken the lead in reaching out to their East Asian counterparts in broader security discussions and in formally institutionalizing an ongoing dialogue in the form of the ASEAN Regional Forum (ARF).[51] Both East and Southeast Asian countries now recognize the desirability of establishing such a regional framework to discuss security issues of common concern.[52] In effect, in the post–Cold War extended security environment, the distinction between "East Asian" and "Southeast

Asian" security issues has lost some of its subregional relevance.[53] This transition would be more thoroughgoing were it not for the determinedly "East Asian" cultural identities of China and Japan, and were it not for their condescending tendencies that arouse cross-regional suspicions in Southeast Asia.

As a consequence of these altered circumstances the new security reality in the Asia-Pacific region has led Asian actors to attempt to manage tensions through preventive diplomacy. However, the problem of China, the future roles of Japan and India, and the nexus of problems on the Korean peninsula can be managed—from the perspective of virtually all contemporary Asian leaders—only within the context of a wider Asia-Pacific security framework that also engages the United States.[54] Nevertheless, the problems involved in building and operating a new security framework—from both Asian and American perspectives—are taxing.[55] First, the region has existing "double-containment" bilateral security relationships between the United States and, for example, Japan and South Korea, which would seem to conflict with a multilateral security structure. Second, the region's well-known diversity in ideology, forms of government, culture, religion, language, and geography belies any easy application of a European-style security framework. Experience elsewhere suggests that security frameworks are more a product of consensus than of diversity and that such diversity could well frustrate collective action rather than permitting it. Third, given the central role accorded to the United States in contemporary regional security thinking, the undeniable ideological underpinnings of American foreign, defense, and international economic policies suggest enduring disputes between the United States and Asia's protected, relatively closed, and often repressive societies. Finally, the European experience in Bosnia indicates that conflict cannot be resolved unless there is agreement between the major actors, or unless their interests are threatened, or unless they are directly engaged. Conflicts between second-tier players which may threaten the security environment may not be readily addressed by a multilateral structure that depends on such major power activism.

On the other hand, some of the forces that had earlier reshaped the security environment in post–Cold War Europe now also seem to be at work in the Asia-Pacific region: the end of the Cold War has transformed perceptions and definitions of the "threat," and is reconfiguring key elements of regional actors' economic, national security, and regional strategic priorities. With attitudes toward communism no longer treated as the defining rod, Asian powers have been unleashed to pursue relations based on calculations of their national interest and their determination of the shifting balance of power in the region. They are no longer restricted to reactive options and are helping to reshape the rules of the game. For example, Indonesia, Brunei, and Singapore have all reestablished relations with China; South Korea has established diplomatic ties to Russia, China, and Vietnam; North Korea is exploring its diplomatic options vis-à-vis the United States and Japan; India has renewed its interest in Southeast Asia; and Taiwan has creatively used its role as a regional foreign investment powerhouse. Even Vietnam and the United States—despite the legacy of their bitter war—have taken a major step toward full diplomatic relations with the opening of liaison offices and an agreement to exchange diplomats.[56] All these examples serve to illustrate the flowering of national strategies in the looser and more unpredictable security environment created by the demise of the Cold War.

Part of the dynamic at work reflects the broad trends also refashioning economic relations in the region. Just as substantial economic interdependence in East and Southeast Asia has become a hallmark of the waning years of this century, so too have the security horizons of East and Southeast Asia become interdependent. In reality, across a range of matters at differing levels, Asia is caught up in an unfolding process of "Asianization,"[57] a process fed by a curious mixture of arrogance, optimism, and unease. Further reductions in America's military presence in the region, and a further erosion of America's relative economic importance to the region, promise to accelerate Asianization, although present conditions would seem to preclude its ultimate realization. Equally important, the post–Cold War era makes it possible to envision such a shift in the United States' regional engagement in terms that would have been considered unthinkable in the relatively inflexible Cold War years.

Part of the impetus for creating new Asian regional security structures stems right from the incomplete termination of the Cold War in Asia. Unlike in Europe, communism is not dead in Asia. With surviving communist regimes in China, North Korea, Laos, and Vietnam, the process of completely supplanting the "old order" of American-devised security arrangements with radically redesigned structures is likely to remain partially stalled. In effect, the Asia-Pacific region is still in a transitional phase and may well confront the turbulence of both continuing Cold War legacies and the new post–Cold War troubles centered on ethnic and religious strife, border disputes, and nationalist demands. Ironically, the continuation of the Cold War (albeit in an attenuated form without the Soviet Union as a threat) in the Asia-Pacific region may have perversely kept a lid for now on a potentially bubbling cauldron of problems in the region analogous to the graphic chaos of the Balkans in post–Cold War Europe.

The potential for strife and conflict from post–Cold War territorial disputes, ethnic conflicts, and challenges to sovereignty is very real. Many of these disputes had no genuine connection to the Cold War's roots and thus remain ongoing despite the end of the Cold War. The list of unresolved territorial disputes in East Asia is topped by the dispute between traditionally suspicious and militarily powerful neighbors, Russia and Japan, over the Kurile Islands.[58] Territorial disputes include those between Japan and Korea over the Liancourt Rocks in the Sea of Japan, and a recurring debate between Japanese and Korean nationalists over whether to call that body of water the Sea of Japan (*Nihonkai*) or the East Sea (*Tong hae*). Other important territorial disputes include frictions between Japan and China over the Senkaku Islands in the East China Sea; between China and India in the Himalayan border region; between China, Taiwan, Vietnam, Brunei, Malaysia, and the Philippines over the Spratly Islands; between China and Vietnam over the Paracels; between China and South Korea over territorial water borders, between China and Vietnam over border territories; between Vietnam and Malaysia over offshore borders; between the Philippines and Malaysia over Sabah; and between Malaysia and Indonesia over islands in the Celebes Sea.

Similarly, internal ethnic tensions and revolts continue to fester—the difficulties in the Philippines involving both communist and Muslim insurgents, the separatist movement in Sabah, the Bougainville secessionist movement in Papua, New Guinea, the resistance in East Timor to Indonesia rule, the Aceh independence movement in Sumatra, continuing conflict in Cambodia, and a series of ethnic rebellions in Burma, to name only some of the better-known challenges. Finally, and most durably from the Cold War, divided sovereignty disputes are of course the hallmark of the Korean peninsula and the China–Taiwan contestation.

Taken together, the spectrum of conflict is broad and its geographic reach sweeping in the Asia-Pacific region. Although many of these conflicts are unlikely to lead to interstate conflict—some will be resolved through protracted negotiation while others will remain internal matters—nevertheless the number of interstate disputes feeding mistrust, tension, and misunderstanding portend a region unlikely to remain tranquil. In fact, when those remaining outposts of the former Cold War (i.e., Korea and China–Taiwan) are actually resolved, it may no longer be possible to camouflage the end of the Cold War in ways that today help to keep a lid on other regional tensions.

It is noteworthy that many of the conflicts and sources of tensions noted above involve disputes over maritime boundaries and offshore territorial claims. These conflict issues are significant factors shaping the defense modernization programs now under way in East and Southeast Asia.[59] Taken together, regional concerns—the drawdown of American forces; the growth of Japanese, Chinese, and Indian naval powers; the requirements for building a sovereign defense capability; and the ability to pay for new weapons systems derived from the ongoing economic boom in most of the region—are all driving the requirement for greater maritime defense capabilities, including short- and long-range surface and submarine ships and advanced maritime reconnaissance aircraft. Simultaneously, they are also creating a regional demand for longer-range aircraft capable of projecting power great distances from national shores.

Moreover, new developments arising from the Third United Nations Conference on the Law of the Sea (UNCLOS III), including the promulgation of 200-mile Exclusive Economic Zones (EEZs) "has generated requirements for surveillance and power-projection capabilities over resource-rich areas which, for many states in the region, are greater than their land areas."[60] Indeed, throughout the region, security concerns increasingly address economic and environmental issues. Traditionally economic security has involved the protection of sea lines of communication. Now it is broadened to include the protection of fish stocks and other marine resources (especially real or potential oil and natural gas deposits).[61] Given the tremendous maritime-borne trade in the Asia-Pacific region, it is not surprising that very real concerns also exist over illegal activity, including piracy, smuggling, and unlicensed fishing.[62] Once again, this generates new requirements for maritime surveillance and enforcement capabilities.

Furthermore, environmental issues risk becoming an increasing source of interstate disputes. Southeast Asia has already had firsthand experience of major oil spills and other offshore pollution spilling over national boundaries, while acid rain spurred by China's rapid economic growth has become a matter of serious concern in Japan and elsewhere in East Asia.[63] Large-scale interstate population movements in response to environmental degradation cannot be ruled out, and promise to add to the pressure to acquire appropriate maritime policing and defense capabilities.[64]

Given the seemingly close nexus between stability and economic success, the eruption of these types of conflicts could well bring incalculable costs to Asia's economic dynamism. In reality, the basis for optimism in the region, derived from its stunning economic success, may rest on a troubling security foundation.[65] One of the consequences of economic success, namely, the ability to allocate ever greater resources to the acquisition of sophisticated weapons and other attributes of defense modernization, may at times exacerbate a sense of vulnerability and threat in neighbors, thereby further heightening the prospects for conflict.[66] Arms races, where they exist, are typically powered by two driving forces: security perceptions and the ability to acquire new weapons. It is too early to detect whether the region, or large parts of it, are entering the process of interactive arms acquisitions characteristic of an "arms race." Nevertheless, with its above-average economic growth, indeed startling growth in many cases, and given the new and old uncertainties over the contours of the new post–Cold War regional security order, it is not surprising that military expenditures in East and Southeast Asia register a comparatively high rate of growth.

Military Expenditures and Defense Modernization in the Asia-Pacific Region

By the mid-1990s, the Asia-Pacific region had undertaken sustained defense modernization and weapons acquisitions programs for over a decade. The end of the Cold War did not mark the end of this cycle. Indeed, in many countries in the region, the rate of military expenditures accelerated from the late 1980s to the present.

The noted Australian defense analyst, Desmond Ball, has commented that through the mid- and late 1980s, regional defense spending increased at an "unprecedented rate."[67] As Table 4.1 indicates, given the decline in defense spending in the United States, Europe, and

Table 4.1

Military Expenditures: World Shares and Growth (in percentages)

	World Share		Real Growth Rate	
	1981	1991	1981-91	1987-91
World	100.0	100.0	0.1	-3.7
Developed	79.9	76.7	0.1	-5.2
Developing	20.1	23.3	0.1	2.5
Region				
Africa	1.5	1.5	-1.1	-3.1
East Asia	*9.6*	*11.5*	*1.6*	*2.4*
Europe, all	54.7	47.0	-1.0	-6.4
NATO Europe	16.6	18.1	0.7	-0.2
Warsaw Pact	36.3	26.6	-2.0	-10.1
Other Europe	1.8	2.2	0.9	2.6
Latin America	1.5	1.5	-0.2	-4.7
Middle East	6.4	8.5	-0.9	9.3
North America	24.9	28.1	1.5	-4.0
Oceania	0.6	0.8	2.0	0.4
South Asia	0.7	1.1	4.7	-0.3
Organization				
NATO, all	41.4	46.2	1.2	-2.6
Warsaw Pact	36.3	26.6	-2.0	-10.1
OPEC	5.6	7.9	-0.7	10.6
OECD	45.3	51.6	1.4.	-2.2

Source: U.S. Arms Control and Disarmament Agency (ACDA), *World Military Expenditures and Arms Transfers 1991–92* (Washington, D.C.: U.S. ACDA, March 1994), p. 2.

the former Soviet Union since the end of the 1980s, this has resulted in a sharp jump in the Asian share of world military expenditures. The Middle East and East Asia are virtually alone in registering an increase in the real rate of growth of military expenditures.

Table 4.2 examines global and regional arms imports. As the data indicate, Asia's share of world expenditure on arms transfers rose from 9.8 percent in 1982 to 14.4 percent in 1991. This relative ranking would have been much higher in the absence of the Persian Gulf War, which distorts the picture for the Middle East. The largest importers in the Asia-Pacific region during the latter half of the decade were Vietnam, Japan, Taiwan, and South and North Korea.[68]

Given the widely differing economic profiles and security

Table 4.2

Arms Imports: World Shares and Growth (in percentages)

	World Share		Real Growth Rate	
	1981	1991	1981-91	1987-91
World	100.0	100.0	−6.9	−21.5
Developed	21.2	24.7	−5.5	−19.0
Developing	78.8	75.3	−7.2	−21.9
Region				
Africa	17.5	3.5	−18.4	−39.1
East Asia	*9.8*	*14.4*	*−3.2*	*−20.2*
Europe, all	19.5	16.1	−7.2	−24.4
NATO Europe	8.4	14.6	−0.7	−12.4
Warsaw Pact	10.0	0.9	−20.3	−52.2
Other Europe	1.1	0.6	−8.3	−35.6
Latin America	8.1	3.8	−11.4	−29.3
Middle East	35.9	41.4	−7.7	−18.6
North America	2.8	8.2	1.1	−10.8
Oceania	1.3	1.0	−2.9	−32.5
South Asia	4.9	11.4	4.4	−14.5
Organization				
NATO, all	11.1	22.8	−0.1	−11.8
Warsaw Pact	10.0	0.9	−20.3	−52.2
OPEC	32.4	36.7	−8.0	−16.5
OECD	14.8	27.5	−0.4	−13.2

Source: U.S. Arms Control and Disarmament Agency, *World Military Expenditures and Arms Transfers, 1991-92* (Washington, D.C.: U.S. ACDA, March 1994), p. 8.

challenges confronting the disparate grouping of countries making up the region, it is not surprising that there are significant differences in the total and in the rates of growth of defense expenditures in the region. Defense budgets are typically considerably higher in Northeast Asia than in Southeast Asia (official defense budgets range from $10 billion to $40 billion, in contrast to $1.5 billion to $3 billion). Moreover, defense budgets in Northeast Asia grow at faster rate than is common in Southeast Asia. In South Korea, for example, the defense budget was 7.8 percent higher in 1993 than in 1992 ($12.06 billion versus $11.19 billion).[69] Taiwan's defense ministry has proposed a record $10.6 billion defense budget for 1995–96 (or 24.5 percent of the entire national budget), a total only marginally behind that of South Korea.[70] In China, the increase in official defense spending for 1994

Table 4.3

Armed Forces: World Shares and Growth (in percentages)

	World Share		Real Growth Rate	
	1981	1991	1981–91	1987–91
World	100.0	100.0	0.0	–2.2
Developed	37.1	33.3	–1.1	–4.6
Developing	62.9	66.7	0.6	–1.0
Region				
Africa	5.2	6.3	1.8	–1.3
East Asia	*32.8*	*31.0*	*–0.7*	*0.0*
Europe, all	34.2	29.4	–1.5	–5.4
NATO Europe	13.1	13.0	–0.4	–1.9
Warsaw Pact	19.2	14.8	–2.2	–8.0
Other Europe	1.8	1.5	–2.1	–5.4
Latin America	5.9	6.0	–0.8	–3.6
Middle East	6.9	9.8	5.3	–0.5
North America	8.0	8.5	0.2	–1.7
Oceania	0.3	0.3	–0.3	–0.5
South Asia	6.7	8.8	2.0	–0.6
Organization				
NATO, all	21.1	21.5	–0.2	–1.8
Warsaw Pact	19.2	14.8	–2.2	–8.0
OPEC	5.3	7.5	5.5	–1.6
OECD	23.0	23.4	–0.2	–1.8

Source: U.S. Arms Control and Disarmament Agency, *World Military Expenditures and Arms Transfers, 1991-92* (Washington: U.S. ACDA, March, 1994), p. 5.

was 22 percent,[71] and 1994 was the fifth consecutive year of double-digit increases.[72]

As Table 4.3 indicates, East Asia accounts for the largest share of world armed forces, 31 percent in 1991. China, North Korea, Vietnam, South Korea, and Taiwan account for 82 percent of the region's military manpower.[73] Two striking features are revealed in the table: first, there was a modest decline in regional armed forces over the decade; and, second, during the second half of the period covered, no further declines took place, making this region unlike every other region of the world. This is all the more interesting in light of China's substantial reduction of PLA forces over the last two years of the decade (a drop of 700,000 personnel). Although China's armed forces are declining in size, they remain the largest in the world, and are about the size of the combined armies of North and South Korea, Vietnam, and Taiwan. North Korea's armed forces grew to 1.2 million in the early 1990s, making it the world's largest army relative to the country's population.

Although this analysis is not an appropriate place to discuss in detail the numerous and varied new weapons systems being acquired in the region, some general illustrations of the type of defense modernization now under way may be helpful. As the data and analysis above indicate, from Seoul to Singapore through to New Delhi, regional defense planners are in the process of acquiring sophisticated weapons and electronic systems for air, sea, and land combat, including state-of-the-art long-range missiles. A brief examination of these acquisitions serves to confirm the nature of threats and potential conflicts analyzed above.

First, most countries in the region are acquiring large numbers of advanced multirole fighters, that is, fighters with maritime attack capabilities as well as defense capabilities. Ball cites data indicating that about 3,000 new fighters and strike aircraft will be obtained during the 1990s by Asia-Pacific countries, while nearly the same number of existing aircraft will be upgraded with new avionics and armaments.[74] Approximately 1,500 of these new fighters will be deployed by four Northeast Asian air forces—the air forces of China (about 550 fighters), Taiwan (446), Japan (400), and South Korea (160). In Southeast Asia, the ASEAN countries are likely to acquire 300 new fighters this decade, while in South Asia, India and Pakistan will likely acquire around 1,000 such aircraft. In most instances, these fighters are being equipped for antiship operations.

Second, over 120 maritime reconnaissance aircraft are being acquired in the regime, effectively doubling the present number of these aircraft. The Japan Maritime Self-Defense Force alone plans to acquire up to seventy-four P-3c long-range maritime patrol aircraft, while South Korea is acquiring eight to ten P-3c's. Such aircraft are equipped with antiship missiles. In Southeast Asia, Singapore, Thailand, Malaysia, Indonesia, and Brunei are all modernizing their airborne surface surveillance capabilities.

Third, nearly 200 new major surface combatants are planned for procurement in East Asia through the 1990s, with another fifty being seriously considered. These include the light aircraft carrier being acquired by Thailand; four (and possibly eight) *Aegis* destroyers being acquired by Japan; more than 100 new frigates and more than 100 corvettes. In addition, probably more than 200 minor surface combatants will also be procured in the region.

Fourth, adding to the stock of submarines, more than three dozen new submarines are planned for acquisition during the 1990s. In Northeast Asia, Japan is in the process of building another dozen submarines, South Korea is acquiring at least nine Type 209s, and Taiwan is seeking to acquire between six and ten submarines. In Southeast Asia, only Indonesia currently has a submarine capability, and it intends to acquire three additional Type 209s in 1995–96 to join its existing force. Malaysia has decided to acquire two to four submarines later in the 1990s, while Singapore and Thailand have a submarine option under serious consideration.

It should be noted that each of these types of weapons systems involves strike capabilities with offensive aspects. Although each nation is responding to its own assessment of its threat environment, these brief illustrations of some of the new weapons systems being acquired in the region—spanning fighter aircraft, submarines, and long-range antiship systems—are indicative of the new thresholds being reached in the region and possibly new challenges to maintaining regional stability. In the case of Southeast Asia, where the sense of change is greater than in East Asia, the acquisition of these types of weapons should be seen largely as a response to the new and unpredictable post–Cold War circumstances confronting most governments. With an uncertain role for the United States in maintaining regional security, and given the evolving rivalry for hegemony between Japan, China, and India, Southeast Asian defense planners have little option but to enhance their own capability to deter conflict. During the Cold War, Southeast Asian defense establishments were largely oriented toward counterinsurgency, as the most significant threat was seen as an internal one. Now, having largely defeated internal armed opposition (with the most notable exception being the Philippines), and given post–Cold War realities, defense planners are in the process of creating more conventional military establishments geared to meeting external threats.[75] In effect, Southeast Asia military modernization is increasingly taking on characteristics already in place in Northeast Asia, another reflection of the extended security horizon evolving in the region.

The United States and Asian Security:
Prospects and Options

The United States has been adjusting to the post–Cold War era in Asia during the later portion of the Bush administration and during the Clinton administration. Despite the collective best efforts of these administrations, they have not produced a truly coherent U.S. security policy for the region or for its component parts. Their attempts to do so[76] are extraordinarily cautious—not to say timid. This may have been warranted in terms of President George Bush's preference for "prudence," but it is not warranted in terms of President Bill Clinton's frequent emphasis on "new paradigms" that can address new challenges. These recent efforts on the part of the U.S. bureaucracy may well suffice in an Asia where Asian leaders prefer to see the United States' grand strategy respond to sudden changes at a glacial pace, so that Asia is not caught off guard and can have ample time to adjust to possible American moves. In keeping with the nautical flavor of the maritime-oriented U.S. strategy in the Western Pacific, the United States is akin to an aircraft carrier—large, strong, intimidating, but very slow to change course. This suited many Asians just fine during the Cold War, and they still prefer to keep the United States on a steady, predictable course designed to assure stability in the region.

These desires by Asia's leaders are reciprocated by most U.S. leaders, who are, in turn, tacitly supported by the American people. It is quite possible, perhaps probable, that this harmony of purpose will prevail for some time to come. However, the post–Cold War era's uncertainties and latent stresses also create circumstances in which Americans can contemplate relatively dramatic new policy options that would permit the United States to do things differently and/or to stop doing some things. Once the American public and their representatives in Washington begin to internalize the scope of the changes occurring in Asia—and how they could be accentuated by the eradication of Cold War remnants in Asia—they may choose to engage in a serious reassessment of U.S. policy priorities in Asia. This prospect is underscored by the political volatility expressed by the American electorate, first in 1992, when they dumped the once highly popular Bush administration in favor of Clinton while dabbling with a serious third-party alternative, and then in the 1994 mid-term congressional elections, when they rejected the Clinton administration in favor of a sharp swing to the right. These domestic political considerations could turn out to be a transient phenomenon, in which case they will scarcely matter to Asia's reliance on the United States.

On the other hand, the volatility of American politics could auger for a more profound shift in the posture of the United States in world affairs. It is impossible to predict with any assurance such possible trends. What is crucial for present analytical purposes, however, is that Asian leaders must recognize that there is a possible new variable at work in the Asia-Pacific balance of power, namely post–Cold War uncertainties about the long-term constancy of the U.S. commitment to the region. These uncertainties do not stem from foreign, defense, or economic policy logic; rather, they emanate from the inner dynamics of American society. In one sense, these issues have been present throughout the Cold War years, but—as is true of once constrained Asian tensions—the end of the Cold War also has unleashed these American domestic factors. This is an important and functionally "new" element in the calculus of Asia-Pacific power. Not only do Americans have to pay far more nuanced attention to what Asians say and do in a more flexible context, but also Asians must learn to live with a less predictable United States. As this learning process evolves, all the states of the Asia-Pacific region will be compelled to adjust to the full consequences of the end of the Cold War and its corollaries for the region's peace and security.

Notes

1. Many aspects of the economic transformation by countries in the region reflect startling changes. From the world's largest country to one of its smallest, the data on economic performance in the region are spectacular. Thus China has been registering double-digit growth year after year for half a decade. In the case of Singapore, between 1966 and 1990, its economy grew a remarkable 8.5 percent per year, three times as fast as the United States, and per capita income grew at a 6.6 percent rate, roughly doubling every decade.

2. Analysts need to exercise care in accepting the longevity of economic trends in the region. In a cautionary assessment, the noted economist Paul Krugman warns of the danger of simply extrapolating the pace of regional growth into a projection of future growth. He sees regional growth as running into diminishing returns and inevitably slowing down. See Paul Krugman, "The Myth of Asia's Miracle," *Foreign Affairs*, Vol. 73 (6), November–December 1994, pp. 62–78. Though we will not enter into the debate concerning future economic pros-

pects for the region, the implications for regional security of sharply varying growth rates deserves further attention: for example, it is certainly conceivable that the cessation of growth or indeed simply a prolonged marked slowdown in "hypergrowth economies" could prove to be very unsettling for regional peace.

3. Robert A. Manning and Paula Stern, "The Myth of the Pacific Community," *Foreign Affairs*, Vol. 73, (6) November–December 1994, p. 80. As Manning and Stern point out: "To put the region's economy in context, the East Asian economies in 1960 comprised 4 percent of the world's GNP. By 1991 they comprised some 25 percent of the world's GNP (roughly equal to that of the United States). By the year 2000, they are projected to account for a third of the world's GNP. Already, the seven leading East Asian economies have 41 percent of global bank reserves, up from 17 percent in 1980. The average savings rate of Asian economies is 30 percent, compared to 8 percent for the G-7 economies. According to World Bank estimates, Asia will account for half of the global GNP growth and half of the global trade growth in the decade from 1990–2000" (Manning and Stern, "The Myth of the Pacific Community," p. 81).

4. Robert A. Manning, " The Challenge of Geoeconomics," in Michael D. Bellows, ed., *Asia in the 21st Century: Evolving Strategic Priorities* (Washington D.C.: National Defense University Press, 1994), pp. 115–31. Economic integration as measured by trade flows is increasing in the Asia-Pacific region. By one account, 43 percent of "East Asia's" exports went to other "East Asian" countries in 1993, significantly higher than the 32 percent a decade earlier. *The Economist*, November 19, 1994, p. 15.

5. Michael T. Klare, "The Next Great Arms Race," *Foreign Affairs*, Vol. 72 (3), Summer 1993, pp. 136–52.

6. International Institute for Strategic Studies (IISS), *The Military Balance, 1993–1994* (London: IISS, Brasseys), p. 148.

7. IISS, *The Military Balance, 1993–1994*, p. 158.

8. Desmond Ball, "A New Era in Confidence Building: The Second-Track Process in the Asia/Pacific Region," *Security Dialogue*, Vol. 25 (2), 1994, p. 159.

9. Satoshi Morimoto, "The Japanese Self-Defense Force: Its Role and Missions in the Post–Cold War Period," in Bellows, ed., *Asia in the 21st Century*, pp. 171–88. In an especially forthright manner, Morimoto comments: "Whereas on the European front it is easy to explain why there has been a noticeable reduction in the threat posed by FSU (Former Soviet Union) military forces, there has been no basic strategic change in Northeast Asia. The FSU is still accumulating large numbers of military forces in the region and is continuing with its gradual military modernization. In addition, conventional weapons are still being transferred to the Asian front from the European front. . . . unlike in Europe, there is no buffer zone in Northeast Asia. Based on the evidence, it would seem that any perceived reduction in the threat posed by Russian forces in Northeast Asia is groundless" (p. 174). See also Michael J. Green and Richard J. Samuels, "Recalculating Autonomy: Japan's Choices in the New World Order," *NBR Analysis*, Vol. 5 (4), December 1994, pp. 13–19. Finally, Eugene Brown points out that Japanese wariness over a heavily armed Russia is based on four central post–Cold War issues: (1) the reliability of command and control over the arsenals of the FSU; (2) the problem of arms proliferation; (3) the unresolved status of the Northern Territories; and (4) the overall Asian strategy being pursued by Boris Yeltsin

(Eugene Brown, "Japanese Security Policy in the Post–Cold War Era," *Asian Survey*, Vol. XXXIV [5], May 1994, p. 433). Also see Clare Hollingworth, "Japan's Defence Worries Grow," *Asia-Pacific Defence Reporter*, April–May 1994, pp. 9–10.

10. *Far Eastern Economic Review*, July 28, 1994, p. 16.

11. A full translation is given in Patrick M. Cronin and Michael J. Green, *Redefining the US–Japan Alliance: Tokyo's National Defense Program* (Washington, D.C.: Institute for National Strategic Studies, National Defense University, November 1994), pp. 21–60.

12. See Steve Glain, "Long-Term Focus on Japan Skews Korea Military Plans," *The Asian Wall Street Journal Weekly*, January 23, 1995, p. 9.

13. *The Korea Herald*, May 7, 1994, p. 3.

14. E.A. Olsen examined that trend more thoroughly in "Korean Security: Is Japan's 'Comprehensive Security' Model a Viable Alternative?" in Doug Bandow and Ted Galen Carpenter, eds., *The U.S.-South Korean Alliance; Time for a Change* (New Brunswick, N.J.: Transaction Publishers, 1992).

15. *The Korea Herald*, May 25, 1993, p. 2.

16. *Far Eastern Economic Review*, May 12, 1994, p. 38, and July 28, 1994, pp. 22–23.

17. For example, see David Winterford, "Chinese Naval Planning and Maritime Interests in the South China Sea: Implications for U.S. and Regional Security Policies," *The Journal of American–East Asian Relations*, Vol. 2 (4), Winter 1993–94, pp. 369–98; David Shambaugh, "Growing Strong: China's Challenge to Asian Security," *Survival*, Vol. 36 (2), Summer 1994, pp. 43–59; Larry M. Wortzel, "China Pursues Traditional Great-Power Status," *Orbis*, Vol. 78 (2), Spring 1994, pp. 157–75; Alexander Chieh-cheng Huang, "The Chinese Navy's Offshore Active Defense Strategy: Conceptualization and Implications," *Naval War College Review*, Vol. XLVII (3), Summer 1994, pp. 7–32. For a view that stresses that China is neither a "villain" nor a "renegade" but rather "an ambitious country understandably seeking to expand its influence abroad," see Nicholas D. Kristof, "The Rise of China," *Foreign Affairs*, Vol. 72 (5), November–December 1993, pp. 59–74.

18. IISS, *The Military Balance, 1993–1994*, p. 154.

19. "The Military Balance, 1991–1992," *Asia-Pacific Defence Reporter, Annual, 1991–1992*, p. 139.

20. A.W. Grazebrook, "China's Technological Advances," *Asia-Pacific Defence Reporter*, December 1992–January 1993, p. 11.

21. A.W. Grazebrook, "More Ships, More Sailors for Regional Navies," *Asia-Pacific Defence Reporter*, December 1991–January 1992, p. 69.

22. An indication of the general easing of tensions between Beijing and Moscow (despite significant continuing border disputes) is the signing of a five-year renewable agreement that provides for annual military cooperation plans to be drawn up bilaterally each year. Among the areas for cooperation are logistics, communications, and land surveying. In the "spirit of mutualism," the two countries will use maintenance and refueling facilities at each others' airfields "if necessary." They might also undertake joint military exercises in Russian training areas. *Far Eastern Economic Review*, May 26, 1994, p. 24. For a discussion of enduring border tensions, particularly over the right to control parts of the Amur and Ussuri rivers, see *The Economist*, September 3, 1994, pp. 39–40.

23. *The New York Times*, January 2, 1995, p. 2A.

24. Grazebrook argues that "The Chinese preference for the Su-27K naval variant Flanker, with its heavier, higher payload and much longer range than the Fulcrum MiG-29K (and the F/A-18) must be assumed to be indicative of Chinese thinking. That is, the Chinese Navy (like the Chinese Air Force) wanted the heavier, longer range aircraft with the advantages that carries [sic] in operations outside Chinese territory." Grazebrook, "China's Technological Advances," p. 11. According to Jonathan Pollack, Russian President Boris Yeltsin disclosed during his December 1992 visit to China that "weapons contracts between China and Russia had reached $1.8 billion for 1992, with expectations that comparable or even higher levels would be realized in future years" (*Asian Wall Street Journal Weekly*, March 8, 1993, p. 16). For an assessment of China's military capabilities which argues that it has "a limited capability for projecting military power far beyond China's borders," see Gary Klintworth, "China: Myths and Realities," *Asia-Pacific Defence Reporter*, April–May 1994, pp. 13–15.

25. For discussions of early post–Cold War Sino-Russian military ties, and Chinese acquisition of sophisticated missile-guidance and rocket technology and advanced long-range bombers from Russia, see *Far Eastern Economic Review*, September 1992, p. 21, and November 12, 1992, p. 28.

26. China's territorial claims in Southeast Asia cover almost all the South China Sea, including the strategically placed and potentially oil-rich Spratly Islands. China has rejected the right of both Vietnam and the Philippines to grant exploration rights in the area to private oil companies, seeing these as an infringement of China's sovereignty (*Far Eastern Economic Review*, June 30, 1994, pp. 20–21). According to China's foreign ministry, Chinese naval ships blockaded a Vietnamese rig that had been set up in an area claimed by China, and the navy turned back a Vietnamese supply ship (*The Economist*, July 23, 1994, p. 33).

27. This expanded regional reach includes Japan as well. Alarmed by rising Russian arms exports to China, Tokyo is reported to have launched a secret diplomatic initiative to limit Moscow's arms sales to Beijing. Japan is said to have quietly warned Russia that upsetting the military balance in East Asia by strengthening China with high-technology conventional weaponry will hurt Moscow's chances for massive aid from Japan and the West for reconstruction (*Washington Post Weekly*, August 20–26, 1992). Subsequent announcements of new Russian military sales to China suggest that Tokyo's efforts have met with little success.

28. *The Asian Wall Street Journal Weekly*, October 19, 1992.

29. *Far Eastern Economic Review*, September 3, 1992.

30. Robert Scalapino states: "The betting is that China will emerge in the 21st century as a major economic and political force, its influence extending—for better or worse—over the region and perhaps beyond. . . . China's military budget is rising . . . (signaling) a greater strategic reach in the future. And China remains dissatisfied with the status quo" (Robert Scalapino, "Back to the Future," *Far Eastern Economic Review*, May 26, 1994, p. 38).

31. J.N. Mak, "The Chinese Navy and the South China Sea: A Malaysian Assessment," *Pacific Review*, Vol. 4, 1991, p. 153.

32. It is thought that China received older U.S. in-flight refueling from Iran partly in exchange for providing nuclear reactors. Washington continues to warn

Beijing (and Russia) about providing Iran with the technology necessary for production of nuclear weapons. *The New York Times*, January 25, 1995, p. A4.

33. For a discussion of Israeli weapons sales to China and other Asian countries, see *Far Eastern Economic Review*, January 19, 1995, pp. 26–27. It is believed that China recently successfully tested a prototype of aerial refueling technology. The problem of extending the range of China's fighter bombers will also end soon, when a fleet of Chinese-built A-5M *Fantan* and F-8–2 twin-engine fighter-bombers fitted with in-flight refueling ducts are introduced into service.

34. Susan L. Shirk, "Chinese Views on Asia-Pacific Regional Security Cooperation," *NBR Analysis*, Vol. 5, (5), December 1994, p. 11.

35. Reflecting the reality of China's new power and influence in the region, at the inaugural meeting of the ASEAN Regional Forum in 1994, Southeast Asian nations individually moved toward accommodating China's views of its territorial claims in the South China Sea by rejecting an Indonesian proposal to put a large portion of China's claims on hold. *Far Eastern Economic Review*, August 11, 1994, p. 18.

36. Growing maritime tensions also exist between the U.S. Pacific Fleet and the Chinese navy. In October 1994, the American aircraft carrier *USS Kitty Hawk* confronted a Chinese nuclear submarine and Chinese air force fighters in the Yellow Sea. *Los Angeles Times*, December 14, 1994, p. 10.

37. *Far Eastern Economic Review*, September 22, 1994, pp. 17–20.

38. *Far Eastern Economic Review*, June 23, 1994, p. 29.

39. *Far Eastern Economic Review*, June 23, 1994, p. 29.

40. J. Mohan Malik, "Sino-Indian Rivalry in Myanmar: Implications for Regional Security," *Contemporary Southeast Asia*, Vol. 16 (2), September 1994, 137–56.

41. It should be noted that Sino-Burmese ties are rooted in economics, and arms sales as well as security links. It is the totality of China's influence that seems to worry two of its neighbors, Thailand and India. See *The Economist*, October 8, 1994, p. 35–36.

42. Leszek Buszynski, "ASEAN National Security in the Post–Cold War Era," in Bellows, ed., *Asia in the 21st Century*, p. 96. Moreover, India's naval buildup was initially of concern to Southeast Asia when the Maldive Islands operation of 1988 demonstrated New Delhi's ability for rapid intervention.

43. Signaling the post–Cold War warming in relations between India and the United States, U.S. Secretary of Commerce Ron Brown and Defense Secretary William Perry each paid prominent visits to India in January 1995, with the result that New Delhi and Washington concluded major economic and defense agreements, including an agreement concerning intelligence exchanges and joint military training and exercises. See *Far Eastern Economic Review*, January 26, 1995, pp. 14–16; *The Asian Wall Street Journal Weekly*, January 23, 1995, p. 4; and *The New York Times*, January 13, 1995, p. A6.

44. Michael Richardson, "Rapprochement between ASEAN and India," *Asia-Pacific Defence Reporter*, April-May 1994, pp. 12–13.

45. Malik, "Sino-Indian Rivalry in Myanmar," p. 147.

46. Malik, "Sino-Indian Rivalry in Myanmar," p. 153. For a somewhat softer view, albeit still foreseeing a deeply troubled bilateral relationship, see Surjit Mansigh, "India-China Relations in the Post–Cold War Era," *Asian Survey*, Vol.

XXXIV (3), March 1994, pp. 285–300. For an analysis of post–Cold War Sino-Indian relations by a prominent Chinese analyst, see Zheng Ruixiang, "Shifting Obstacles in Sino-Indian Relations," *The Pacific Review*, Vol. 6 (1), 1993, pp. 63–70.

47. For background on the Korean nuclear issue, see O Won-chol, "Nuclear Development in Korea in the 1970s," *Pacific Research*, November 1994, pp. 11–18, and Michael Ertman, "North Korean Arms Capabilities and Implication: Nuclear, Chemical, and Ballistic Missile," *Korea and World Affairs*, Winter 1993, pp. 605–26.

48. Those concerns are addressed in Thomas H. Henriksen and Kyong-soo Lho, eds., *One Korea? Challenges and Prospect for Reunification* (Stanford: The Hoover Institution, 1994).

49. Despite its enormous military power, for the moment, most Asian countries have effectively discounted Russia as a serious threat to their security. Internal conditions—including a debilitated economy, civil-military strife, localized rebellions, and weak political leadership—all leave Moscow with little energy to exert itself beyond its own borders. While it is hardly likely that Russia will remain a minor regional player over the longer term, for the time being it is seen as posing little challenge to most of East and Southeast Asia. Russia's territorial dispute with Japan is, however, a notable exception to this view of a relatively benign Russia.

50. ASEAN in particular has found it necessary to extend its political, diplomatic, economic, *and* security horizons to meet the new challenges of the post–Cold War period if it is to have influence on those factors and actors that affect Southeast Asia. See *Far Eastern Economic Review*, July 28, 1994, p. 24.

51. Michael Antolik, "The ASEAN Regional Forum: The Spirit of Constructive Engagement," *Contemporary Southeast Asia*, Vol. 16 (2), September 1994, pp. 117–36. At the inaugural meeting of ARF (held in Bangkok in July 1994), the potential for conflict over the Spratlys both on the Korean peninsula and in the South China Sea was discussed, signaling the regionwide concerns of the eighteen nations attending. See *Far Eastern Economic Review*, August 4, 1994, pp. 14–15.

52. For an assessment of the regional impetus for new multilateral security structures in the wake of the collapse of the East-West conflict, see Edward A. Olsen and David Winterford, "Asian Multilateralism: Implications for U.S. Policy," *The Korean Journal of Defense Analysis*, Vol. VI (1), Summer 1994, pp. 9–40. For an analysis of prospects for post–Cold War arms control in the Asia-Pacific region, see Edward A. Olsen and David Winterford, "Multilateral Arms Control Regimes in Asia: Prospects and Options," *Asian Perspective*, Vol. 18 (1), Spring–Summer 1994, pp. 5–37.

53. However, Leifer seems somewhat skeptical of the durability or reality of the institutional structures marking the growing interdependence and dialogue in security matters between East and Southeast Asia. He asks, "Does that development indicate a genuine structural adjustment to a new strategic horizon or is it little more than a tinkering with the form of existing regional security arrangements?" (Michael Leifer, "Expanding Horizons in Southeast Asia?" *Southeast Asian Affairs 1994* [Singapore: Institute for Southeast Studies, 1994] p. 3).

54. Buszynski, "ASEAN National Security in the Post–Cold War Era," p. 98.

55. Olsen and Winterford, "Asian Multilateralism: Implications for U.S. Policy," pp. 9–40.

56. *The New York Times*, January 28, 1995, p. A1. Fearing growing Chinese strength in Southeast Asia, Vietnam has also begun to signal an interest in permitting American naval forces to use Cam Ranh Bay. *The New York Times*, November 24, 1994, p. A4.

57. Yoichi Funabashi, "The Asianization of Asia," *Foreign Affairs*, Vol. 72 (5), November–December 1993, pp. 75–85. Also see Hee Kwon Park, "Multilateral Security Cooperation," *The Pacific Review*, Vol. 6 (3), 1993, p. 255.

58. While the end of the Cold War and the severe political and economic problems confronting Russia might be thought to provide new opportunities for solving the issue of the disputed territories between Russia and Japan, "there are plenty of indications that both sides are now further away than ever from solving the dispute" (Yakov Zinberg and Reinhard Drifte, "Chaos in Russia and the Territorial Dispute with Japan," *The Pacific Review*, Vol. 6 [3], 1993, p. 277).

59. Desmond Ball, "Arms and Affluence: Military Acquisitions in the Asia-Pacific Region," *International Security*, Vol. 18 (3), Winter 1993–94, p. 90.

60. Ball, "Arms and Affluence," p. 90.

61. The impact of the newly implemented Law of the Sea Convention on defense and maritime issues is well illustrated by the recent recognition of Indonesia's claim to archipelagic status. In practical terms, it gives Jakarta an additional 3 million square kilometers of territorial waters and jurisdiction over another 3 million square kilometers of EEZs. As a result, the Indonesian government is moving to establish at least three north-south archipelagic sea-lanes that will give it greater control over commercial and military ships passing through its newly delimited waters. Given past Indonesian efforts to close sea-lanes, this new development carries the potential for creating strained relations with countries in and beyond Southeast Asia. *Far Eastern Economic Review*, December 29, 1994, and January 5, 1995, pp. 18–19.

62. The question of official involvement in piracy risks turning an endemic problem into an interstate dispute. Increasingly, regional actors suspect that China, for example, is using "piracy" carried out by naval patrol boats to exercise de facto authority in the waters of East and Southeast Asia. If such acts of extraterritorial sovereignty went unchallenged, the South China and East China seas would effectively be turned into Chinese lakes. Russia has already responded to attacks on Russian vessels by deploying a naval flotilla to the East China Sea, making it known that "pirates" will be confronted by the Russian Navy. While the Russian threat of armed retaliation appears to have been effective in deterring further attacks on Russian ships, it clearly carries the risk of escalating regional tensions and possibly triggering naval battles. For further discussion, see *Far Eastern Economic Review*, June 16, 1994, pp. 22–28.

63. With rising affluence, Asians have become increasingly sensitive to environmental quality. As a potential harbinger of future events, Indonesia has discovered that massive clouds of black smoke from seemingly uncontrolled forest fires on Sumatra and Borneo can readily strain relations with neighboring countries. See *The New York Times*, October 10, 1994, p. A10, and *The Economist*, October 8, 1994, pp. 36–39.

64. For an analysis of the security context of environmental issues in Northeast Asia, see Edward A. Olsen, "Northeast Asian Confidence Building Measures (CBMs): From a Regional Context to the Environmental Frontier," *Technical*

Report NPS-NS-94–002 (Naval Postgraduate School, Monterey, Calif.), October 1994.

65. For a skeptical analysis of the optimistic view that the depth and complexity of economic interdependence is sufficient in the Asia-Pacific region to make the outbreak of war unlikely, see Barry Buzan and Gerald Segal, "Rethinking East Asian Security," *Survival*, Vol. 36 (2), Summer 1994, pp. 3–21.

66. One of the more troubling aspects of current military modernization in the region is the emergence of Russia as a major arms supplier to regional powers. Desperate for foreign exchange, and seeing arms sales as one way to remain an active player in regional affairs, Moscow has sold sophisticated weapons at bargain prices to a growing list of Asian buyers, including China, India, and Malaysia. Buszynski has warned that "the assumption of this role . . . will perpetuate a potentially destructive legacy from the Soviet Union" and confirm preexisting trends in Russian policy toward "a balance of power approach with its emphasis upon power alignments and military strength . . . with the tensions and the conflicts that this approach entails" (Leszek Buszynski, "Russia's Priorities in the Pacific," *The Pacific Review*, Vol. 6 (3), p. 289). Also see Hyon-Sik Yon, "The Russian Security Interests in Northeast Asia," *The Korean Journal of Defense Analysis*, Vol. VI (1), Summer 1994, pp. 155–74. For a discussion of Russia's successful and controversial sale of MiG-29s to Malaysia, see *Far Eastern Economic Review*, June 16, 1994, p. 20. By the same token, American and European arms manufacturers are also aggressively seeking new or additional markets in Asia in order to compensate for sharply reduced defense spending at home. Substantial quantities of "surplus" conventional weapons and supplies from American, European, and Russian inventories further contribute to perpetuation of a buyer's market and cut-rate prices.

67. Ball, "Arms and Affluence," p. 79.

68. U.S. Arms Control and Disarmament Agency, *World Military Expenditures and Arms Transfers 1991–92* (Washington, D.C.: U.S. ACDA, March 1994), p. 12.

69. IISS, *The Military Balance, 1993–1994*, p. 161. By comparison, ASEAN's total defense spending amounts to about $12 billion, which is about the same as South Korea's. Denis Warner, "Arms Race, or Prudent Deterrence?" *Asia-Pacific Defence Reporter*, April–May 1994, p. 11.

70. Alistair McIntosh, "China's Might Casts Shadow over Prosperous Asia," Reuters, December 1, 1994.

71. The size of China's defense budget is particularly difficult to determine given the hidden nature of research and development (R and D) expenditures, as well as revenues from arms sales and PLA-run commercial ventures. Using purchasing power parity, the IISS has recalculated the amount of China's defense spending and suggests that it is an estimated $27 billion to $43 billion. That would rank China third, or possibly second, in the world (and make it rival Russia). *The Economist*, July 9, 1994, p. 39–40. For a discussion of the PLA's business ventures, see *The Economist*, June 11, 1994, p. 29–30.

72. Michael Richardson, "Watchful Eyes on China's Maritime Development," *Asia-Pacific Defence Reporter*, June-July 1994, p. 27.

73. U.S. Arms Control and Disarmament Agency, *World Military Expenditures and Arms Transfers 1991–92*, p. 5.

74. Ball, "Arms and Affluence," p. 98. The next several paragraphs draw heavily on his analysis. See also Warner, "Arms Race, or Prudent Deterrence?" pp. 10–12.

75. Amitav Acharya, "Why the Rush in Arms Upgrading in Southeast Asia?" *Asian Defence Journal*, April 1994, pp. 27–30.

76. See U.S. Department of Defense, *A Strategic Framework for the Asian Pacific Rim: Report to Congress* (July 1992) and *Defense Strategy for the 1990s: The Regional Defense Strategy* (January 1993).

5

Problems and Prospects of Asian Countries and the United States in the New Pacific Community

Sheldon W. Simon and Robert L. Youngblood

As the Asia-Pacific region approaches a new millennium, regional international relations are moving away from Washington-centered bilateralism to a more diffuse multilateral structure. This structure consists of both political-economic and security components, which currently run along separate tracks. Both are quite comprehensive in that almost all the Asia-Pacific states are involved, though they are not completely inclusive. For example, Russia, North Korea, the Indochinese states, and Burma (Myanmar) are not yet members of economic regional groups. Nor are North Korea and Taiwan members of the new regional security gathering. (In all probability, however, India, Burma, Vietnam, Laos, and Cambodia will join both types of Asia-Pacific organizations by the turn of the century.)

Economic regionalism in the Asia-Pacific region, in contrast to Europe, has been driven by market forces rather than politics. The European Community (EC) evolved over a 35-year period through top-down political decisions. Economies were linked through negotiations among Western European governments. In the Asia-Pacific region, economic regionalism has been a product of market forces through which capital from Japan, the United States, and Europe has

Prepared for the Center for Asia Pacific Studies of Pacific States University, Los Angeles, December 1994.

created linkages among Asian economies via transnational corporations and technology transfer. Again, unlike Europe, this market-led
regionalism is open to interaction with states outside the Asia-Pacific
region on the basis of reciprocity. The European model is rejected as
too rigid, institutionalist, and discriminatory.[1]

Open economic regionalism in East Asia is partially driven by fears
that other regionalisms will be closed. Asian states fear being shut out
of the North American Free Trade Agreement (NAFTA) as well as the
European Union (EU). They are attracted, rather, to the concept of
global free trade as embodied in the General Agreement on Tariffs and
Trade (GATT) and its successor, the World Trade Organization
(WTO). Within their own region, Asian states have initiated policy
consultations as well as some coordination to establish such common
goals as the gradual elimination of trade barriers. They hope to accomplish these tasks through ASEAN Free Trade Area (AFTA) negotiations and Asia Pacific Economic Cooperation (APEC) forum plans. At
this stage, however, no member state is willing to consider sharing
authority with a supranational mechanism that could make the kinds of
binding decisions that the EU makes.

One of the most striking features of Asian economic growth has
been mutual economic penetration. In the aggregate this has led to
remarkable rates of economic growth in the Pacific over the past 15
years, but it has also led to friction with respect to the distribution of
trade benefits, particularly between the United States and Japan, and
the United States and the newly industrializing economies (NIEs).
America has been running large annual deficits with the Asia-Pacific
region—currently around $80 billion to $90 billion—since the early
1980s. To meliorate this financial drain, Washington has pressed its
Asian trading partners to open their markets further to U.S. products,
in the Japanese case even insisting that some U.S. exports be guaranteed shares of Japan's market (government procurement, automobile
parts, computer chips). Bilateral negotiations with Japan, China, South
Korea, and Thailand, in particular, have created political tensions that
threaten to undermine the generally favorable U.S. relationship with
Asia in the post–Cold War period.

Despite these frictions, Asia-Pacific economies are of vital importance to the United States. American trade across the Pacific is one and
a half times its counterpart with Europe. Exports to APEC countries
account for 2.6 million jobs in the U.S. economy. Approximately 50

percent of U.S. exports are sent to Asia; about 60 percent of U.S. imports come from that region; and 30 percent of U.S. overseas investment goes to APEC countries.[2]

The Declining U.S. Position in the Asia-Pacific Region

As a declining hegemon, the United States plans to sustain important political, security, and economic positions in the western Pacific. However, it can no longer accomplish these ends either unilaterally or through exclusively bilateral means. Its allies now share the costs of maintaining forward-deployed U.S. forces on their soil, with Japan paying virtually all local costs after 1995 and the Republic of Korea (ROK) paying approximately 35 percent of these costs.[3]

Since trade drives American foreign policy on the Pacific rim issues in the post–Cold War era, the U.S. Department of Commerce and the Office of the U.S. Trade Representative seem to take precedence over both the Department of State and the Department of Defense. Thus, the Clinton administration places the need to protect foreign patents, copyrights, and intellectual property at the top of its foreign policy agenda in dealing with Thailand, Indonesia, China, and the ROK. It also presses for more open markets throughout the region. The United States believes that the Pacific's economic dynamism is at least partly based on the export emphasis of virtually all its economies. Unlike Europe, Asia does not so far appear to be sliding toward protectionism or inward-looking regionalism. Washington hopes to ensure that this economic openness continues. President Bill Clinton has consciously used the American military presence as a lever to open regional markets further for U.S. products. At the November 1993 APEC summit in Seattle, he stated: "We do not intend to bear the cost of our military presence in Asia and the burdens of regional leadership only to be shut out of the benefits of growth that stability brings."[4] Thus, under Clinton, the United States has brandished its security role as a good for which improved trade and investment access should be exchanged.

Another point of contention between the United States and several of its Asian partners—which will be covered in some detail in the second part of this monograph—is Washington's emphasis on human rights as a condition for economic assistance and favorable political relations. Increasingly, U.S. aid is allocated to nongovernmental organizations (NGOs) in recipient countries. Many of these NGOs are in conflict with their governments. In Indonesia, for example, $320,000 was recently given to the Indonesian Legal Aid Institute, one of the country's leading NGOs in the promotion of democratic reform. Such actions, though small in scale and impact, are seen by some as interference in Jakarta's internal affairs.[5]

Further complicating this issue is the fact that the U.S. vision of human rights is derived from North American and European histories which emphasize the rights of the individual vis-à-vis governments. Asian experiences reverse these priorities, insisting that benefits for the collective (society) must come ahead of the individual and that government's primary responsibility and a basic "human right" must be economic development. In addition, U.S. efforts to link workers' rights and environmental issues to trade are challenged in Asia as a form of American protectionism. Better wages and working conditions are seen as a way of raising costs and lowering the competitiveness of Asian products.[6]

Finally, it should be noted that the ability to use access to the American market as leverage is declining. By the early 1990s, 43 percent of Asia's exports were sent to other Asian states. Relative dependence on the U.S. market declined from 30 percent in 1986 to only 21 percent in 1991[7]—all the more reason for the United States to remember that "get-tough" unilateralism will not fit in an era of economic globalization and regional multilateralism.

APEC and Open Regionalism

APEC represents the culmination of a process of market-oriented, outward-looking policy reforms that began in the ASEAN economies in the 1980s. These reforms ultimately convinced the association's most skeptical member—Indonesia—that an Asia-wide economic consultative body had become a necessity. Because the market economies of East Asia are trade-dependent, APEC was launched in 1989 in support of the GATT process of *open regionalism*, a commitment to nondiscrimination or the offer of most favored nation (MFN) treatment to all trade partners either inside or outside APEC who are willing to reciprocate. Thus, APEC has been more concerned with the health of global trade than with the creation of an East Asian trade bloc.[8]

Indeed, most APEC members, with the exception of the United

States, Australia, Singapore, and possibly Indonesia, prefer that the organization confine its activities to discussions of trade and investment liberalization and related studies. There is little sentiment to institutionalize this forum by creating a permanent bureaucracy or allocating decisions on these matters to the membership as a group. Thus, APEC has no decision-making capability. Nevertheless, it has established ten working groups capped by a distinguished array of well-known economists and other intellectuals drawn from its members. This Eminent Persons Group (EPG) has taken two years to devise a free trade blueprint for the region, a recommendation guaranteed to generate controversy. The other working groups are less controversial. They have already produced useful reports on APEC investment patterns and a tariff database for all members.[9]

The United States may have a different agenda for APEC, however. The Clinton administration's concentration on opening Asian markets is seen by Washington as APEC's primary utility. If there is a regional commitment to trade liberalization through APEC, then U.S. efforts to deal with bilateral trade imbalances with Japan, China, and Thailand should be eased. However, any special U.S. bilateral trade arrangements may be at the expense of other APEC partners. This occurred in Japan's negotiations concerning both U.S. beef at the expense of Australia and American plywood at the expense of Indonesia and Malaysia.[10] U.S. behavior reinforces the apprehensions of the ASEAN countries that Washington is out to hijack APEC and turn it into a free trade area that will be dominated by the large economies.

Certainly, the August 1994 Second EPG Report for the November 1994 APEC meeting in Jakarta could be read in this light. It called for regionwide trade and investment liberalization in three phases, with industrial countries eliminating all barriers by 2010, the NIEs by 2015, and finally the less developed states by 2020. The EPG Report also took note of potential conflicts between APEC and the practices of such subregional groups as AFTA and NAFTA, urging that these bodies equalize the preference arrangements they offer members of their subgroups with the larger APEC.[11] This is in keeping with APEC's commitment to open regionalism: equal benefits to outsiders providing they reciprocate. Parallel recommendations are being made for investment policy through a separate APEC committee report which requested that members provide nondiscriminatory treatment to foreign investments, that is, treat foreign investors the same as domestic investors. This recommendation is also consonant with GATT principles.[12]

EPG free trade proposals are interpreted as particularly advantageous to the United States because they call for reciprocity, a procedure the United States has advocated in bilateral negotiations with Asian trade partners. Reciprocity would require trade partners to open their markets to each other on an equal basis. As U.S. negotiators insist, this would level the playing field. Thai officials, reflecting the concerns of other ASEAN states, reacted cautiously, however, fearful that equal treatment for foreigners would drive some local industries out of business. Malaysia and the Philippines have openly criticized the EPG proposals, claiming that, if implemented, they would move APEC toward a trade bloc, diminishing ASEAN's importance within the larger Pacific group.[13] Nevertheless, with Indonesian President Suharto's support, the free trade timetable has prevailed, even though it may be inconsistent with GATT principles against discrimination and despite Malaysian Prime Minister Mahathir bin Mohamad's objection to APEC's becoming a trade bloc instead of a "loose forum."[14]

Subregionalism: AFTA and the EAEC

A major reason for ASEAN reticence over Pacific-wide free trade is the belief that it would supersede ASEAN's own free trade area. Similarly, Malaysia's East Asian Economic Caucus (EAEC) initiative has been stalled by Washington's objection that it would split APEC into Asian and non-Asian components. At its July 1994 Foreign Ministers meeting, the ASEAN communique virtually ignored the EAEC. This stalemate appears unresolvable, since Japan has stated it cannot support the caucus unless the United States removes its objection.[15]

The successful conclusion of the Uruguay Round of GATT negotiations has accelerated the AFTA timetable of tariff reductions in order to keep ASEAN consistent with the new WTO. AFTA negotiators have shortened the time from fifteen to ten years so that intra-ASEAN tariffs on industrial and agricultural goods will be reduced to a maximum of 5 percent by 2003. These reductions combined with new subregional economic cooperation—among Indonesia, Malaysia, and Singapore; among the Philippines, Indonesia, and Malaysia; and between the Mekong River states of Thailand and Indochina—should help to make Southeast Asia an attractive investment region. Moreover, the ASEAN economic ministers have also agreed to expand AFTA's coverage to include raw agricultural products and the services sector. Thus expanded, AFTA should cover virtually all intra-ASEAN trade, which currently accounts for 20 percent of the total trade of ASEAN members.[16]

The primary obstacle to harmonious American participation in Pacific economic regionalism remains the EAEC. Prime Minister Mahathir has downgraded his original 1990 proposal, which would have created a separate ASEAN-led bargaining group for Asia-Pacific economic diplomacy, to a more modest consultative group within APEC. EAEC proponents have also sought to reassure North America and Australia that the caucus would remain committed to an open multilateral trading system. Other potential EAEC members, such as South Korea, Singapore, and, of course, Japan, would also ensure that the group did not create a protectionist bloc within APEC. Washington's continued objection, therefore, may be overdrawn. The United States could earn considerable goodwill within the region by endorsing the EAEC. Such an endorsement would be an effective followup to America's renewal of China's MFN status. Moreover, the real target for EAEC proponents may be less the United States than Japan. That is, the EAEC may well be a device to open Tokyo's market to Asian exporters rather than a way of diminishing the importance of the non-Asian members of APEC.

Regionalism and Asian Security

The second track of Asia-Pacific regionalism in the post–Cold War period lies in the political-security realm. Pacific-wide security discussions are a new phenomenon. They evolved in the aftermath of the Cold War and emerged from the U.S. military drawdown in the Pacific. While American forces remain in fixed bases in both Japan and Korea, they have left the Philippines in Southeast Asia, even though the ASEAN states did not desire a complete U.S. departure from the region. In fact, six ASEAN states in varying degrees have become involved in helping the United States maintain a low-profile air and naval presence in their vicinity through a relationship known as "places not bases."[17] Memoranda of understanding have been signed bilaterally with all ASEAN members—except the Philippines and Vietnam—through which U.S. ships and planes in small numbers have rights of access to specific ports and airfields for repair, provisioning, and joint exercises. Through these arrangements, the United States remains the dominant sea and air power throughout the Western Pacific and not just in Northeast Asia, where its only bases are located. The low-key U.S. presence in Southeast Asia is designed to alleviate local anxieties about putative regional threats without compromising sovereignty or offending nationalist sentiments. Nevertheless, U.S. efforts in late 1994 to discuss with Thailand and Indonesia the prospect of permanent, offshore prepositioned military supplies in their vicinity were rejected as a vestige of the old Cold War dependence on outsiders for regional security. That era has ended.

Although a U.S. presence remains, it is no longer a sufficient guarantee of security, nor is it appropriate for such concerns as territorial disputes, local arms buildups, and ethnic tensions. Only discussions among the region's members can address these concerns effectively. These discussions seek to develop a habit of dialogue and transparency among regional actors, thus providing reassurance about intentions even as military capabilities increase.[18] South Korea's establishment of diplomatic relations with three of its former adversaries (China, Russia, and Vietnam) is an example of efforts to establish this new dialogue of reassurance even as the ROK gradually builds a military capacity for *regional*—not just peninsular—action.

ASEAN's decision to become the core of an Asian-Pacific security discussion forum emerged from two realizations: first, that the region's economic linkages to Northeast Asia meant that developments in the North Pacific directly affected Southeast Asia, and second, that it was desirable to preempt the organization of a Pacific-wide security group in order to have some control over its agenda. ASEAN feared the prospect of being subordinated to the United States, Japan, Korea, and China if any combination of the latter initiated regional dialogue before ASEAN could.

Initially through Post-Ministerial Conferences (PMCs) and then through the ARF (discussed below), ASEAN and its dialogue partners have developed an Asiawide discussion agenda for the 1990s, the primary aim of which seems to be *transparency*. Various sorts of information—on arms transfers, acquisitions, and indigenous arms production; on military deployments and exercises; and on defense doctrines—are fair game for a cooperative security dialogue. This agenda was originally developed by government-funded think tanks in the ASEAN states, consisting primarily of academic researchers whose recommendations were then transferred for action to the official level.[19] The ultimate purpose of transparency is, of course, reassurance. Accumulated mutual confidence is a prerequisite to resolution of harder issues, such as territorial and resource disputes. That ASEAN, an organization which has assiduously avoided any semblance of security responsibilities since its inception, should emerge as the primary institution for wide-ranging Pacific security discussion is a real measure of how much change the post–Cold War world has induced in Asia. ASEAN is founding a new regional security order centered on itself to at least partially replace (some would say to supplement) the old system, based on bilateral security ties with the United States.[20] Emblematic of this new arrangement is the fact that the 1976 ASEAN Treaty of Amity and Cooperation has become the basis of security ties among neighbors. The Indochina states are adhering to it as a first step toward joining ASEAN itself.

An additional explanation for Asian decisions to create their own security mechanisms is a growing realization that America's post–Cold War foreign policy goals may not be entirely compatible with Asian political developments. The Clinton administration has placed democracy and human rights near the top of its global agenda. This means that Washington has become increasingly concerned with how Asian states are governed. From the target government's viewpoint, this comes perilously close to direct interference in its internal politics and a challenge to its governing elites. Insofar as this human rights concern focuses on labor conditions, it is also seen as an effort to raise business costs in the region and/or to justify U.S. protectionism against Asian products. Either way, Washington's human rights agenda is one more indication that the purely military security concerns of the Cold War have ended and that a much more complex U.S. relationship with the Asia-Pacific region has begun.[21]

The Asian country whose security intentions seem the most imponderable is China. On the one hand, even traditional adversaries such as Malaysia, Indonesia, and the ROK see the People's Republic of China (PRC) as a newly awakened capitalist giant with which trade and investment provide mutual profitability. On the other hand, the PRC is perceived to be a regional great power inexorably developing economic and military capabilities which will permit Beijing to restore its traditional influence over the region. In general, the Asian states have responded by trying to encourage China's outward-looking commercial policies in hopes of nurturing a political-business elite with a strong stake in maintaining regional stability.

A litmus test for the PRC's intentions is its policy toward the future of the potentially oil-rich Spratly archipelago in the South China Sea. China remains the only holdout among six claimants (the others are Vietnam, Malaysia, Taiwan, Brunei, and the Philippines) by refusing to endorse a pledge to refrain from using force to settle incompatible claims. Moreover, it has also refused to engage in multilateral discussions about creating a development regime for the Spratlys, though it appears to have endorsed the idea in principle.

China has focused its Spratly confrontation on Vietnam, thereby hoping not to antagonize the ASEAN states. However, Vietnam will soon join ASEAN. Late 1995 is the projected date, and Hanoi immediately agreed to the 1992 ASEAN declaration on the South China Sea asking all parties to the dispute to exercise restraint and settle their differences peacefully. Therefore, China lost its diplomatic gambit with the association, which sees Beijing and not Hanoi as a threat to the region. This alignment on the South China Sea reverses the situation of the 1980s, when Vietnam was the predator and China was one of the region's protectors against a Moscow-Hanoi alliance.

Nevertheless, Chinese specialists insist that Vietnam is at fault, having sunk 80 to 100 oil wells in the South China Sea area claimed by Beijing. Of the Social Republic of Vietnam's annual 35 million barrels of offshore crude oil production, China alleges that most come from disputed areas. To prevent further Vietnamese drilling in a block given by China to the U.S.-based Crestone corporation, the PRC's navy has deployed warships to interdict resupply of Hanoi's rig.[22] Competitive exploration and drilling in overlapping blocks is one of the most dangerous features of the Spratly conflict. Military confrontation between Hanoi and Beijing occurred in 1988. It could occur again.

Trends in Defense Cooperation

China and Vietnam are not the only states along the Pacific rim with mutual suspicions of each other's intentions. Indeed, the single most important obstacle to the creation of a genuine Asia-Pacific security concert is a persistent absence of trust among neighbors. Illustrative of this anxiety was a recent complaint by an Indonesian parliamentary official that Malaysia's military exercises featuring the capture of an island by that country's new rapid deployment force could be interpreted as an indirect threat to Indonesia because of island disputes between the two countries. Singapore and Thailand were also reported to express concern, for they too have unresolved territorial claims against Malaysia.[23] All this despite the fact that these states are close collaborators within ASEAN on security issues.

Malaysian defense acquisitions are fairly typical of arms buildups throughout the Pacific over the past decade, as economic prosperity has permitted the region's militaries to acquire modern air and naval components. Unlike the period through the early 1980s, East Asian armed forces are expanding their tasks beyond counterinsurgency and border protection to control of air and sea spaces in their vicinities. These new capabilities have become particularly important since the 1982 Law of the Sea Treaty was activated in November 1994. Under this new maritime regime, littoral states acquire a 200-mile exclusive economic zone (EEZ), the protection of which depends on possession of an oceangoing navy and a long-range air force.

In this context, Malaysia has taken delivery of Russian MiG-29s and American FA-18D fighters as well as two new British frigates. In the pipeline are submarines, three-dimensional defense radars, and a new fleet of fast patrol boats. All are justified in terms of developing an EEZ defense capability. Malaysian officials do not stop there, however. Defense Minister Datuk Sri Najib Tun Razak notes that "our added capability means we are contributing to regional security. A stronger Malaysia in military terms means a stronger ASEAN." Moreover, similar upgrades by Singapore, Indonesia, Thailand, Australia, and (farther away) South Korea are all acceptable so long as they exclude weapons of mass destruction. Minister Najib has also reiterated the importance of a continued American military presence and regular joint exercises with regional forces so that they can work together on a bilateral basis.[24]

Other forms of defense cooperation are emerging, too. A major breakthrough in Philippine-Malaysian relations has occurred, considerably easing the long-term enmity that had prevailed between the two countries over an unresolved Philippine claim to Sabah. In a move indicative of Malaysia's willingness to see the claim essentially as an issue in domestic Philippine politics rather than as a problem between the two states, Minister Najib and Philippine Defense Secretary Renato de Villa concluded a bilateral defense cooperation pact in September 1994. The agreement provides for regular joint military exercises, an exchange of military information to encourage transparency, and the possible joint use of each other's defense locations. This joint use would include repair and service, thus providing for the repair of Philippine C-130 transport aircraft at Malaysian facilities.[25]

Japan, too, may be moving gradually toward a regional defense capability. A summer 1994 high-level advisory committee report to the Japanese government recommended not only a greater commitment to U.N. peacekeeping operations but also improved surface warfare, sealift, and air defense capabilities through the acquisition of air-refueling tankers. These capabilities would provide Japan with longer-range deployment opportunities.[26] As if to underline these new considerations, for the first time, Japan and South Korea began to plan for training exchanges. The two countries' navies exercised *jointly* for the first time, in the six-nation Rim of the Pacific (RIMPAC) exercises near Hawaii.[27]

ASEAN Regional Forum

As the Cold War wound down in the 1980s, alternative security logics to Realism's confrontational approach began to be explored. The old idea of a *concert* of countries was resurrected, though on a regional rather than a global basis. The Conference on Security and Cooperation in Europe (CSCE) was revitalized as a device to bridge the North Atlantic Treaty Organization (NATO) and the now-defunct Warsaw Pact. In Asia, discussions were initiated in nonofficial think tanks to explore security arrangements *with* rather than against states.[28] These new dialogues, many of which included government participants in their private capacity, emulated such Track Two economic communities as the Pacific Economic Cooperation Council (PECC) and the Pacific Basin Economic Council (PBEC). That is, they conceptualized security in a broad manner, going beyond narrow military considerations to economic development and commercial linkages—all the while emphasizing cooperative approaches.

During the 1980s, as discussed above, East Asian states also experienced sustained economic growth. Resources became available to expand defense establishments beyond counterinsurgency and close-in territorial defense to the protection of adjacent sea and air space out to the 200-nautical-mile EEZ enunciated in the 1982 Law of the Sea Treaty. Overlapping maritime jurisdictions and the need to collaborate on fishery, poaching, and antipiracy led to intense discussions in such Track Two regional groups as the ASEAN Institutes of Security and International Studies (ISIS).[29] These discussions included academic policy specialists from throughout the region, addressing issues that were considered too sensitive for official meetings. The ASEAN-based forums laid the groundwork for subsequent governmental negotiations on such issues as collaboration in the exploitation of South China Sea resources and peaceful settlement of the Spratly islands claims.

The ASEAN Regional Forum (ARF) evolved gradually from ASEAN ISIS meetings into the ASEAN Post-Ministerial Conferences, which inaugurated security discussions in 1992. The next step was the first Senior Officials Meeting (SOM) in July 1993, which, in turn, announced the creation of the annual Regional Forum, to begin the following year. Most states along the Pacific rim were included; the few exceptions were North Korea, Vietnam, Cambodia, and Burma. Particularly noteworthy has been Japan's enthusiastic participation— the first time Tokyo has engaged in multilateral security discussions. This new policy may symbolize a break from the Yoshida Doctrine's exclusive reliance on the United States in all security matters. It may constitute the beginning of an independent Japanese voice in Asian security matters. Japanese security analysts have recently written of cooperative security arrangements that will supplement the Japan-U.S. Security Treaty: "Japan may need, for example, to provide such cooperation as transportation and rear support for the United States guarding the major shipping lanes."[30] Thus, the presence of U.S. bases in Japan will be seen more directly as a Japanese contribution to regional stability.

In its early stages, the ARF will probably not go much beyond a venue for the discussion of security transparency and confidence-building measures (CBMs). Regional problems that were addressed by the ASEAN Senior Officers Meeting in March 1994, before the July ARF, included Cambodia, South China Sea issues, relations with Burma, and nuclear issues on the Korean peninsula. The SOM's recommendation to the ARF was to be as inclusive as possible, that is, to engage disputants in proactive negotiations, when feasible, to resolve international disputes. Singapore's *Straits Times* perhaps best articulated the Asia-Pacific region's hope for the new forum on March 2, 1994:

> What the region needs is a permanent forum to facilitate consultative processes, promote confidence-building measures, and whenever necessary, set up the machinery to investigate disputes. This implies, of course, constant dialogue and interaction so that members acquire a better appreciation of each other's security concerns.

The 1994 Bangkok ARF took several important steps: (1) It established the forum as an annual event. (2) It endorsed ASEAN's Treaty of Amity and Cooperation as a code of conduct among ARF members, thus formalizing a kind of nonaggression undertaking among them. This was understood to be a CBM and a basis for political cooperation. (3) Studies were commissioned for the next ARF (scheduled for 1995 in Brunei), including studies on nuclear nonproliferation, further CBM prospects, the creation of a regional peacekeeping training center, exchanges of nonclassified military information, antipiracy issues, and preventive diplomacy.[31] These topics are so broad-gauged that they could cover virtually all possible security issues along the Pacific rim.

Some countries proffered specific security issues, reflecting their own priorities. The ROK proposed consideration of a Northeast Asia security cooperation forum that would parallel Southeast Asian security discussions. Australia presented a paper on defense cooperation among the region's militaries which could induce "habits of cooperation" and lead to a "framework for regional security." An ASEAN report called for the exchange of defense white papers as a transparency measure. Japan and the Philippines proposed a regional arms register. While Vietnam requested multilateral negotiations on the South China Sea, the Chinese contribution was limited to an expression of interest in scientific cooperation around the Spratly Islands.[32]

Among the more important of these suggestions was the South Korean plan for a ministerial-level security forum for Northeast Asia, which would include the two Koreas, Japan, China, Russia, and the United States. Like the Regional Forum, the Northeast Asia subgroup would first focus on CBMs and preventive diplomacy based on nonaggression and nonintervention agreements. With progress toward the settlement of the Korean nuclear standoff achieved in October 1994, prospects for a Northeast Asian security dialogue may be improving.

Such a dialogue would provide a mechanism for bringing Russia back into regional security discussions, as well as a way of linking Japan and both Koreas in political discourse for the first time. China may be the least interested in such an arrangement, however. Beijing has preferred to deal with security matters on a bilateral basis and has not responded positively to transparency proposals such as foreign observers at People's Liberation Army military maneuvers or joint exercises.[33]

Equally indicative of security problems facing the Asia-Pacific region are issues that were dropped from the Bangkok ARF statement because they were considered too controversial or premature. These included the creation of a regional security studies center, the exchange of military observers among neighbors, the sharing of defense white papers, and the establishment of a maritime database which would facilitate the protection of sea-lanes. Nor was the future of either Cambodia or Burma mentioned in the final statement, though the situation in both countries was discussed in the ARF meeting. Dissensus prevailed, with Thailand opposing any effort to assist in the development of a more professional Cambodian army, while the United States and Australia argued that assistance to that army might be necessary if the Khmer Rouge were to be defeated and internal security restored.[34] For Thailand, a more stable Cambodia could mean a neighbor less susceptible to Thai economic interests and political pressure.

The Future of Asia-Pacific Multilateralism

The United States will remain an important player in Asia's political economy and security future. However, it will be seen increasingly as an outsider, as the nations of the Asia-Pacific region turn more and more to each other for trade and investment. The U.S. market can no longer be the primary engine of growth for Asia-Pacific development. As a heavily indebted mature economy, it cannot absorb the export surpluses that characterized Asian development in the Cold War era. Thus, Asian states are increasingly turning to one another as both suppliers and markets. Japan's trade surplus with the rest of Asia exceeded its surplus with the United States for the first time in 1993. Taiwan, the ROK, Singapore, and even Malaysia are becoming major investors in their neighbors' development. Japan's direct investment in Southeast Asia has soared in the 1990s, as the strong yen (*endaka*) has led a number of manufacturers to locate in other parts of the region. These economic dynamics are occurring outside the U.S. relationship with the Asia-Pacific region.

Along the security dimension, while a U.S. naval and air presence in the Pacific remains welcome for its calming and deterrent effects, its importance for the settlement of local conflicts over South China Sea jurisdictional claims, Cambodia's future, Burma's fate, illegal migration among neighbors, and a host of other political tensions is marginal. Regional political and security disputes will be negotiated in regional forums, such as ASEAN, or handled exclusively among the disputants. Any American role in dispute settlement will, once again, be marginal. So, although the United States continues to be the number one Pacific power, its economic and security roles in the Asian portion of the Pacific are inexorably declining.

The Challenges of Human Rights, Population Growth, and Environmental Degradation

Not since the presidency of Jimmy Carter have human rights been so emphasized in the conduct of American foreign policy as during the first two years of the Clinton administration.[35] The perils of insisting that certain performance standards on human rights be met as a condition for economic and political relations with the United States, however, are manifest in President Bill Clinton's decision in May 1994 to renew the MFN trading privileges of China, despite Beijing's continued occupation of Tibet, repression of internal dissent, and harsh treatment of political prisoners. Moreover, the debate surrounding Clinton's retreat on MFN issues underscores the complexity involved in attempts to achieve agreement on international standards of human rights between (and among) nations with different political systems and at different stages of development, while concomitantly attempting to resolve important economic and political issues.

Perhaps nowhere in the world is a rigid linking of trading (or other) privileges with human rights more complicated for the United States than in East and Southeast Asia. With 2 billion people, or approximately two-fifths of earth's population, the region is currently the world's most dynamic area of economic growth (see Table 5.1). China's gross domestic product (GDP) grew at more than 13 percent in 1992–93 and is expected to grow at 11.5 percent in 1994 before dropping to 9 percent in 1995, while the combined growth rate for Indonesia, Malaysia, the Philippines, and Thailand was 6.3 percent in 1993, despite the sluggishness of the Philippine economy. The Asian Development Bank projects that Malaysia, Thailand, and Singapore will have growth rates above 8 percent in 1994–95, and forecasts that the Philippine economy will jump from 4.6 percent in 1994 to 6.2 percent in 1995.[36] Overall, Asia's growth rate is more than twice that of the world (7.5 percent in Asia versus 2.3 percent world growth in 1993), and over the past four years, per capita income has grown in Asia at double the rate of other regions.[37]

The countries that make up APEC, including all of Asia's most robust economies, account for more than 40 percent of world trade and make up nearly half of the world's gross product.[38] In 1992, East Asia and the Pacific accounted for 41 percent and 29 percent, respectively, of all U.S. imports and exports, but, with the exception of Brunei, the United States had a negative balance of trade with ASEAN countries and with China, Hong Kong, Japan, South Korea, and Taiwan.[39] Without doubt, as President Clinton emphasized during the APEC meeting in November 1994, trade relations with Asia are crucial to future expansion of the U.S. economy. At the same time, however, the Clinton administration, nongovernmental organizations, and others have grave concern about human rights abuses in Asia.

Asian Human Rights in U.S. Policy

Across the region adherence to international standards of human rights is quite variable. Only Japan and South Korea were ranked as "free" by Freedom House, a nonprofit human rights organization based in New York City, in its 1993 survey of freedom in the world. Burma, China, Indonesia, Laos, North Korea, and Vietnam were classified as "not free," while Cambodia, Malaysia, the Philippines, Singapore, Taiwan, and Thailand were categorized as "partly free."[40] The 1993 Human Rights Reports of the U.S. Department of State agreed substantially with the Freedom House ratings. The State Department noted that Burma "took only limited steps to correct longstanding, serious human rights violations"; that China continued to commit "widespread and well-documented human rights abuses, including torture, forced confessions, and arbitrary detention"; and that Indonesia engaged in "extrajudicial arrests and detention, torture of those in custody, and [used] excessively violent techniques for dealing with suspected criminals or perceived troublemakers." The one-party communist states of Laos and Vietnam were similarly criticized for limiting civil liberties and continuing to violate human rights, including at least one extrajudicial killing in Laos and the employment of arbitrary arrest and detention in both countries.[41]

The Asian countries categorized by Freedom House as "partly free" also received trenchant scrutiny by the State Department. Malaysia and Singapore were criticized for using their internal security acts against political opponents and for limiting freedom of the press and of assembly. Although Cambodia, the Philippines, Taiwan, and Thailand received credit for improving human rights, a variety of problems continued to plague these countries. Among the violations cited were: racial violence against Vietnamese in Cambodia; "extrajudicial killings, disappearances, arbitrary arrests, torture, and harassment of suspected insurgents and their supporters" in the Philippines; physical abuse of prisoners in Taiwan; and the "summary executions and physical abuse of detainees" in Thailand.[42]

Considerable corroborating evidence lends credence to the conclusions of the State Department's report and suggests that improvements in human rights conditions will evolve slowly and unevenly in Asia. Examples from three different regimes are illustrative. China continues to arrest advocates of labor, political, and religious reform and, despite persistent external criticism, to relocate thousands of Han Chinese in Tibet, threatening to destroy the region's cultural uniqueness.[43] Indonesia is also chary about allowing political dissent and self-determination. In June 1994, following a period of greater press freedom, the Suharto government closed three newspapers—*Detik, Editor,* and *Tempo*—for violating so-called ethical standards of reporting, which prohibit the publication of anything considered injurious to the nation,[44] and in November 1994, Muchtar Pakpahan, leader of *Serikat Buruh Sejatrhera Indonesia* (SBSI), Indonesia's largest independent trade union, was sentenced to three years in prison for inciting strikes and riots in Medan, Sumatra, the previous April, although he was not in Medan at the time.[45] In addition, incidents of military repression in Aceh, Irian Jaya, and especially East Timor—which Indonesia invaded in 1975, resulting in an estimated 200,000 deaths—continued to be reported in 1993 and 1994.[46]

Even Singapore, the most urbanized and developed country in Southeast Asia, with the region's highest per capita income, maintained its reputation for harshness against convicted criminals and political dissenters in 1994. In May, American teenager Michael Fay received four lashes of a cane and four months in jail upon conviction for vandalism, and in September, Dutch businessman Johannes van Damme was hanged for possession of heroin.[47] Both sentences were carried out despite pleas for leniency by human rights groups. That Singapore remains intolerant of political dissent was reaffirmed in November 1994 when contempt-of-court charges were filed against Christopher Lingle, a visiting American scholar at the National University of Singapore. Lingle was cited because he had written an article critical of authoritarian governments in Asia, which was published in the *International Herald Tribune* (Singapore).[48] Singapore was not named in the article.

Intermittently since the Carter administration, the White House and Congress, acting either together or separately, have sanctioned or threatened to sanction Asian governments for human rights violations. Following the June 1989 Tiananmen massacre, the United States joined other nations in condemning China, imposing a combination of symbolic and substantive penalties that included the suspension of military transfers, the termination of all high-level official contacts, and the deferral of Beijing's loan applications to international lending institutions.[49] In July 1994, because of continued human rights violations in East Timor, Congress voted to limit arms sales to Indonesia and to retain a ban on U.S. military training of Indonesian officers which had been put into effect after the November 12, 1991, Santa Cruz massacre in Dili, East Timor.[50] Washington also signaled Thailand in August 1994 that funds for the Joint U.S. Military Advisory Group (JUSMAG), namely support for the International Military Education Training (IMET) program, in Bangkok would be terminated if the Thai government were discovered assisting the Khmer Rouge in Cambodia or blocking support for Burmese prodemocracy forces.[51] President Clinton expressed repugnance about Singapore's caning of Michael Fay, while the State Department protested the attempt by Singapore police to intimidate Christopher Lingle.

Increasingly, the views and actions of the United States on human rights have come under attack in Asia. Given a history of repressing native Americans and holding blacks in slavery, and a contemporary society marked by economic inequality and high crime, U.S. pronouncements on human rights are often seen as sanctimonious. America is no longer accepted uncritically as *the* model for a just society.[52] Following the May 1992 riots in Los Angles resulting from the Rodney King verdict, China's press contrasted its own low official crime rate with violence and racial discrimination in the United States, noting that China performs better on many measures of human rights.[53] A year later at the Asian-Pacific human rights conference in Bangkok, Jin Yongjian, the head of China's delegation, encouraged "solidarity" among Asian nations on human rights and warned against "one country" using human rights "to launch political attacks against other countries." Similarly, Thailand's foreign minister, Prasong Soonsiri, castigated Western nations for their "self-righteous and censorious attitude" on human rights.[54] The prevalence of drugs, guns, murders, homelessness, and unemployment has also prompted Singapore's senior minister, Lee Kuan Yew, to criticize Washington's human rights leadership. Lee maintains that too much individual freedom in the absence of social responsibility has contributed to the "breakdown of civil society" in the United States and that only in a well-ordered society (like Singapore) can citizens have "maximum enjoyment" of freedoms.[55]

The charge against Washington of human rights hypocrisy also extends to the international arena. In Asia, for example, the Central Intelligence Agency (CIA) has meddled in domestic politics, the United States backed the genocidal Pol Pot regime in the United Nations, and Washington did nothing when Indonesia invaded East Timor in 1975. Criticisms of the United States about these kinds of lapses periodically surface, and explanations that such behavior was justified in the past because of the Cold War are seen as duplicitous.[56]

As citizens of former colonies or countries exploited by the West during the past 500 years, many Asians consider human rights criticism from Washington (and the West) to be a form of neocolonialism. In 1991, Prime Minister Mahathir of Malaysia asserted that the use of human rights and environmentalism was an attempt to "reimpose colonial rule,"[57] while in 1994, Rafidah Aziz, Malaysia's minister of international trade and industry, accused the United States of being "patronizing" and "egocentric" for coupling trading privileges with human rights, labor, and environmental conditions.[58] The neocolonialism charge is coupled with a concern that Washington may use human rights criticism as a means for remaining economically dominant and, concomitantly, retarding Asian development.[59] Thus, with the exception of Japan, Asian delegates to the March 1993 Asia-Pacific human rights conference in Bangkok opposed any linking of human rights performance with development assistance,[60] and in July 1994, Asian foreign ministers spoke against tying conditions of labor to trade.[61]

The primacy of economic development is underscored by the fact that Asian leaders often place equal or greater emphasis on economic rights as opposed to civil and political rights, arguing that the right to subsistence takes precedence over all other rights. Malaysian foreign minister Ahmad Badawi and others have argued that human rights and democracy have little meaning in a context of economic deprivation and political instability. With tens of millions below the poverty line, countries like China and Indonesia have championed economic rights over political rights,[62] while rapidly developing nations like Malaysia, Singapore, and Thailand have been leery about allowing demands for civil and political rights to stall economic development. The championing of civil and political rights over economic, social, and cultural rights, to many Asians, also contains overtones of neocolonialism:

> By equating human rights to civil and political rights, the rich and powerful in the North hope to avoid coming to grips with those economic, social, and cultural challenges that could well threaten their privileged positions in the existing world order. What the rich and powerful do not want is a struggle for economic transformation presented as a human rights struggle, a struggle for human dignity. If . . . the discourse on human rights is confined to civil and political rights, it will be much easier to put governments in the South on trial for alleged violations of freedom of expression or freedom of assembly. Consequently governments in the South will be on the defensive. If economic rights become the central issue, it is not inconceivable that the North, which dominates the global economy, will be in the dock.[63]

Closely associated with the notion of neocolonial economic subordination is a fear that U.S. interpretations of human rights represent a thin edge of a cultural imperialism wedge. Malaysian and Singaporean leaders have been particularly critical of American (and Western) cultural influences, especially popular music, styles of dress, television programs, and newspaper stories.[64] Both governments repress reports from the Western media, and neither has yet allowed the establishment of independent human rights–monitoring bodies affiliated with Amnesty International or Human Rights Watch/Asia. The rejection of

Western-style democracy, materialism, and American pop culture in favor of Confucianist values respecting authority and order has been a frequent theme of Lee Kuan Yew in recent years. At the March 1993 human rights meeting in Bangkok, other Asian leaders emphasized indigenous varieties of human rights and democracy that value the rights of society over the rights of the individual, and argued that unique historical, cultural, socioeconomic, and political circumstances perforce result in different interpretations and applications of universal human rights standards.[65]

The degree of sensitivity to what Asian governments consider undesirable external influences—including the activities of foreign human rights monitors—and infringement upon national sovereignty is clear in China's human rights policies and in the final declaration of the March 1993 Bangkok meeting. China rejects all attempts to intervene on human rights issues on grounds that such issues are solely "within the domestic jurisdiction of a country" and that the internationally accepted principles of national "sovereignty and noninterference in internal affairs are applicable . . . to all fields of international relations," including "the field of human rights."[66] The delegates to the Bangkok conference likewise condemned "any attempt to use human rights as a conditionality for extending development assistance" and upheld "the principles of respect for national sovereignty and territorial integrity as well as noninterference in the internal affairs of States, and the nonuse of human rights as an instrument of political pressure."[67]

Many nongovernmental organizations (NGOs) took issue with positions that were held at the Bangkok conference and at the June 14–25, 1993, U.N. World Conference on Human Rights in Vienna. In essence, at these conferences, universally accepted standards of human rights were declared open to different interpretations based upon a country's history, culture, politics, and stage of development. NGO representatives worried that the "cultural uniqueness" argument was a license for ignoring rights abuses and justifying authoritarian government.[68] While sympathetic to NGO concerns, John Shattuck, the U.S. head delegate in Vienna, proclaimed—with reservations—the Vienna Declaration and Program of Action a "strong, forward-looking document that reaffirms the universality of human rights and the basic principles" that America "has stood for."[69] Shattuck's reservations about the success of the Vienna conference and the conflict surrounding Clinton's decision to de-link trade from human rights performance in extending

MFN trading rights to China reflect current reality for the United States in grappling with approaches to upholding the basic principles of human rights in a complex world.

By approaching what can be accomplished on the human rights front in the post–Cold War world with pragmatism, the Clinton administration may have discovered the best long-term solution to achieving adherence to international standards of human rights. Speeches by Asian leaders, positions taken by Asian delegates to international forums, and documents such as the Bangkok and Vienna declarations reflect animosities and suspicions that suggest Washington should be judicious in how it approaches Asian governments on human rights questions. This does not mean that the United States should abandon its human rights ideals and goals. Instead, the U.S. government should attempt to diversify sources of pressure on countries with poor human rights records by supporting the efforts of NGOs, cooperating with like-minded allies such as Australia, the Philippines, and the European Community; and remaining open to suggestions of Asian governments on how best to improve human rights in the Asian region. The Clinton administration and Congress have already taken steps in these directions. Congress included $500,000 in the 1995 Foreign Assistance Appropriations Bill for human rights and environmental NGOs in Indonesia,[70] and in November 1994, Secretary of State Warren Christopher assured Thailand that IMET funding would not be terminated precipitously.[71] Similarly, Christopher suggested that the Clinton administration is prepared to consider adopting ASEAN's "constructive engagement" policy vis-à-vis Burma if the State Law and Order Restoration Council (SLORC) is serious about political reform, human rights, and countering illegal narcotics.[72]

Human Rights Implications for U.S. Policy

By taking a pragmatic approach to human rights improvement in Asia, the Clinton administration has already achieved several important goals. First, the de-linking of trade and human rights paved the way for former Secretary of Commerce Ronald Brown's successful trade mission to China in August 1994. In addition to the $5 billion in contracts signed during Brown's trip, there are prospects that U.S. business will be able to bid on huge infrastructure projects in the future.[73] Second,

China agreed in October 1994 to discontinue exporting medium-range (300 kilometer) M-11 surface-to-surface missiles in return for the right to purchase previously banned high-technology products from the United States.[74] Third, and perhaps most important, China approved the nuclear-free Korean peninsula agreement between the United States and North Korea.[75] As North Korea's closest ally, Beijing was in a position to have torpedoed the arrangement had relations with Washington been soured over the termination of MFN.

A more conciliatory approach to Burma also may provide dividends for U.S. policy in Southeast Asia. Already the SLORC has held political discussions, in September and October 1994, with Aung San Suu Kyi, the detained leader of the National League for Democracy and the 1991 Nobel Peace Prize laureate. In November 1994, the SLORC signaled a willingness to allow hospital visits by the International Committee of the Red Cross. Burma has also attended ASEAN meetings as an observer. Likewise significant are the appearance of stress fractures in Rangoon-Beijing relations. Many ordinary Burmese resent the fact that Chinese businessmen dominate cross-border trade and are deeply ensconced in the economy of Mandalay, Burma's second-largest city, while some sectors of the military worry that Rangoon's political and military dependence on Beijing may turn Burma into a colony of China. Countering China's growing influence in Burma is among the reasons for ASEAN's "constructive engagement" policy, Japan's renewal of development assistance, and the Clinton administration's willingness to rethink its Burma policy.[76]

Not only are good relations with Asia important for U.S. business expansion and for resolving immediate political crises such as the nuclear confrontation with North Korea, but also they may become crucial in avoiding future confrontations resulting from population growth and competition for scarce resources. To be sure, population size and growth have contributed to human rights abuses as Asian governments have attempted to develop rapidly. The need to provide for large, growing populations has been a major reason for Asian governments' emphasis upon sustenance as a more fundamental right than civil and political freedoms. China alone has more than 80 million people below the poverty line, close to 100 million migrant workers, and an estimated 130 million superfluous peasants ready to leave the farm for better jobs.[77]

Looming Population and Environmental Challenges:
Lessons from the Philippines and China

The magnitude of Asia's potential population problem is summarized in Table 5.1. With a population of approximately 2 billion at the beginning of the 1990s, East and Southeast Asia may grow by another 1 billion by 2019 and may more than double by the middle of the next century, reaching 4.4 billion.[78] Given current growth patterns, the populations of seven nations—Burma, Cambodia, Laos, Malaysia, North Korea, the Philippines, and Vietnam—will more than triple in size by 2050. China and Indonesia, the region's two largest populations, could together total more than 3 billion. Even slow-population-growth countries like the Republic of China, Singapore, and Thailand are projected to double by 2050. Japan, with the slowest rate of growth, could add another 30 million people, reaching a total population of 158 million.

Despite the fact that Asia may more than double in population by 2050, not all governments viewed their population rates as too high, as column 6 in Table 5.1 indicates. Cambodia, Laos, North Korea, and Singapore considered their rates too low, while Brunei, Burma, Japan, Malaysia, and Thailand were satisfied with 1985–90 growth rates. Fortunately, the governments of the region's largest countries, namely China, Indonesia, the Philippines, South Korea, and Vietnam, ranked their population growth rates as too high. Official dissatisfaction, however, does not necessarily translate into effective population policy, nor does it significantly reduce short- and medium-term economic and political problems associated with high growth.

The Philippines is an example of the debilitative effects of rapid population increase in a context of slow growth and dwindling resources, while China, with its huge population, represents a potentially disruptive factor in the Pacific region should economic development falter or political instability ensue in the post–Deng Xiao Ping period.

The magnitude of the Philippines' population problem is underscored by the fact that the 2.48 percent growth rate shown in Table 5.1 may be conservative; other estimates indicate a growth rate of 2.7 percent, which, if accurate and not reduced, could result in a total population of nearly 320 million by 2050.[79] Even with the government's growth rate figure of 2.4 percent, 1.4 million children are added to the population annually, resulting in a population of nearly 120 million people by the year 2018.[80] The population density of 560 in-

Table 5.1.

Asian Population Growth (in millions)[a]

	Total 1989	Growth Rate %	Doubling Time	Total in 2019	Total in 2050	Government Perception of Growth[b]
East Asia						
Japan	124,017	0.4	177	139,795	158,211	2
Korea, N.	22,402	2.36	30	45,102	92,947	1
Korea, S.	43,064	1.19	59	61,410	88,615	3
PRC	1,119,876	1.39	51	1,694,430	2,599,396	3
ROC	20,866	1.1	51	28,972	40,669	N/A
Subtotal	1,330,225			1,969,709	2,979,838	
Southeast Asia						
Brunei	398	6.3	14	2,488	16,535	2
Burma	40,814	2.09	34	75,911	144,140	2
Cambodia	8,044	2.48	28	16,774	35,847	1
Indonesia	177,615	1.62	43	287,644	473,380	3
Laos	3,970	2.49	28	8,303	17,798	1
Malaysia	16,944	2.31	30	33,617	68,237	2
Philippines	60,878	2.48	28	126,950	271,298	3
Singapore	2,673	1.09	64	3,700	5,178	1
Thailand	54,856	1.53	46	86,508	138,510	2
Vietnam	65,684	2.24	31	127,669	253,706	3
Subtotal	431,876			769,564	1,424,629	
Total	1,762,101			2,739,273	4,404,467	

[a]Calculated from Nafis Sadik (ed.), *Population Policies and Programmes: Lessons Learned from Two Decades of Experience*. New York: New York University Press, 1991, Annex - Table 1, pp. 395–96. Growth rate percentages are based on the years 1985-90. Figures for Japan, Republic of China (ROC), and Brunei started in 1991 and were taken from *PC Globe Maps 'n Facts*. Novato, Calif.: Broderbund Software, Inc., 1993.
[b]Government perceptions of population growth rate were taken from Sadik, *Population Policies and Programmes*, Annex - Table 2, pp. 400–1. 1 = Rate is too low; 2 = Rate is satisfactory; and 3 = Rate is too high.

habitants per square mile is exceeded only by Singapore among Southeast Asian nations. If population growth continues unchecked, the Philippines will quickly surpass Japan's 845 inhabitants per square mile, to rival the population density of Bangladesh (2,063 inhabitants per square mile), a country the Philippines is increasingly compared to, often unfavorably, on levels of poverty.

The "compound-interest formula" characteristic of the above figures suggests an alarmist, doomsday future for the Philippines and other Asian countries with rapidly expanding populations. This view, however, is disputed by those who argue that population growth fosters economic development and technological innovations, resulting in the discovery and exploitation of new natural and man-made resources, and that men and women, as rational beings, will adjust birth rates when necessary to avoid catastrophe.[81] Optimists find support in a 1990 report by the National Economic and Development Authority (NEDA) that reported Filipinos living better under the Aquino administration than ever before, and also in the current economic growth projections of the Ramos administration.[82] Other data, especially on poverty, dispute the conclusion of the NEDA analysis and suggest that economic growth must be sustained to have a significant impact on the lives of the poor.

An increase in income inequality and a rise in the number of Filipino families below the poverty threshold over the past twenty years has been exacerbated by high population growth, especially in the absence of a fundamental restructuring of the economy. The percentage of total family income of the poorest 40 percent of the population dropped from 11.9 percent in 1971 to 9.3 percent in 1981, while the total family income of the top 10 percent of families increased from 36.9 percent to 42 percent.[83] Similarly, the percentage of families below the poverty line grew from 44.9 percent to 53.2 percent between 1971 and 1975, according to a World Bank study, and climbed to 59 percent by 1985.[84] Although the percentages of families below the poverty threshold fell to 49.5 percent by 1988, the National Statistics Office (NSO) reported that seven regions of the country—Bicol; the Western, Central, and Eastern Visayas; and Western, Northern, and Southern Mindanao—had higher poverty percentages than the national rate, with the incidence of poverty in Bicol and the Western and Eastern Visaysas above 60 percent.[85]

Optimism about declining poverty rates, however, is tempered by other information. National survey data from 1983 to 1990 suggest that poverty rates are highly volatile, bouncing up and down in response to short-term economic conditions, and that by 1989 the poverty rates were again rising, along with inflation rates.[86] Moreover, in 1991 Jesus Estanislao, the secretary of finance, downplayed the significance of the reported drop in poverty in 1988 because of the vulnerability of the Philippine economy to external forces.[87] In July 1991, the Food and Nutrition Institute reported that more than 90 pesos a day (P2,737 per month) was needed to "meet the food threshold" of a family of six, while the Center for Research and Communication maintained in March 1990 that a family of five living in Metro Manila needed P6,600 a month "to enjoy basic comfort and [a] humane existence," a goal the poor just dream of achieving.[88] Because only 30 percent of the population have incomes at or above 90 pesos a day, millions of Filipinos suffer from malnutrition, and an estimated 1.61 million pre-school-age children are "severely underweight."[89] Compounding the high incidence of poverty are an annual 800,000 increase in the labor force and high levels of unemployment and underemployment, which averaged 15 and 36 percent, respectively, during the 1980s.[90]

Rapid population growth has also contributed to a surge of migrants to urban areas in search of work. The NSO estimates that 26.2 million people live in urban areas today, a figure that is expected to increase to 36.3 million by the year 2000.[91] The influx of rural migrants has concomitantly given rise to the growth of slums and homelessness. Nationwide an estimated 11 million—approximately 17 percent of the population—reside in squatter settlements. At least one out of four inhabitants of Metro Manila is a squatter, and squatters may compose more than half of the city's population by the year 2000.[92] Manila proper has the dubious distinction of having the largest slum in Asia but, unfortunately, is not the only city in the country with a large area of squalor.[93] Expanding urbanization has been accompanied by a degradation of basic services, resulting in electrical blackouts, increased pollution, inadequate housing, traffic snarls, poor garbage disposal, and water shortages. Around Metro Manila, another result has been the conversion of large rice-growing zones to housing projects, further reducing rice production.[94]

Rapid population growth and government promotion of lowland plantation agriculture to help pay the large foreign debt ($30 billion in 1992) have enlarged the number of landless agricultural workers. Millions have migrated to urban areas or abroad, while millions more have moved to hilly upland areas that are agriculturally marginal and environmentally vulnerable. By 1988, 14.4 million lived in the rural uplands, and by 2020, 42 million are expected to reside in these areas.[95] The result has been increased ecological destruction and civil strife, as soil erosion and reduced agricultural productivity have further heightened competition for land and sustenance.[96]

The magnitude of the population cum environment problem in the Philippines is readily grasped in forest reduction and soil erosion figures. At the turn of the century, most of the Philippines' 60 million hectares was covered by forests, and following World War II, two-thirds of the country remained forested. Since 1950, however, forest cover has disappeared so rapidly that current estimates of forested lands range from 6.8 to 7.3 million hectares. At the present rate of destruction, estimated between 91,000 and 320,000 hectares per year, the most valuable virgin forests, both commercially and biotically, will be gone by the turn of the century.[97]

Soil erosion, which is related to deforestation, is equally widespread and often severe. The Magat watershed on Luzon Island, which is suffering an erosion rate of 219 tons per hectare per year, is typical of many Philippine watersheds.[98] Yet a loss of 50 tons per hectare per year in tropical countries, according to some experts, imposes unacceptably high social and economic costs relative to the availability of alternative land. By the late 1980s, more than 90,000 square kilometers of land were so severely eroded that they were unfit for agricultural crops.[99]

Widespread deforestation, upland migration and farming, and watershed erosion have also contributed to severe downstream problems in the Philippines. Perhaps the most dramatic recent catastrophe resulting from the degradation of watershed was the November 1991 flood in Ormoc, Leyte, which killed an estimated 8,000 and left 120,000 homeless.[100] Less publicized are the erratic water flows and rapid siltation of dams and reservoirs used for irrigation and electrical generation, the destruction of habitat for tribal Filipinos, the depletion of fisheries, the debasement of forest biodiversity, and the potential loss of tourism because of damage to coastal marine life.[101]

Population pressures and environmental degradation in the Philippines, while acute, are not unique in East and Southeast Asia. Although China's family-planning program has reduced the population growth rate from 2.61 percent in 1965–70 to 1.39 percent in 1985–90, no one realistically expects China to achieve the target of zero population growth by the year 2000.[102] On the contrary, economic reform measures and family planning policy changes contributed to an upsurge of births in the late 1980s, prompting an official crackdown that by 1992 led to a steep decline in births. Nevertheless, population experts suspect that part of the decline was due to underreporting, while recent anecdotal reports suggest that many Chinese couples are readily circumventing the one-child policy. Regardless of short-term ups and downs in the fertility rate, China in 1994 had an estimated internal migrant population of more than 100 million. Its workforce is expected to rise from 727 million in 1990 to 858 million by the year 2000.[103]

The large internal migrant population and the necessity for the Chinese economy to employ another 131 million new workers by the year 2000 could complicate Washington-Beijing relations. Currently an estimated 100,000 Chinese enter the United States illegally each year. While the figure is modest in comparison to the number of illegal aliens from Mexico and Latin America, stalled economic development, political instability after the death of Deng Xiao Ping, or deteriorating U.S.-China relations over issues such as human rights could exacerbate the problem by "pushing" more Chinese to the United States in search of work, or could result in China's becoming intransigent about taking apprehended illegal nationals back. Even under the best of economic and political circumstances in China, the number of illegal Chinese entering the United States will probably increase in the short term and may, because of the current anti-immigrant climate in the United States, cause a strain in relations.[104]

Just as difficulties arising from population growth are manifest in the Philippines, China, and elsewhere in Asia, as Table 5.1 suggests, so too is environmental degradation. In 1992, the World Health Organization (WHO) ranked the air pollution of Beijing, along with four other Asian capitals, among the world's dirtiest,[105] and in 1994, the World Bank issued an alarming report about environmental damage caused by rapid economic growth. Throughout China's urban areas, untreated wastewater flows directly into lakes and rivers due to a lack of adequate sewage treatment, and at least 7 million tons of untreated industrial and domestic sewage is emptied daily into the Huaihe, China's fourth largest river. Moreover, part of the 15 million tons a year of sulfur dioxide discharged into the atmosphere by China's factories ends up as acid rain in Japan and creates a 1,000-mile-long smog trail over the Pacific Ocean.[106]

Leaving aside a discussion of Japan, South Korea, and Taiwan, population growth and development policies in Southeast Asian countries (apart from the Philippines) have also resulted in significant environmental damage.[107] Rapid deforestation in Burma, Indonesia, Malaysia, Thailand, and Vietnam are creating problems similar to those already experienced by the Philippines, while the pollution of the atmosphere and water in Bangkok, Jakarta, and Manila mirrors that of Beijing and other major industrial centers in China.[108] Numerous examples underscore the magnitude and diversity of the problem. Uncontrollable forest fires in Sumatra and Kalimantan have blanketed Singapore and parts of Malaysia in dense smoke for weeks in recent years; illegal logging in Burma, Malaysia, and Thailand has displaced tribal groups, threatening some with extinction; and unregulated marine development has contributed to the loss of fisheries and coral reefs throughout Southeast Asia.[109]

When questioned, especially by Westerners, about ecological damage resulting from uncontrolled development, Asian leaders have often responded irritably. At the Rio Conference in July 1992, for example, President Suharto of Indonesia castigated the industrialized nations for attempting to set world standards of environmental behavior without candidly admitting they are the world's worst polluters.[110] Malaysian Prime Minister Mahathir bin Mohamad was even more blunt, saying:

> [The] rich will not accept a progressive and meaningful cutback in their emission of carbon dioxide and other greenhouse gases because it will be a cost to them and retard their progress. Yet they expect the poor peoples of the developing countries to stifle even their minute growth as if it will cost them nothing.
>
> [And] when the rich chopped down their own forests, built their poison-belching factories and scoured the world for cheap resources, the poor said nothing. Indeed they paid for the development of the rich. Now the rich claim a right to regulate the development of the poor countries. And yet any suggestion that the rich compensate the poor adequately is regarded as outrageous. As colonies we were exploited. Now as independent nations we are to be equally exploited.[111]

Similar reactions were expressed at a U.N.-sponsored meeting on development in October 1994. Diplomats from developing countries, including Indonesia, Malaysia, and the Philippines, worried that Western-imposed labor and environmental standards were becoming conditions for receiving developmental assistance—"even while the developed countries continue to threaten the environment through their unsustainable production and consumption patterns"—and that such conditions were nothing more than another form of protectionism.[112]

Population and the Environment: Implications for U.S. Policy

Because of the potentially serious long-term consequences of population growth in East and Southeast Asia, the United States should continue, where possible and appropriate, to assist Asian governments in population management. Such assistance should be extended both multilaterally and bilaterally. By restoring U.S. contributions to the U.N. population program and by providing assistance for family planning in the Philippines, President Clinton has already reversed the "growth-is-good" policy of the Reagan and Bush administrations and signaled a willingness to help President Fidel Ramos lower population growth in the Philippines. The Clinton administration also took a pro–family-planning stance in September 1994 at the United Nations Conference on Population and Development in Cairo, Egypt. Domestic controversy over abortion and strong opposition abroad to family planning, primarily from the Vatican and from fundamentalist Muslims, suggest that Washington should remain flexible and sensitive in offering advice and assistance in different cultural contexts. At the same time, the U.S. government must not lose sight of the consequences of the world's population increasing annually by 94 million, rising at current growth rates from 5.7 billion today to a projected 10 billion by the year 2050, with a sizable portion of the increase in Asia.

Just as it should be alert to the consequences of population growth, the U.S. government should also be concerned about the amount of environmental destruction taking place in Asia; but while most Asian governments recognize the need to control population growth, Asian leaders are often testy about foreign criticism of ecological degradation. The refusal of George President Bush in 1992 to sign the biodiversity treaty and Washington's weakening of the world climate control pact, for example, prompted a storm of anti-American sentiment at the United Nations Conference on Environment and Development in Rio de Janeiro in June 1992. Also, wrangling over how to provide aid in exchange for forestry protection guarantees inflamed Asian leaders like Prime Minister Mahathir, who joined delegates from other developing nations in scrapping a strong declaration on forest preservation.[113]

The growing seriousness of ecological destruction, coupled with its status as a sensitive issue, requires that Washington demonstrate leadership and cooperativeness in addressing environmental issues. As one of the world's largest producers of waste, the U.S. government should concentrate on remaining at the forefront of environmental protection efforts by continuing to enforce tough environmental standards and seeking ways to help industry develop new environment-friendly technologies. An example of the possibilities is the recent Clinton administration agreement with Detroit to combine government technologies and funding with automobile industry expertise to produce a superefficient "clean car" by the year 2003.[114] The arrangement makes sense from a number of perspectives, but especially because, if successful, the project will give the United States added international credibility in the environmental area and will provide technological innovations that will be marketable abroad.

Finally, because population and environmental issues vary in contentiousness from country to country, the U.S. government should work within existing international organizations such as the U.N. and, where appropriate, with American and Asian NGOs engaged in population planning and environmental protection. Within the past decade, NGO activity on the environment has mushroomed in Thailand and the Philippines. Just assisting Asian and American NGOs in staying informed about population and environmental developments in the Pacific region would be of enormous help. Perhaps a good first step might consist of establishing a category on the Voice of America's Internet connection for the distribution of information on population and the environment, and lobbying the United Nations to distribute and archive similar information electronically.

U.S. Pragmatism on Human Rights, Population Growth, and Environmental Destruction

Attempting to resolve differences about human rights, population growth, and environmental degradation through nonacrimonious dialogue promises to pay the highest dividends to U.S. policy in Asia for the foreseeable future. Confrontation on these issues will not only hurt America's strategic interests in Asia, but also damage U.S. prospects for increasing trade and investment in the region. The economic stakes are enormous. China alone is expected to import $1,000 billion worth of goods between now and the year 2000; by the end of the decade, it is projected to invest $233 billion on infrastructure projects, $35 billion of which will be raised abroad.[115] The future well-being of the U.S. economy hinges on reducing the trade deficit with Asia by increased exports and investments in the region.

A gloomier scenario also compels U.S. pragmatism on human rights and concern for population growth and environmental degradation. Experts such as Thomas Homer-Dixon make a persuasive argument that, should population growth and environmental destruction outstrip balanced economic development, the resulting scarcities would contribute to increased civil disorder. The guerrilla war between the military and the Communist New People's Army in the Philippines is fundamentally a conflict over scarce resources within the context of a rapidly expanding population compounded by uneven economic development. More ominous, however, is the fact that the "received wisdom" on China underscores the tremendous economic development of its coastal provinces while overlooking "environmental pressures [that] may cause the country's fragmentation."[116] The interests of the United States clearly lie with assisting China and other Asian states in becoming increasingly prosperous, stable, and, if possible, democratic.

Notes

1. For recent discussions of these distinctions, see Tsuneo Akaha, "Asia-Pacific Regionalism: The Economic Dimension," paper prepared for the International Studies Association—West meeting, The University of Washington, Seattle, October 15, 1994; and Richard Higgott, "Introduction: Ideas, Identity and Policy Coordination in the Asia Pacific," *The Pacific Review* 7, no. 4 (1994): 1–20.

2. *Asahi Shimbun* (Tokyo), 8 July and 6 November 1993.

3. For an extended assessment of the U.S. position in the Pacific, see Sheldon W. Simon, "U.S. Policy and the Future of Asian-Pacific Security," *The Australian Journal of International Affairs* 47, no. 2 (October 1993): pp. 250–62.

4. Quoted by *Kyodo* (Tokyo) 19 November 1993, in FBIS, *Daily Report East Asia*, 23 November 1993, 4.

5. Nigel Holloway, "Seed Money," *Far Eastern Economic Review*, 18 August 1994, 18.

6. Statement by Singapore Foreign Minister S. Jayakumar, quoted in *The Straits Times*, 28 July 1994.

7. Sean Randolph's presentation in The Heritage Foundation's Asian Studies Center Symposium: *The New "Malaise": Clinton Adrift in Asia* (Washington, D.C.: The Heritage Lectures, 21 June 1994), 15.

8. Richard A. Wilson, "APEC: The Next Step toward a New Pacific Community," *CAPA Report No. 12* (San Francisco: The Asia Foundation, November 1993).

9. Mohammed Ariff, "The Multilateralization of Pacific-Asia," paper prepared for the Fourth Defense Services Asia Conference, Kuala Lumpur, 21–22 April 1994, 3.

10. Ariff, "The Multilateralization of Pacific-Asia," 11.

11. "APEC Set to Consider Ambitious Plan to Create World's Most Open Trade Area," *The Asian Wall Street Journal Weekly*, 8 August 1994, 4.

12. *Kyodo*, 10 September 1994, in FBIS, *Daily Report East Asia*, 12 September 1994, 2.

13. *The Nation* (Bangkok), 7 September 1994, in FBIS *Daily Report East Asia*, 7 September 1994, 80; *Kyodo*, 21 September 1994, in FBIS, *Daily Report East Asia,* 21 September 1994, 2–3; and *The Bangkok Post*, 24 September 1994, in FBIS, *Daily Report East Asia,* 26 September 1994, 2.

14. *The Asian Wall Street Journal Weekly*, 26 September 1994, 2.

15. *Kyodo*, 23 July 1994, in FBIS, *Daily Report East Asia*, 25 July 1994, 8–9.

16. Adam Schwarz, "Local Heroes," *Far Eastern Economic Review*, 6 October 1994, 14–15.

17. The evolution of this new U.S. security relationship with Southeast Asia is discussed by Donald K. Emmerson in "U.S. Policy Themes in Southeast Asia in the 1990s," in *Southeast Asia in the "New World Order": Rethinking the Political Economy of a Dynamic Region*, eds. David Wurfel and Bruce Burton (Basingstoke, England: Macmillan Press, 1995).

18. Hee Kwan Park, "Multilateral Security Cooperation," *The Pacific Review* 6, no. 3 (1993): 253.

19. David Dewitt, "Common, Comprehensive, and Cooperative Security," *The Pacific Review* 7, no. 1 (1994): especially 9–11.

20. Donald Crone, "New Bilateral Roles for ASEAN," in *Southeast Asia in the "New World Order,"* Wurfel and Burton, eds. Also see Sheldon W. Simon, "Realism and Neoliberalism: International Relations Theory and Southeast Asian Security," *The Pacific Review* 8, no. 1 (1995).

21. See Sheldon W. Simon, "East Asian Security: The Playing Field Has Changed," *Asian Survey*, 34 (December 1994); and Charles McGregor, "Southeast Asia's New Security Challenges," *The Pacific Review* 6, no. 3 (1993): 269.

22. "Dispute over South China Sea Provides a Test for China's Regional Intentions," *The Asian Wall Street Journal Weekly*, 25 July 1994, 12.

23. *Antara* (Jakarta) 10 October 1994, in FBIS, *Daily Report East Asia*, 11 October 1994, 84.

24. Interview with Malaysian Defense Minister Najib in *The Sunday Times* (Singapore), 24 July 1994.

25. *The Sunday Chronicle* (Manila), 25 September 1994.

26. Kensuke Ebata, "More Active Security Role Urged for Japan," *Jane's Defense Weekly*, 27 August 1994, 4.

27. *Kyodo*, 14 June 1994, in FBIS, *Daily Report East Asia*, 14 June 1994, 8–9.

28. For a review of these security studies, see Paul Evans, ed., *Studying Asia Pacific Security* (Jakarta: University of Toronto, York University Joint Center of Asia Pacific Studies, and Center for Strategic and International Studies, 1994).

29. The most recent review of ASEAN ISIS activities may be found in Pauline Kerr, "Security Dialogue in Asia Pacific," *The Pacific Review* 7, no. 4 (1994). This consortium of private, though often government-sponsored, think tanks was formed in 1988, and included all ASEAN states except Brunei.

30. Satoshi Morimoto, "The Future of Japan-U.S. Security," *Secutarian* (Tokyo), 1 July 1994, in FBIS, *Daily Report East Asia*, 20 October 1994, 15–16.

31. *Kyodo*, 25 July 1994, in FBIS, *Daily Report East Asia*, 26 July 1994, 9.

32. These proposals are summarized in *The Bangkok Post*, 25 July 1994, in FBIS, *Daily Report East Asia*, 25 July 1994, 17–18.

33. Nayan Chanda, "ASEAN: Gentle Giant," *Far Eastern Economic Review*, 4 August 1994, 16.

34. A review of the ARF Cambodia debate was carried by *Kyodo*, 26 July 1994, in FBIS, *Daily Report East Asia*, 26 July 1994, 13.

35. Robert Youngblood would like to thank JoAnne Dukeshire for assistance in gathering information for "The Challenges of Human Rights, Population Growth, and Environmental Degradation" section in this chapter, pp. 158–59.

36. "Asian Economic Growth Continues Despite Sluggish Global Environment, ESCAP 1993 Economic Survey Says," ESCAP/211, 29 December 1993; and "Asian Economy Expected to Post 7.8," *Kyodo* (Manila), 26 October 1994.

37. Rexie Reyes, "Asia to Outpace World Growth Despite China Dip," *Reuters* (Manila), 26 October 1994.

38. Brian Johns, "Openness to Investment Is U.S. Priority for Pacific Rim Pact," *The Journal of Commerce Knight-Ridder/Tribune Business News*, 26 October 1994.

39. Computed from John Bresnan, *From Dominoes to Dynamos: The Transformation of Southeast Asia* (New York: Council on Foreign Relations Press, 1994), tables 7–9, 31–33.

40. Jim Wolf, "Survey Cites Big Jump in Repression Worldwide," *Reuters* (Washington), December 16, 1993. The ratings were based on twenty-four questions assessing civil liberties and political rights citizens enjoy, and as such were not measures of government performance on human rights.

41. U.S. Department of State, *Country Reports on Human Rights Practices for 1993, Report Submitted to the Committee on Foreign Affairs, U.S. House of Representatives and the Committee on Foreign Relations, U.S. Senate, February 1994* (Washington, D.C.: U.S. Government Printing Office, 1994), 577–768.

42. U.S. Department of State, *Country Reports on Human Rights Practices for 1993.*

43. Patrick E. Tyler, "Abuses of Rights Persist in China Despite U.S. Pleas," *The New York Times*, 29 August 1994, A1–A2; and Bernard Krurup, "Tibet's Importance for China Leads to Draconian Rule," *Deutsche Presse Agentur*, 6 November 1994.

44. William Branigin, "Indonesia Cracking Down on Media," *Washington Post*, 10 August 1994. What angered the government was a series of articles questioning the purchase and renovation of thirty-nine former East German ships in connection with·an estimated $1.1 billion expansion of the Indonesian Navy.

45. Merrill Goozner, "Indonesia Finds Independent Labor Leader Is an Outlaw," *Chicago Tribune*, 12 November 1994; and Bob Mantiri, "Indonesia-Human Rights: Clinton Urged to Put Pressure on Jakarta," *Inter Press Service* (Brussels), 10 November 1994. Pakpahan maintained that "provocateurs" started the riot; and Human Rights Watch/Asia (formerly Asia Watch) claimed that the trial was a pretense for dismantling SBSI.

46. Canada-Asia Working Group, "Human Rights in Asia, Submission Prepared for the 50th Session of the United Nations Commission on Human Rights, Geneva, 31 January–11 March 1994," *Currents* 16 (February 1994): 19–28.

47. "Fewer Lashes for Teen-Ager in Singapore," *San Jose Mercury News,* 19 June 1994, 13A; and "Dutch Businessman Hanged in Singapore, He Was Caught with 9.4 Pounds of Heroin," *San Jose Mercury News,* 23 September 1994, 19A.

48. Philip Shenon, "Economist Fears Imprisonment if He Goes to Singapore, *The New York Times*, 6 November 1994; and "American Charged with Contempt of Court," *Associated Press* (Singapore), 18 November 1994. The *International Herald Tribune* (Singapore) Private Ltd., and the *Tribune's* Singapore correspondent were also charged in the suit.

49. See Peter Van Ness, "Australia's Human Rights Delegation to China, 1991: A Case Study," in *Australia's Human Rights Diplomacy*, by Ian Russell, Peter Van Ness, and Beng-Huat Chua, The Australian Foreign Policy Publications Program, Department of International Relations, Research School of Pacific Studies (Canberra: The Australian National University, 1992), 49–85.

50. Charles Scheiner, "Congress Limits Arms Sales and Military Training for Indonesia," *ETAN/US's Network News*, no. 11, November 1994.

51. *BurmaNet News*, 26 August 1994.

52. Peter Van Ness, "China's Human Rights Diplomacy: The Theoretical Foundations of the Chinese Communist Party's Response to Western Condemnation of China's Human Rights Practices," Working Paper No. 141, Peace Research Centre, Research School of Pacific Studies (Canberra: Australian National University, 1993), 6–7.

53. Van Ness, "Australia's Human Rights Delegation to China, 1991," 78; Lincoln Kaye, "From the Glass House: China Chides U.S. on Riots, Defends Own Record," *Far Eastern Economic Review*, 21 May 1992, 26–27; and Lincoln Kaye, "Peking in Defense of Its Humanitarian Record: The Rights Stuff," *Far Eastern Economic Review*, 14 November 1991, 13.

54. *China News Digest* (Global Service) IV, 1 April 1993.

55. Fareed Zakaria, "Culture Is Destiny: A Conversation with Lee Kuan Yew," *Foreign Affairs*, 73 (March–April 1994): 111.

56. See, for example, Satyanarayan Sivaraman, "Cambodia: The Khmer Rouge Has Not Changed Its Spots," *Inter Press Service* (Bangkok), 7 November 1994; and Van Ness, "China's Human Rights Diplomacy," 7.

57. As quoted in Van Ness, "Australia's Human Rights Delegation to China, 1991," 76.

58. Michael Zielenziger, "Malaysian Trade Minister Gives U.S. a World Lesson," *San Jose Mercury News*, 12 June 1994, 12A.

59. "China's Jiang Says Poor Countries Must Counter West," *Kyodo News Service*, 18 November 1994.

60. "Final Declaration of the Regional Meeting for Asia of the World Confer-

ence on Human Rights of 2 April 1993," *Human Rights Law Journal* 14 (November 1993): 370–71.

61. Denis D. Gray, "Asians Criticize Linkage of Labor Conditions and Trade," *Associated Press* (Bangkok), 23 July 1994.

62. "Asian 'Democracy' Is Debated," *Associated Press* (Bangkok), 28 July 1994.

63. Chandra Muzaffar, "The New World Order: Gold or God," *24 Hours*, February 1992, Special Supplement, p. 31, as quoted in Van Ness, "Australia's Human Rights Delegation to China, 1991," 78.

64. See, for example, "Malaysia PM Blasts West," *Associated Press*, 6 December 1994.

65. Gordon Fairclough, "Standing Firm: Asia Sticks to Its View of Human Rights," *Far Eastern Economic Review*, 15 April 1993, 22; and Thalif Deen, "Asia Split on Political, Economic Rights," *Inter Press Service* (Vienna), 20 June 1993.

66. *Human Rights in China* (Beijing: Information Office of the State Council, November 1991), in *Australia's Human Rights Diplomacy*, by Russell, Van Ness, and Beng-Huat Chua, Appendix A, 141.

67. "Final Declaration of the Regional Meeting for Asia of the World Conference on Human Rights of 2 April 1993," *Human Rights Law Journal* 14 (November 1993): 370.

68. *China News Digest* (Global Service) IV, 4 April 1993; and Lina Cabaero, "Asian NGOs Hold Forum on Human Rights and National Security at World Conference on Human Rights," *NGO News* (Vienna), 19 June 1993.

69. Steve Pagani, "World Conference Adopts New Document on Human Rights," *Reuters* (Vienna), 26 June 1993.

70. Charles Scheiner, "Congress Limits Arms Sales and Military Training for Indonesia," *ETAN/US's Network News*, no. 11 (November 1994).

71. "U.S. Promises More Support for Thai Military Students," *Bangkok Post*, 18 November 1994, reprinted in *BurmaNet News*, 18 November 1994.

72. Elaine Sciolino, "U.S. to Adopt Policy of Conciliation with Burmese," *New York Times News Service,* 17 November 1994; and "Burma's Diplomatic Winter May be Lifting," *The Nation* (Bangkok), 18 November 1994, reprinted in *BurmaNet News*, 18 November 1994.

73. "Commerce Chief Hails Trip to China, Human Rights Talks Set for Next Month," *San Jose Mercury News,* 31 August 1994, 6A.

74. Rajiv Chandra, "China-United States: Strengthening Military Ties," *Inter Press Service* (Beijing), 14 October 1994.

75. Robin MacNeil, interview with Secretary of Defense William Perry, 25 October 1994; and "Text of Clinton News Conference in Indonesia," *Federal News Service*, 14 November 1994.

76. Satyanarayan Sivaraman, "Burma-China: Rangoon's China Connection," *Inter Press Service*, 10 November 1994; and "Japan Said to Resume Burma Aid," *Bangkok Post*, 5 November 1994, reprinted in *BurmaNet News*, 12 November 1994.

77. "Asian 'Democracy' Is Debated," *Associated Press* (Bangkok), 28 July 1994; and "In China, Harsh Working Conditions in Factories," *London Observer Service*, 22 November 1994.

78. Because population growth rates are expected to change, the projection of current rates to the years 2019 and 2050 may be viewed as simplistic. Nevertheless, as no Asian nation has yet reached zero population growth, a worst-case analysis focuses attention on the perils of uncontrolled population increases.

79. The 2.7 estimate comes from PC Globe, Version 4.0. The Philippine Population Institute estimates that the actual rate is 2.8 percent, the highest in Southeast Asia. "Getting Serious about Baby Boom," *Manila Chronicle*, 2 April 1990, 4.

80. The more conservative projections by the Department of Health (DOH) show that the population grew 529.9 percent, from 7.64 million in 1903 to 48.1 million in 1980. Given the current growth rate (2.4 percent), it is expected to reach nearly 120 million by the year 2018. Nerissa M. Quizon, "Philippines' Population to Double by 2010s—DOH," *Business Star*, 26 February 1990, 2.

81. Julian Simon, *The Ultimate Resource* (Princeton, N.J.: Princeton University Press, 1981). For a gloomy view of the effects of population growth on environment and society, see Paul Ehrlich and Anne Ehrlich, *The Population Explosion* (London: Hutchinson, 1990).

82. "NEDA Says Filipinos Are Better Off Today," *Business Star*, 3 April 1990, 10.

83. Ma. Cristina G. Ginson, "Philippine Labor and the Economic Recovery Program," *Pulso 1*, no. 3 (1985): 181, table 1; and Ellen H. Palanca, "Poverty and Inequality: Trends and Causes," in *Philippines after 1972: A Multidisciplinary Perspective, Budhi Papers VI*, ed. Ramon C. Reyes (Manila: Ateneo de Manila University, 1985): 109, table 5.

84. International Bank for Reconstruction and Development (World Bank), "Poverty, Basic Needs, and Employment: A Review and Assessment," confidential first draft (Washington, D.C., January 1980), table 1.10, 36 (typewritten); and Mahar Mangahas, "On Poverty Comparisons," *Manila Chronicle*, 31 July 1989, 4–5.

85. Catalino Hernandez, "More Filipinos Are Living below the Poverty Line," *Manila Chronicle*, 2 May 1990, 7. See also Ruth M. Esquillo, "The Dilemma of the Rural Poor," *Manila Chronicle*, 15 August 1989, 5.

86. See Mahar Mangahas, "On Poverty Comparisons," *Manila Chronicle*, 31 July 1989, 4–5; "Taxation, Inflation and Poverty," *Manila Chronicle*, 4 June 1990, 4; and Juan V. Sarmiento, Jr., "Inflation Leaps to 21%," *Philippine Daily Inquirer*, 5 February 1991, 11.

87. Rigoberto Tigiao, "Reality Is Hidden Underground," *Far Eastern Economic Review*, 13 June 1991, 38–39.

88. Elizabeth Perez, "Family of Six Needs at Least P90/Day for Food," *New Chronicle*, 2 July 1991, 1, 10; and *Business Star*, 20 March 1990, 1, 6.

89. Perez, "Family of Six Needs at Least P90/Day for Food."

90. Robert Daniel T. Ela, "Poverty Is Worse: Economy Cannot Grow Because of Low Productivity," *Business Star*, 7 October 1991, 8; and *Business Star*, 23 March 1990, 1, 3.

91. Antonieta IG. Zablan, "Synergizing Rural and Urban Policies," *Manila Chronicle*, 5 March 1990, 5.

92. "United Notions," *Manila Chronicle*, 17 September 1988; and Dennis Murphy, "The Slum Problem Can Be Solved," *Manila Chronicle*, 21 October 1990, 10.

93. *Asia Focus*, 27 February 1991, 2.

94. *Asia Focus*, 16 January 1991, 5.

95. Norman Myers, "Environmental Degradation and Some Economic Consequences in the Philippines," *Environmental Conservation* 15 (Autumn 1988): 207.

96. Thomas F. Homer-Dixon, "Environmental Changes as Causes of Acute Conflict," *International Security* 16 (Fall 1991): 83

97. Gareth Porter with Delfin J. Ganapin, Jr., *Resources, Population, and the Philippines' Future: A Case Study*, World Resources Institute Paper No. 4 (Washington D.C.: World Resources Institute, 1988), 24; James N. Anderson, "Lands at Risk, People at Risk: Perspectives on Tropical Forest Transformations in the Philippines," in *Lands at Risk in the Third World: Local Level Perspectives*, eds. Peter D. Little and Michael M. Horowitz, with A. Endre Nyerges (Boulder, Colo.: Westview Press, 1987), 250; and Myers, "Environmental Degradation," 206.

98. Thomas F. Homer-Dixon, "Environmental Scarcities and Violent Conflict: Evidence from Cases," *International Security* 19 (Summer 1994): 24

99. Myers, "Environmental Degradation," 208.

100. Julio C. Teehankee, "The State, Illegal Logging, and Environmental NGOs in the Philippines," *Kasarinlan* 9 (Third Quarter, 1993): 20–21.

101. See, for example, James F. Eder, "Deforestation and Detribalization in the Philippines: The Palawan Case," *Population and Environment: A Journal of Interdisciplinary Studies* 12 (Winter 1990): 99–115; James Clad and Marites D. Vitug, "The Politics of Plunder," *Far Eastern Economic Review*, 24 November 1988, 48–52; Robin Broad and John Cavanagh, "Marcos's Ghost," *The Amicus Journal* 11 (Fall 1989): 18–29; Paul Mincher, "The Philippine Energy Crisis," *The Ecologist* 23 (November–December 1993): 228–33; and Myers, "Environmental Degradation," 208–11.

102. Nafis Sadik, ed., *Population Policies and Programmes: Lessons Learned from Two Decades of Experience* (New York: New York University Press, 1991), 310–13.

103. Tyrene White, "Two Kinds of Production: The Evolution of China's Family Planning Policy in the 1980s," in *The New Politics of Population: Conflict and Consensus in Family Planning*, by Jason L. Finkle and C. Alison McIntosh (New York: Oxford University Press, 1994), 137–58; Nicholas D. Kristof, "China's Crackdown on Births: A Stunning, and Harsh, Success," *The New York Times*, 25 April 1993, 1, 12; and Loretta Tofani, "For Many in China, Government Is No Longer the Boss," *Knight-Ridder News Service*, 4 November 1994.

104. For an analysis of factors in international migration, see Philip L. Martin, "Migration and Trade: Challenges for the 1990s," available electronically via the gopher at (dual.ucdavis.edu) under *Migration News, Working Papers*, ciip.txt.

105. "U.N.: Air Getting Fouler in Third World Cities," *San Jose Mercury News*, 2 December 1992, 1A. The cities were Bangkok, Jakarta, Manila, and Seoul.

106. Song Dian Tang, "China City's Smog Hides Community in Noxious Haze," *Arizona Republic*, 10 November 1994, A16; and Geoffrey Murray, "Massive Environmental Cleanup Urged in China," *Kyodo News Service* (Beijing), 11 November 1994.

107. For a discussion of the environmental costs of rapid development in South Korea and Taiwan, consult Walden Bello and Stephanie Rosenfeld, *Dragons in Distress: Asia's Miracle Economies in Crisis* (San Francisco: The Institute for Food and Development Policy, 1990).

108. Theodore Panayotou, "The Environment in Southeast Asia: Problems and Policies," *Environmental Science and Technology* 27 (November 1993): 2270–74; and Arthur E. Bruestle, "East Asia's Urban Environment," *Environmental Science and Technology* 27 (November 1993): 2280–84.

109. See, inter alia, "Pollution Worsens in Singapore, Malaysia," *Deutsche Press Agentur* (Singapore), 28 September 1994; S. C. Chin et al., *Logging against the Natives of Sarawak* (Kuala Lumpur: Institute of Social Analysis, 1992); Dhira Phantumvanit and Khunying Suthawan Sathirathai, "Thailand: Degradation and Development in a Resource-Rich Land," *Environment* 30 (January–February 1988): 10–15, 30–32; Isagani de Castro, "Environment-Asia: Pollution and Over-fishing Kill Seas," *Inter Press Service* (Manila), 7 October 1994; and Doug Tsuruoka, "Vanishing Coral Reefs," *Far Eastern Economic Review*, 7 January 1993, 24–25.

110. "Statement by His Excellency President Soeharto of the Republic of Indonesia at the United Nations Conference on Environment and Development, Rio de Janeiro, 12 June 1992," *ASEAN Economic Bulletin* 9 (July 1992): 101–5.

111. "Statement by His Excellency Prime Minister Dr. Mahathir Mohamad of Malaysia at the United Nations Conference on Environment and Development, Rio de Janeiro, 13 June 1992," *ASEAN Economic Bulletin* 9 (July 1992): 107–8.

112. Thalif Deen, "Development: Third World Warns against Hidden Conditions for Aid," *Inter Press Service* (United Nations), 1 October 1994.

113. "Forests Treaty Diluted in Rio: Developing Nations Reportedly Oppose U.S. Bid for Tougher Pact," *San Jose Mercury News*, 9 June 1992, 4A; and "Bush's Summit Showdown: Stands Defiant against Treaty; 'Open Checkbook' Is Closed, He Says," *San Jose Mercury News*, 11 June 1992, 1A.

114. Amory B. Lovins and L. Hunter Lovins, "Reinventing the Wheels," *The Atlantic Monthly Online*, January 1995.

115. "China Reports Big Deals in U.S. Trade Mission," *Reuters* (Beijing), 21 April 1994; and Rajiv Chandra, "Development China; Tottering Infrastructure Gets a Boost," *Inter Press Service*, 26 September 1994.

116. Thomas Homer-Dixon, "Environmental Scarcities and Violent Conflict," 37.

6

Cultural Relations between Korea and the United States in the 1990s

Ralph C. Hassig and Ruth H. Chung

The term "cultural relations" is open to many interpretations, depending on how the terms "culture" and "relations" are defined. Conceptualized in the broader, more inclusive sense, culture is everything that people have, think, and do as a consequence of being members of a given society. Culture provides people with meanings to explain their world and rules to guide their behavior and confer value on their lives. Culture in the broader sense forms the basis for political and economic relations, which are susceptible to subjective prescriptions and interpretations, and thus are rarely conducted in an entirely rational manner.

In international relations the term "cultural relations" is usually given a more restrictive interpretation, referring to the *social* relations of two peoples. Considered in this sense culture "has usually been relegated to a residual category" after consideration of political and economic relations (Kim Kyong-Dong, 1986, p. 2). In this essay we will follow convention and define cultural relations in terms of the social relations that parallel political and economic relations (and for that matter any other types of relations one may wish to consider). Cultural relations, then, are influenced by political and economic relations, and in turn influence them.

What does it mean to say that relations exist between two nations or cultures? Cultural relations can be viewed simply as the mutual attitudes of two societies, even in the absence of contact between those societies. As we shall see, the Korean-American relationship has existed largely in terms of images transmitted by the media: Relatively few Americans and Koreans have had meaningful personal contact with each other. Closer than media contact is sojourner contact, such as that shared by a host people with tourists, foreign students, business-people, and soldiers stationed abroad. The most intimate contact is experienced by immigrants, for example Korean immigrants in America, who are immersed in another culture.

We begin our exploration of cultural relations by examining the images that Koreans and Americans have developed of each other, primarily through media exposure, for it is these past images that guide cultural relations in the present and the future. We then take up the case of Korean immigrants in the United States, who must deal with cultural relations on a long-term basis. Their experience can enlighten us about the nature of cultural relations between the two nations.

Korean-American Cultural Relations

A Brief History of Korean-American Contact

Korean-American relations have an uneven history. The United States literally forced itself upon Korea in the nineteenth century, only to abandon Korea to the Japanese in the early years of the twentieth century. The United States took a limited interest in Korea after the Japanese were defeated, but ended up having to fight the North Koreans and the Chinese to keep South Korea out of the hands of Kim Il Sung. Now that the Cold War is over, it is unclear what America's role in Korea will be.

The Americans' earliest contact with Korea came about accidentally, when American trading ships were blown onto the Korean coast. The Korean kingdom pursued a policy of international isolation, and stranded sailors were given safe passage north to the Manchurian border. When the merchant ship *General Sherman* attempted to sail into Korean waters in 1866, it was set afire and all hands perished. Subsequent attempts to ascertain the fate of the ship and its crew were successfully rebuffed by the Koreans until a squadron of U.S. naval vessels defeated Korean forces in 1871, forcing them ultimately to come to terms with the West, as the Japanese had already been forced to do. In 1882 diplomatic relations were established between the Kingdom of Korea and the United States. Contact between the two nations was limited to missionaries, a few traders, and the necessary diplomatic corps. In 1905 the Japanese claimed Korea as a protectorate, and the United States, which had little interest in the small kingdom, acceded to their claim. Throughout the next half-century, Korean-American contact remained limited, as American missionaries gradually left Korea and diplomatic contacts shifted from the Koreans to the Japanese officials administering the country.

The era of American-Korean contact began in earnest in September 1945, when U.S. forces landed in Korea to accept the Japanese surrender. The Americans tried to stabilize the political situation, in part by working with Koreans who had collaborated with the Japanese administration, a decision that was expeditious but highly unpopular with the Korean people. Unable to reach an agreement with the Soviets, who controlled the northern half of the country, on how to reunify Korea, the United States placed the Korean question before the United Nations, which subsequently oversaw elections in the southern half of the peninsula. Within a year of the inauguration of Syngman Rhee as the first South Korean president, virtually all American troops had been withdrawn from Korea. In January 1950, Secretary of State Dean Acheson in a public speech drew the outer line of defense for the United States as running through Japan and leaving Korea outside the defensive perimeter, a decision that was probably responsible in part for Kim Il Sung's decision to invade South Korea. The South Koreans saw Acheson's speech as yet another abandonment of Korea.

In a sudden reversal of foreign policy, the United States sent troops back to Korea after North Korea invaded South Korea on June 25, 1950. During the course of the Korean War, which lasted until 1953, some 360,000 American troops fought the North Koreans and their Chinese allies. Overnight, South Korea had become an integral part of the U.S. alliance against communism. The American troops that remained in South Korea after the war (still numbering some 60,000 in 1957 and declining to approximately 40,000 by the mid-1970s) constituted the main point of contact between American culture and Korean culture. For the most part, the troops stayed on or near their bases, but American goods leaked out to the Korean economy, and U.S. armed forces radio and television broadcasts were enjoyed by the average Korean citizen. The United States also extended economic and military support to hasten South Korea's recovery from the Korean War. American businesspeople went to Korea, and so did the Peace Corps, in the 1960s. Many Koreans emigrated to the United States, and Korean orphans were adopted by American families. A large proportion of Koreans in top government positions received their university education in the United States.

The military/security relationship remained the most important link between the two countries for many years. The relationship provided the United States with a bulwark against communist expansion in Asia, and the South Koreans enjoyed American protection from further North Korean attacks. In 1977, when President Jimmy Carter proposed withdrawing the remaining U.S. ground troops from Korea, the decision was seen by the South Koreans as yet another attempt to abandon them. President Carter's decision was so unpopular in the United States, in South Korea, and in Japan that he reversed it following his return from a visit to South Korea, after only a few thousand troops had been withdrawn. Approximately 37,000 troops still remained in South Korea in 1996.

Since the mid-1980s, nonmilitary contact between Korea and the United States has increased. Korean emigration and travel to the United States rose as the Korean government relaxed travel restrictions. Business links expanded and American tourism increased, especially with the 1988 Seoul Olympics. By the 1990s, South Korea had become the United States' seventh largest trading partner, and South Korean–branded goods were widely available in the American market. Korean immigrants became a visible business presence in larger American cities. Although the demise of communism reduced the need for U.S. overseas troop deployments to counter communist threats, North Korea's nuclear program and its belligerent posture toward South Korea were perceived as a continuing threat to U.S. and South Korean security, justifying the maintenance of a close bilateral security relationship.

American Perceptions of Korea

Donald S. Macdonald (1986) argues that Americans' images of Korea are a product of five factors, with American ignorance of Korea leading the list (followed by historical tradition, current events as conveyed by the mass media, the impact of Asia as a whole, and the influence of Americans with firsthand knowledge of Korea). Americans know relatively little about Korea. In a survey of American attitudes toward Korea, Eun Ho Lee, Hyung-chan Kim, and Yong Soon Yim (1991) found that 34 percent of their respondents, who were drawn from the general population, admitted to not being knowledgeable about Korea, with 53 percent claiming to be "somewhat knowledgeable." Although 96 percent of the respondents could identify the capital of South Korea, only 17 percent knew the name of the South Korean president, Roh Tae Woo. Fifty-seven percent believed (correctly) that South Korea was a U.S. ally; 24 percent did not know, and the remainder thought South Korea was allied with either China or Russia! In an earlier survey of college-educated Americans (Watts, 1982), 76 percent correctly identified the location of Korea as "a peninsula with a common land boundary with communist China"; other respondents agreed with the (false) statements that Korea had a common land boundary with Japan (9 percent) or that Korea was an island (9 percent). Five percent admitted they did not know where Korea was.

Relatively few Americans know Korea from personal contact, and most of those who have firsthand experience gained it as soldiers during the Korean War or as troops living on American bases in Korea. In the survey by Eun Ho Lee, Hyung-chan Kim, and Yong Soon Yim (1991), only 9 percent claimed firsthand contact with Koreans, compared to 66 percent who knew Korea only from newspapers and television. This is not to say that American attitudes toward Korea are necessarily inaccurate, but they are likely to be either simplistic or, as Watts (1982) discovered, ambiguous or "mushy."

When Americans are asked to describe the Korean people, their responses tap several, rather stereotypical dimensions. Respondents in the survey by Eun Ho Lee, Hyung-chan Kim, and Yong Soon Yim believed that Koreans were more industrious, self-disciplined, group-oriented, and reserved than Americans. When Watts asked his respondents to choose between polar attributes, Koreans were described as group-oriented (71 percent) more often than individualistic (19 percent), hard-working (70 percent) rather than lazy (23 percent), and as more imitative (60 percent) than creative (30 percent). Other majority attributes chosen were disciplined (54 percent), humble (53 percent), loyal (51 percent), peaceful (50 percent), straightforward (46 percent), and competitive (46 percent). Most of these adjectives are on the positive end of the scale. The image that the relatively uninformed American public seems to have of Koreans is a stereotypical Orientalist image of Koreans as human ants—industrious, disciplined, and group-oriented. In the Watts (1982) study, the Japanese and the Vietnamese were described in similar terms, although the Japanese were perceived to be more industrious and the Vietnamese were thought to be more hostile toward Americans (in 1976).

It is interesting to compare these Korean images with the impressions of 189 American missionaries, Peace Corps workers, soldiers, and assorted other American residents in Korea who were surveyed by W.E. Biernatzki in 1976 (reported in Eun Ho Lee, Hyungchan Kim, and Yong Soon Yim, 1991). From a list of forty-five traits, Koreans were most often described in the following terms: respectful of authority, nationalistic, patriotic, likable, group-oriented, ritualistic, courteous, racially biased, trustworthy, and cooperative—on balance an admirable set of qualities. The images of discipline and group orientation are consistent with those found in other studies, although industriousness did not emerge as one of the ten most frequently mentioned traits. The American residents did comment on the friendliness of their Korean neighbors and on their patriotism and nationalism. Assuming there is a kernel of truth to these foreign stereotypes and on-the-scene impressions, the Korean traits diverge in some important respects from those usually attributed to Americans.

Most Americans and Koreans know each other only through the news and entertainment media, which present information selectively and often in distorted form. Two complaints that Koreans make about U.S. news coverage of their country are that it is too limited and too negative. These complaints are also voiced by other developing and newly industrializing nations (Chang, Shoemaker, and Brendlinger, 1987). Research on international news flows suggests that the extent of one nation's news coverage of another is correlated with the distance between the two countries, cultural similarity, the population size of the country of news origin, the strength of trade ties between the two countries, and the gross national product (GNP) of the country of news origin. The strongest finding is that "elite" nations—the major powers—receive the most news coverage (Kariel and Rosenvall, 1984). Chang, Shoemaker, and Brendlinger found that the international news stories that get published in the American press tend to concentrate on foreign news events that deviate from American norms and that have the potential for effecting a change in the foreign nation.

A number of factors correlate with favorable public opinion toward a foreign country. Nincic and Russett (1979) found that shared national interests and, to a lesser extent, similarities correlated with favorable public opinion. Their study defined "shared interests" as the number of American military personnel and bases in a foreign country and the amount of trade and direct investment. "Similarity" was defined in terms of race, religion, level of economic activity, and political system. Tims and Miller (1986) investigated the relation between attitudes toward a foreign country and perceptions of that country. In their study, conducted in Belgium, perceptions of shared interests and, to a lesser extent, perceptions of national similarity predicted favorable attitudes, consistent with Nincic and Russett's finding of a positive correlation between favorable attitudes and objective measures of similarity and interests. Tims and Miller defined shared interests by answers to the question "Do you think the basic interests of our country [Belgium] and the United States are in very much agreement?" Perceived similarity was assessed by questions asking how similar Belgium and the United States were in terms of "the overall quality of life in each country" and "the ability of each country to provide an adequate standard of living for most of its people." A third correlate of favorable opinion in the Tims and Miller study was perceived trust in another country, as indicated by responses to the question "In the event that Belgium's security was threatened . . . how much trust do you feel we can have in the United States to come to our defense?" The trust dimension may be largely irrelevant to American perceptions of Korea, but it is central to Korean perceptions of America. Tims and Miller note that the three factors of shared interests, similarity, and trust have also been found to predict liking between groups and between individuals.

Another factor in the Tims and Miller study (1986) is of particular interest from the perspective of international news coverage. The Belgian respondents were asked to give their impression of American positions on a variety of policy issues, such as U.S. support for the North Atlantic Treaty Organization (NATO), nuclear nonproliferation, and energy problems. A number of policy perceptions, including the foregoing, also predicted attitudes toward the United States. This policy dimension is different from the interest, similarity, and trust dimensions in at least one important respect: Policy issues change as international events unfold. As Tims and Miller note, however, it is unclear whether news events have an immediate, a delayed, and/or a permanent effect on public opinion.

Looking at American coverage of Korean news from the perspective of these studies, we note that Korea is not one of the great powers, nor is it close to the United States in terms of either physical distance or cultural similarity. Korea's population of some 40 million and its GNP should put it in the middle distance of American perceptions, and Korea's trading relationship should bring it even closer to America's attention. Yet Korea's geostrategic position as a medium-power country sandwiched between major powers may detract from Korea's importance to the news media and to the American public.

In terms of the perception of shared interests, the U.S.–South Korean alliance against communism would appear to have provided a strong bond until the recent collapse of most communist governments. On closer examination, however, the security alliance may be an imperfect example of shared interests. For South Korea, the alliance is primarily valued as a means to defend against North Korean aggression. For the United States, the alliance enlists South Korea as a proxy to fight global communism on its Asian flank. The American interest is primarily international; the Korean interest is local.

Current events, as reported in the American press, have often not improved South Korea's image. The "Koreagate" scandal, Korean student protests, and more recently the North Korean nuclear issue have received considerable press coverage, none of it particularly good for South Korea's image. It has long been acknowledged that the press has considerable power in shaping public opinion. For this reason it is enlightening to consider the results of several studies that have investigated the images of Korea that are held by editors of the American press.

In 1988 and 1989, Seong Hyong Lee (1992) asked managing and foreign editors of major American newspapers to record their impressions of South Korea. In order of descending frequency, the editorial impressions were of Korea's economic growth, the Korean War, riots and demonstrations, South Korean–North Korean division and conflict, the Olympics, military rule, and President Roh's political liberalization. The television series *M*A*S*H* (based on Robert Altman's film of the same name) also received frequent mention. Unfavorable impressions outnumbered favorable impressions by 51 percent to 43 percent.

Perceptions of the Korean people were somewhat more favorable than perceptions of their country, with approximately an equal number of positive and negative impressions (47 percent versus 46 percent, respectively). The Korean people were characterized as hardworking and industrious, radical and protesting, dynamic and dedicated, poor and underpaid, and stubborn and uncompromising. Compared with the impressions held by the general public, the editors' impressions are more focused on newsworthy items. The Koreans are still seen as industrious, but that trait does not lend itself to good news copy. More newsworthy is their relative poverty and the fiery protests of the Korean students.

As a news event, the 1988 Seoul Olympics was the biggest thing to happen to South Korea in many years. Although it was widely acknowledged that the games were hosted in a world-class manner, they had a limited impact on American attitudes toward Korea. In Seong Hyong Lee's study (1992) of American editors' perceptions of Korea as a country, favorable perceptions increased by 5 percent, to 43 percent, and unfavorable perceptions decreased by 6 percent, to 52 percent, after the games. Favorable perceptions of the Korean people increased by 8 percent, to 48 percent, but unfavorable perceptions also increased by 1 percent, to 46 percent. Neutral perceptions decreased from 16 percent to 7 percent, indicating that the American editors were at least forming a clearer picture of the Korean people.

In terms of public relations, the Seoul Olympics were something of a disappointment to the Koreans. Americans tended to see the Olympics primarily as a sporting event which happened to be held in Seoul. The Koreans tried to showcase their country, but the American media viewed Korea by American standards. In newspaper reports Seoul was described as "bustling, hustling, smiling," "a model of planning, both madcap and meticulous," "brawny, rough-and-tumble, rollicking," "everywhere one is grabbed by shoves and shouts and smells and smiles," "a rough-and-ready version of Japan" (see citations in Hassig and Oh, 1989). On balance, the Olympics convinced Americans that the Koreans were more than technically competent to stage the games, but the Koreans' unreasonable hope that only the best side of their country would receive news coverage was disappointed, and their frustration at this disappointment may have harmed their image in the end.

Are American perceptions of South Korea improving? Certainly the image of South Korea has improved since the days of the nineteenth century, when missionaries and travelers often described Koreans as dirty, childish heathens (e.g., see Eun Ho Lee, Hyung-chan Kim, and Yong Soon Yim, 1991). But in recent years it is not clear that there has been a dramatic change in American affection for Korea. William

Watts (cited in Clark, 1993) has conducted a series of surveys of American attitudes toward Korea. Between 1979 and 1992, the American evaluation of Korea actually declined, although not as much as American evaluations of Japan and China. This may be an example of what Watts calls the "Asia Factor" in American perceptions of Korea: Korea tends to be viewed as an undifferentiated part of Asia. Perceptions are also slow to change. In Watts's 1992 survey (cited in Clark, 1993, pp. 196–98), the Korean War was still the most salient image Americans had of Korea.

Watts's "Asia Factor" in American perceptions suggests that South Korea's image may be influenced by American perceptions of North Korea. The North Korean nuclear challenge has received extensive press coverage since 1992, when North Korea, in violation of the provisions of a nuclear safeguards accord that it had belatedly signed with the International Atomic Energy Agency (IAEA), refused to allow special inspections of suspected nuclear sites. In the face of American-led international pressure, North Korea went so far as to announce its withdrawal from the Nuclear Non-Proliferation Treaty (NPT) in June 1993, setting the stage for a series of confrontations and negotiations that have recently culminated in a compromise framework agreement between North Korea and the United States. In a survey of editorial coverage of the North Korea nuclear issue, Jin K. Kim (1994) selected a sample from the 650 editorial items listed between January 1991 and June 1994 in the Nexis database under the key words "nuclear" and "Korea." South Korea tended to be left out of the coverage (which may be all to the good); most attention was directed to the threat that North Korea posed to the United States, especially by way of its challenge to the international nonproliferation regime. Not only did the nuclear issue invite criticism of North Korea's nuclear policy, but also it elicited more general criticisms of North Korea as being an irrational, unpredictable, and violent state.

In Seong Hyong Lee's (1994) companion piece to his research on American editors' perceptions of South Korea, the most frequent editorial impressions of North Korea as a country were that it was a totalitarian dictatorship and a military and nuclear threat, and that it was communist, isolated, and economically backward. The North Korean people fared better. They were seen as victimized, oppressed, poor, hardworking, and regimented, but dangerous and ready to fight—that is, poor, hardworking ants cornered in their colony. The interesting question in regard to American perceptions of North Korea is whether these perceptions might be assimilated to impressions of South Korea, or whether Americans contrast the two Koreas to the benefit of South Korea's image. A possible answer is that the entire Korean peninsula will be viewed as a problem area for the United States.

Although it may be risky to draw a composite picture of Korea from the limited evidence presented above, it seems fair to say that Americans view Korea and Koreans with a mixture of admiration for their industrious accomplishments, suspicion about their devotion to the group, and pity and disdain for Korea's relative poverty. Koreans are viewed as representatives of an Asian culture that remains strange to most Americans, whose roots lie in European civilizations. Finally, Korea is seen as a small country in a conflict-prone part of the world, far from the daily concerns of most Americans.

Korean Perceptions of the United States

Over the years, Korean attitudes toward the United States have changed. Donald Clark (1993), who has spent much of his life in South Korea, summarizes this change by recalling that, in the 1950s, the standard greeting used by Korean children was, "Hello!" In the 1960s, it was, "Hello! You are a monkey!" In the 1970s, it was a similar verbal greeting, perhaps accompanied by a flying rock. In the 1980s, however, it was, "*Miguknom*" ("American S.O.B."). Koreans are sensitive to American opinion and behavior because the U.S.-Korean relationship is more important to them than it is to Americans.

Beginning with the Korean War, U.S.-Korean relations have been heavily influenced by mutual concerns for national security. The United States has provided Korea with economic and military aid and the support of the U.S.-Korean security alliance. Korea in turn has provided the United States with a forward base from which to confront communism. This relationship has often been misinterpreted by both the Korean and the American publics, who have tended to believe the official rhetoric that the two nations are linked by "bonds of friendship," a phrase of uncertain meaning when applied to nation-states. Koreans have subscribed to the friendship theory even more strongly than Americans, looking on the United States as a benevolent older brother.

In fact, many Americans are less than willing to come to the defense of South Korea, or any other country for that matter. In a 1980 survey,

51 percent of a Gallup sample of Americans (and also 51 percent of a college-educated subsample) said they opposed coming to South Korea's defense again if it were attacked by North Korea (Watts, 1982). In May 1994, a CNN-Gallup poll found that 56 percent of American men but only 31 percent of women favored sending U.S. troops to help South Korea if it was invaded by North Korea (USA Snapshots, 1994). It is not unrealistic for Koreans to conclude that Americans, benevolent though they may sometimes be, are motivated primarily by their own interests in Asia, regardless of the best interests of Korea.

A more realistic, and thus more critical, view of the U.S.-Korean relationship has been fostered by the Korean younger generation, especially those who grew up after the Korean War and who doubt the need for American protection from North Korean aggression. A mood of anti-Americanism, especially among college students, literally exploded on the scene in May 1980, when Korean army troops, "released" by the U.S. command in Korea, were sent to the city of Kwangju by General (soon to become President) Chun Doo Hwan to put down an uprising against Chun's virtual military coup. The United States was accused of supporting yet another military dictator in order to further its own security interests, trampling on the democratic desires of the Korean people. Student protests continued throughout Chun's seven-year term and on into the administration of his successor and fellow coup leader, President Roh Tae Woo (see Keun-Hyuk Choi, Tai-Huan Kim, and Chan-Rai Cho, 1991).

Korean perceptions of Americans are ambivalent. American power has saved Korea from military defeat and played an important role in pulling Korea out of poverty. At the same time, American influence has pervaded all aspects of Korean life, like a heavy blanket that both protects and smothers. In a 1955 survey of university student opinion, the American people were described as aggressive, practical, creative, selfish, money-oriented, and arrogant (Ch'a Chae-ho, 1992; reported in Kim Kyong-Dong, 1993). In a 1992 survey of student opinion, the most frequent perceptions were free-spirited, individualistic, selfish, rational, arrogant, and practical (Ch'a Chae-ho and Ch'oe In-ch'ol, 1992; reported in Kim Kyong-Dong, 1993). In a 1988 national sample, Ch'a Chae-ho discovered the following perceptions: individualistic, freedom-loving, selfish, scientific, rational, arrogant, and open-minded. In short, Americans are admired for their individualism and practicality, but disliked for the materialistic lifestyle and the superior attitude that are two consequences of their practical successes.

Much has been written about the negative sentiment toward America that has become more evident in Korea in recent years. The sentiment, which is much more broad-based than the student radical movement, has been variously described as an expression of nationalism, anti-Americanism, anti-pro-Americanism, and critical knowledge (see Clark, 1991). To the extent that this sentiment is applied to the United States as a country or to Americans in general, it may have limited meaning. Kim Kyong-Dong (1993) presents the results of four Korean newspaper surveys conducted between 1980 and 1989, which showed that, for Koreans, the United States and Switzerland were the two countries liked most (university students typically rate the United States much lower). That Switzerland is rated so highly, despite having virtually no relationship with Korea, suggests that the favorable opinions derive from the perception that the Swiss are a neutral people who mind their own business. Americans, on the other hand, are seen as both helpful and meddlesome (e.g., see survey data from Taik Sup Auh, 1990).

The ambivalent Korean view of the United States is brought into focus by Kim Kyong-Dong (1993) in an interesting tabular presentation (based on data from Taik Sup Auh, 1986, and Hy-sop Lim, 1982) of what Korean students like and dislike about the United States. American military assistance is appreciated, while the role played by the U.S. military in dividing Korea is criticized. American economic assistance is valued, but Korea's excessive dependence on the United States is deplored. The United States receives credit for introducing democratic institutions to Korea but is blamed for weakening traditional Korean values and culture. The influence of the United States in modern science and technology is extolled, but the materialistic culture it makes possible is criticized.

Negative perceptions of the United States seem to revolve around a handful of controversial issues that appear in survey after survey. Perhaps the strongest Korean accusation is that in its crusade against communism the United States has supported a series of military-led authoritarian governments in Korea; or to borrow the delicate phraseology of former U.S. Ambassador William Gleysteen, "The United States has been associated . . . with two governments [Park Chung Hee's and Chun Doo Hwan's] that have come to power by unorthodox means" (quoted in Jinwung Kim, 1989, p. 759). The United States, along with the former Soviet Union, is also blamed for dividing the Korean nation, as well as for perpetuating the division by stationing American troops on Korean soil and providing American political support for anticommunist governments in South Korea. The United States has also been accused of influencing the South Korean economy, formerly in terms of making Korea dependent on the American economy, and more recently for pressuring Korea to open its market to American products. Finally, many Koreans have objected to the influx of American culture, both the degraded GI variant that American soldiers (mostly infantry troops) bring to Korea and the broader materialistic culture communicated by the American print and electronic media that have penetrated Korea.

These criticisms have existed in some form, especially in the minds of the younger generation, at least since the 1960s, but attitudes toward the United States have been focused by several historical flashpoints in U.S.-Korean relations. The Kwangju uprising, discussed above, was one such flashpoint. Another was the Olympics, which in terms of public relations was a disappointment to the Koreans, who blamed the American media for biased reporting. A third is the domestic debate in 1994 leading up to Korea's ratification of the General Agreement on Terms and Tariffs (GATT) and the decision of the Kim Young Sam government to begin opening the rice market to imports.

There is no single explanation for the fact that Koreans are becoming more critical of the United States. As memories of the Korean War fade, South Koreans' appreciation of the role of the United States as a security shield is also fading. The perception that the Cold War has ended, and specifically that the contest between South Korea and North Korea has been won by the South, reinforces a belief that the United States is no longer needed to protect South Korea and is in fact a hindrance to Korean unification. With increased economic success, Koreans have gained greater confidence in their ability to handle their own economic affairs and to provide for their own defense. A greater number of Koreans have had the opportunity to travel abroad, enabling them to compare cultures and to see at first hand the good and the bad points of each culture. Seen up close, American society shows signs of fraying around the edges, if not actually rotting at the core. Many thoughtful Koreans are no longer convinced that America provides the best model for Korean society, and there has been a concomitant emergence of interest in traditional Korean cultural norms and values, which often conflict with Western values. Korean youth are overcoming their feeling of inferiority to the West in general, and to America in particular.

Cultures in Contact

Members of different cultures have the best chance of knowing each other when they engage in face-to-face contact, and such intercultural contact is likely to increase in the future (e.g., Brislin, 1981). Increased intercultural contact, however, does not necessarily promote intercultural harmony. When cultures meet, differences become more salient, and often what is different is disliked simply for being different. People of different cultures also hold incompatible values that may be a significant source of conflict. Each culture has developed complex patterns of behavior—for example, regarding what to eat, and when and how to eat it—that may not blend with the behavior patterns of another culture. In addition, from a realpolitik perspective, cultures as represented by political and economic groups often find themselves in conflict over scarce resources.

Bochner (1982) has outlined a number of group and contact dimensions that can influence the outcome of intercultural contact, as follows: (1) On whose territory does the contact occur? (2) What is the length of each contact, and what is the frequency of contacts? (3) What is the purpose of the contact? (4) How intimate is the contact? (5) What are the relative status and the relative power of the two cultures? (6) What is their numerical balance? (7) How visible are their cultural characteristics?

No simple relationship links the characteristics of groups and contact situations on the one hand, and the outcome of those contacts on the other. The influence of the objective factors that Bochner lists are mediated by beliefs and perceptions, referred to by such terms as "stereotypes," "social representations," and "cognitive schemata" (Brewer and Kramer, 1985). Groups and contact experiences are to an important degree subjective constructions rather than objective realities. Often the border between cultures is not even clear: "Perceived differences between ethnic groups . . . do not always correspond closely to objective similarities" (Brewer and Kramer, 1985, p. 225). People create their own cultural relations, depending on how they envision these relations. In this section we consider four ways of looking at the closest form of intercultural contact: the immigrant experience.

The Korean-American Immigrant Experience as a Model for U.S.-Korean Cultural Relations

One of the most intensive forms of contact between two cultures occurs when members of one culture have migrated to another, as in the case of Korean immigrants in America. While there are notable differences in cultural relations among independent nations from that of immigrants and the host culture, the latter may provide insights into the former. The issues that may arise in an intensive cultural contact may be a precursor to and an amplification of the issues that may arise between nations. Of particular interest in this section are different models of cultural contact and adaptation, as applied to the Korean immigrant experience, and subsequently to Korean-U.S. cultural relations.

Assimilation Model of Cultural Adaptation

The Korean-American experience is similar to that of other racial and ethnic groups. Like the first immigrants from England who came in search of religious freedom, later immigrants have been drawn to America's shores by the promise of political and religious freedom, as well as by the dream of a better life for themselves and their children. But the process of becoming American is not an easy one, particularly for the immigrant generation. To leave one's culture of origin and to learn the ways of another culture is one of the most difficult human transitions. Scholars have examined the process of becoming American and have articulated models that describe and prescribe the journey.

The earliest and most predominant model of cultural relations in America is the assimilation model. This is based on a unidimensional and unidirectional conceptualization in which the host and immigrant cultures are on opposite ends of a continuum. Immigrants gradually give up their "old" and "inferior" culture and accept the "new" and "superior" American culture. Inability to make this transition is seen as weakness and failure (Oetting and Beauvais, 1991).

The normative definition of American culture has been redefined over the years. Originally, the standard was Anglo-American culture. With increasing migration from other European countries, the Anglo-

American norm gave way to the melting-pot model in the 1800s (Gordon, 1964). According to this model, America is a huge cauldron of ethnicity in which each new group loses its distinctiveness and blends into a generic American culture created from a mix of many cultures. Both Gordon (1964) and Parks (1950) outlined specific stages of assimilation, whereby minority groups go through different stages of assimilation from initial contact and conflict to various forms of accommodation, and finally gain full acceptance, as indicated by intermarriage and participation in key social institutions. However, Blauner (1972) challenged the applicability of these models for non-European immigrants, asserting that the experience of racially distinct groups in America does not follow the melting pot model but rather the model of internal colonialism. The historic evidence of segregation and discrimination of African-Americans and Asian Americans suggests that their "racial uniform" made them unwelcome candidates for the melting pot (Takaki, 1989). Historical references to early Chinese immigrants as "aliens unfit for assimilation" reflected the mentality that led to the enactment of various exclusionary laws against Chinese and other Asian groups. The salience of the racial uniform and the perpetual foreignness of Asian-Americans persist, despite increased integration and visibility in mainstream society.

Many Koreans who immigrated before 1965 followed the assimilation model of adaptation. Parents encouraged their children to forget their Korean language in an attempt to assimilate as quickly as possible. Visible markers of racial and cultural difference were considered to be barriers to upward mobility and acceptance by the mainstream culture. Even after the 1965 Immigration Act and the significant increase in numbers of Koreans and other Asian immigrants, many who live outside large Korean communities operate from this assimilation model.

While the assimilationistic approach may reduce cultural conflict to some extent, it may also require the individual to pay a high psychological cost. Sue and Sue (1971) describe the assimilationist as a "marginal person." Marginal people strive to be 200 percent American; their sense of worth is measured by how well they are accepted by mainstream society. They tend to deny or try to hide the racial and cultural markers that differentiate them from the mainstream culture. Unfortunately, while values and behaviors can be learned or at least feigned, physical features cannot be so easily altered, despite plastic surgery, colored contact lenses, and hair dyes. Marginalists essentially hate themselves in hating that which is Korean or anything that reminds others of their Koreanness.

While it would be difficult to draw an exact parallel from the assimilation model and the marginal person to Korean-U.S. cultural relations, there are some points of resemblance. First, in the years after the Korean War, as South Korea tried to come into its own as a major economic power in Asia, modernization was inseparable from Westernization. American culture became synonymous with American goods. The desire for the material benefits of the American lifestyle existed without full awareness of the values that accompany the lifestyle. Nevertheless, there was a general appreciation for and striving toward consumerism, which seemed to represent American culture. This is not to argue that consumerism is the monopoly of American culture alone, but rather that in this particular historical context, it may have been perceived to be an American and a Western cultural phenomenon, or to be best achieved through these cultural systems. Thus, it can be argued that in the past Koreans have had an assimilationistic attitude toward American and Western culture, particularly with regard to consumerism and economic development.

Pluralistic Models of Cultural Adaptation

In contrast to the assimilation model are three pluralistic perspectives, which emerged in recognition of the diversity of cultures represented in America and the persistence of ethnicity. These pluralistic perspectives represent a shift from an assimilationistic to an acculturation paradigm.

Broadly defined, "acculturation" is the process of change that occurs in two or more cultures as a result of continuous contact between the cultures (Phinney, 1990). The critical distinction between acculturation and assimilation is that, in acculturation, cultural change is conceptualized as a bidirectional process that affects both cultures, rather than as a unidirectional process whereby the minority culture adapts to the majority culture. This shift from an assimilationistic to a pluralistic paradigm occurs in redefining power relations among groups. The pluralistic paradigm includes a fundamental challenge to the notion that the majority and those who migrated earlier have more of a right, by virtue of their size and seniority, to define who and what is American than those who are fewer in number and have arrived more recently.

The Bipolar Model of Cultural Adaptation

The first of the pluralistic approaches, the bipolar model, is a modification of the original unidimensional, unidirectional assimilation model. The bipolar model is still unidimensional in that the Korean and American cultures are placed at opposite ends of a continuum, but each culture is seen as legitimate, without value judgments about its superiority or inferiority. Unidirectionality is replaced by bidirectionality, since either culture is seen as a viable cultural option. Under this model, the ideal is to achieve biculturality, which is defined as maintaining a balance between the two cultures (Keefe and Padilla, 1987).

While the notion of biculturality, as introduced in the bipolar model, is preferable to the rejection of one culture for the other, as in the assimilation model, some limitations remain. First, because cultural adaptation is conceptualized as a linear process, movement toward one culture comes at the expense of the other. Furthermore, conceptualizing biculturality as being the midpoint between two cultural polarities not only creates an artificial and simplistic bifurcation but may also result in dual marginality, since maintaining a balance between two cultures may mean being on the fringes of both cultures. Individuals may not be fully connected to or accepted by either culture.

Another limitation of this model and, in this case, of other models of acculturation as well, is that, while any two cultures may be considered equally valid in the conceptual domain, in reality there is an unequal power dynamic both among nations and certainly between the host and the immigrant cultures. This imbalance of power translates into greater cultural influence. Thus, despite the bidirectional nature of cultural change assumed in the acculturation paradigm, in reality it remains largely unidirectional, with the direction of cultural change in U.S.-Korean cultural relations in favor of American culture. While the impact of Korean culture on America is barely noticeable, except in major metropolitan areas with a significant Korean population, the impact of American culture on Korea has been profound. Despite Korea's historic legacy as a "hermit kingdom," the direction of cultural influence was almost entirely unidirectional. As indicated earlier in this chapter, Americans are still largely ignorant of and indifferent to Korean culture and what happens in Korea, while Koreans are much more cognizant of and concerned about what happens in America.

Despite this reality, the bipolar model is a more accurate reflection of the contemporary Korean-U.S. cultural relations. Koreans no longer idealize American culture, as they did in the postwar era. Even the most desired aspect of American culture, its materialism, is now being criticized. Opinion polls in Korea reveal a general consensus about the negative influence of American culture (J.H. Kim, 1988). With Korea's rising international status and increasing nationalism, many Koreans question and resist the encroachment of American and other Western cultures. The decline of morality and the increase in social problems in America, as seen through the lenses of Hollywood, have added to Koreans' questioning of American culture.

The Orthogonal Model of Cultural Adaptation

The second pluralistic model of cultural adaptation is the orthogonal model (Oetting and Beauvais, 1991; Keefe and Padilla, 1987). According to this model, any two (or more) cultures are placed on separate (orthogonal) dimensions that intersect; thus, Korean and American cultures can be conceptualized on intersecting x and y axes with low to high cultural practices and identification ranges for each culture. Rather than conceptualizing cultural adaptation as a uniform, global, either/or process, this model employs a multidimensional framework for understanding cultural adaptation, and emphasizes the contextual nature of human behavior. The onus of value judgment inherent in comparing cultures is minimized, because adopting elements of one culture does not require rejecting elements of the other culture. Under this model, it is possible to range from a low identification with one or both cultures (marginality) to a high identification with one or both cultures (biculturality).

In the immigrant experience, Korean-Americans practice this model to a large extent. A college student may be assertive, self-expressive, and challenging of authority in the classroom, because these behaviors are rewarded in an academic environment. The same student may act with proper deference and respect for authority in a Korean cultural context, without even being consciously aware of the change in behavior. Such fluidity assumes a level of familiarity with both cultures in order to understand the cultural norms and rules that govern various contexts.

The orthogonal model offers a viable approach to Korean-U.S. cultural relations. Rather than conceptualizing cultural relations as a zero-sum game in which the gain of one culture results in the loss of the other, the goal would be to become literate in ways of the other culture, thereby expanding the range of perceived reality and choices. Selective elements of the other culture that are deemed to be beneficial can be applied in Korea in their appropriate contexts, and vice versa. However, in this process of selective cultural appropriation, it is inevitable that, as cultural values and practices are removed from their original contexts, they may not have the same meaning or effect.

The Transcultural Model of Cultural Adaptation

While much of human behavior is context-specific, a degree of consistency is necessary and desirable. A model of acculturation that strives for such consistency is the transcultural model. This model emphasizes the formation of a new culture that is a synthesis of two or more cultural alternatives. This would necessitate an honest assessment of the strengths and weaknesses of both cultures, with the desire to select and integrate the most positive elements of each (Oetting and Beauvais, 1991). The challenge inherent in this model is that it may be difficult to combine mutually exclusive elements of different cultures.

Cultural contact affords a dynamic opportunity to critically evaluate and reformulate one's own culture. Hoffman (1993) offers an example of how a young couple in Korea successfully forged a synthesis of the Korean culture and the American culture in their ceremony, in their wedding attire, and in the kind of marital relationship they envisioned. Such a synthesis and reinvention of culture is necessary, desirable, and inevitable to some extent. However, the success of such an endeavor, whether on an individual or a collective level, depends on the ability to cope with the tension between the need for change and the resistance to change, and to overcome the arrogance of ethnocentrism and the fear of the unfamiliar.

The inevitability of cultural contact between Korea and the United States affords both opportunities and challenges. With greater contact will come greater knowledge and familiarity with other cultures, leading to a greater sense of predictability and trust. On the other hand, greater contact will lead to an increased sense of difference, resulting in a more polarized sense of "us" and "them." The different models of adaptation suggest some of the ways the contact situation can be approached. If the past is any indication of the future, the history of cultural relations among Asian and European countries suggests that we can at least learn to tolerate each other, and that we can build alliances if they are mutually beneficial. The orthogonal and trans-cultural models hold out the possibility of even greater cultural enrichment and synthesis.

U.S.-Korean Cultural Relations in the 1990s

We have reviewed surveys of intercultural images and opinions held by those who, for the most part, have had little direct intercultural contact. Even Americans and Koreans who have met and worked together usually have only a sample of behavior from which to draw conclusions about an entire people. Koreans and Americans have learned about each other largely through the media. Koreans have incorporated a romantic, idealized image of Americans, often tainted by a more down-to-earth view gained from the presence of American soldiers in Korea. What Americans know of Korea comes disproportionately from news stories about foreign trouble spots, of which Korea has been a prime example. Neither the Koreans' romanticized image nor the Americans' relative ignorance provides a sound basis for a relationship.

In recent years, changes in Korea have signaled the need for a change in Korean-American relations. The old assimilation model of acculturation is no longer applicable. Koreans are becoming more critical and more selective in their cultural imports. The Kwangju uprising, political liberalization, Korea's continued economic success, American trade pressure, increased economic and political nationalism, the opening of relations with the formerly communist states, and heightened expectations for Korean reunification have set the stage for changes. Korean perceptions of the United States have become increasingly realistic and critical: The American economy is seen to be struggling, U.S. military power declining, and American society decaying. Not the stuff that dreams are made of.

What does the future hold? Korea will become less dependent on the United States and more open to influences from other nations. In that sense, Korea will become a more mature country, no longer tied to America's apron strings. The growth of democracy and an improvement in Korea's standard of living seem assured. The Korean market will open wider to foreign goods, services, and investments. Korean culture will become more Westernized, and Korea will join the ranks of the developed nations. Most significantly, Korea will recognize that its security does not depend on the United States. When this realization occurs, the strongest historical link between the two nations will have been broken.

North Korea will develop ties with South Korea, Japan, and the United States, and American troops will be withdrawn from East Asia. The most likely scenario for North Korea is absorption by South Korea. Korea will develop stronger political and economic relations with its Asian neighbors yet remain wary of them. The World Trade Organization (WTO) and Asia-Pacific Economic Cooperation (APEC) will provide a forum for economic and political dialogue among the United States and its Asian neighbors, and institutionalizing negotiations may help to reduce bilateral conflict (Kreisberg, 1990).

Koreans are likely to become more like Americans, Korean nationalism notwithstanding. As a consequence, Korean-U.S. cultural relations should improve, since similarity leads to liking. To the extent that the Korean and the American economies both continue to grow, and to the extent that barriers to trade in both countries fall, shared economic interests may lead to increased liking, although competitive conflicts will surely continue. These two factors—similarity and shared interests—have repeatedly proved to be strong predictors of positive relations on the individual, group, and international levels. However, we would be naive to expect that an era of harmony lies ahead, be it based on bilateral American-Korean relations or multilateral Asia-Pacific relations.

As the traditional security relationship between South Korea and the United States weakens, what will replace it? What else do the two nations have in common? Will the memory of their Cold War battle against communism be enough to secure them a special place in each other's hearts? Samuel Huntington (1993a) has recently offered his thoughts on the future of international relations. In his view, the end of the Cold War spells the end of the alignment of nations on ideological grounds. In the future, alliances and conflicts will be based on loyalty to civilizations, "the highest cultural grouping of people and the broadest level of cultural identity" (p. 24). Korea and the United States fall on different sides of one "fault line of civilization": The United States is in the Western camp and Korea is in the Confucian camp.

What makes Huntington pessimistic about the cooperation among cultures is that civilizations differ in their basic values—for example, "on the relations between God and man, the individual and the group, the citizen and the state, parents and children, husband and wife . . . the relative importance of rights and responsibilities, liberty and authority, equality and hierarchy" (1993a, p. 25). It would be naive to expect that such basic differences will not be the source of intercultural conflict. Moreover, as cultures increasingly come into contact, these differences will become more salient, and thus more troublesome. Huntington advocates pessimistically that the West take a confrontational stance toward other cultures, preparing to defend itself against their onslaught.

Huntington has been criticized for his inadequate conception of civilizations, which he sees as homogeneous within and heterogeneous without. In a collection of rebuttals to his thesis (Comments, 1993), critics argue that Huntington seriously underestimates the influence of modernity and secularism on non-Western cultures, and overestimates the strength of cultural tradition. Close observers of other cultures see a rapid transformation of those cultures in the direction of Western culture, and thus less reason to predict a clash of civilizations. Moreover, these observers contend that, as in the past, states and their citizens will pursue their own best political and economic interests, regardless of what civilization they "belong" to.

Huntington's thesis will be debated for years to come. In his attempt to create a grand paradigm of international relations (see Huntington, 1993b), in which traditional balance-of-power politics can be played out on the civilization level rather than the state level, Huntington may betray a misguided faith in the capacity of political science theory to provide an adequate view of a complex world. Even so, he does us a service by reminding us of the importance of cultural differences—a realpolitik view of cultural relations. Equally important, his views on international relations, which are relatively uninformed in terms of the actual characteristics of nations, highlight the problem of America's ignorance of the rest of the world.

Writing as Americans, we cannot help but be concerned about the ignorance of the American public in general, and the American government in particular, of Korean affairs. Greater knowledge about another culture may not lead to deeper affection for that culture, but it is essential for constructing a working relationship between countries. Koreans are beginning to gain critical knowledge of the United States that will enable them to take an orthogonal or transcultural perspective on Korean-American relations, making a new culture out of the best of the old cultures. It is not clear that there is a similar interest in the United States in learning about Korea. Korean-American relations, on the political, economic, and social levels, are best conceived of as an ongoing task, requiring both peoples to work to overcome their differences in order to live peacefully and prosperously with each other.

Cultural relations intersect political and economic relations. Ultimately all relations are people-to-people relations. Good cultural relations can exert a positive influence on political and economic relations, and vice versa. While North Korean affairs and U.S.–South Korea trade relations may sour bilateral relations, the major threat to the U.S.-Korean relationship is the failure of the United States to recognize the growth of Korea and its Asian neighbors. Unless Americans are ready to accept the concept of a multilateral economic and political global power structure, even though it has not yet arrived, traditional American views of Korea will be the source of serious friction. The Cold War view of Asian nations as spokes in an American security fan must be replaced by a less America-centered conception of Asian nations as mature nations with their own cultural values and their own national interests.

References

Auh, Taik Sup (1986). Korean perceptions of U.S.-Korean relations. In Robert A. Scalapino and Han Sung-joo (eds.), *United States–Korea relations* (pp. 101–11). Berkeley, CA: Institute of East Asian Studies, University of California.
——— (1990). Korean perceptions of the United States. In Robert Sutter and Han Sungjoo (eds.), *Korea-U.S. relations in a changing world* (pp. 85–97). Berkeley, CA: Institute of East Asian Studies, University of California.
Blauner, R. (1972). *Racial oppression in America.* New York: Harper and Row.
Bochner, Stephen (1982). The social psychology of cross-cultural relations. In Stephen Bochner (ed.), *Cultures in contact: Studies in cross-cultural interaction* (pp. 5–44). New York: Pergamon Press.
Brewer, Marilynn B., and Kramer, Roderick M. (1985). The psychology of intergroup attitudes and behavior. *Annual Review of Psychology, 36,* 219–43.
Brislin, Richard W. (1981). Introduction. In Richard W. Brislin (ed.), *Cross-cultural encounters: Face-to-face interaction* (pp. 1–17). New York: Pergamon Press.
Chang, Tsan-Kuo, Shoemaker, Pamela J., and Brendlinger, Nancy (1987). Determinants of international news coverage in the U.S. media. *Communication Research, 14*(4), 396–414.
Choi, Keun-Hyuk; Kim, Tai-Hwan; and Cho, Chan-Rai (1991). The impacts of anti-Americanism on U.S.-Korean relations. *Korea Observer, 22*(3), 311–33.
Clark, Donald N. (1991). Bitter friendship: Understanding anti-Americanism in

South Korea. In Donald N. Clark (ed.), *Korea Briefing, 1991* (pp. 147–67). Boulder, CO: Westview Press.

———— (1993). American attitudes toward Korea. In Donald N. Clark (ed.), *Korea Briefing, 1993* (pp. 185–200). Boulder, CO: Westview Press.

Comments: Responses to Samuel P. Huntington's "The clash of civilizations?" (1993). *Foreign Affairs, 72*(4), 1–26.

Gordon, M. (1964). *Assimilation in American life.* New York: Oxford University Press.

Hassig, Ralph C., and Oh, Kongdan (1989). I read the news today, oh boy! Unpublished manuscript.

Hoffman, Diane M. (1993). Culture, self, and *"uri"*: Anti-Americanism in contemporary South Korea. *Journal of Northeast Asian Studies, 12*(2), 3–20.

Huntington, Samuel P. (1993a). The clash of civilizations? *Foreign Affairs, 72*(3), 22–49.

———— (1993b). If not civilizations, what? *Foreign Affairs, 72*(5), 186–94.

Kariel, Herbert G., and Rosenvall, Lynn A. (1984). Factors influencing international news flow. *Journalism Quarterly, 61*(3), 509–16, 666.

Keefe, S., and Padilla, A. (1987). *Chicano ethnicity.* Albuquerque, NM: University of New Mexico Press.

Kim, J.H. (1988). Vortex of misunderstanding: Changing Korean perceptions. In R. Scalapino and H.K. Kim (eds.), *Korea-U.S. relations: The politics of trade and security.* Berkeley, CA: Institute for East Asian Studies, University of California.

Kim, Jin K. (1994, October). *Editorial coverage of the North Korean nuclear weapons development issue in U.S. dailies, 1991–1994.* Paper presented at the Fifth Academic Conference of the Korean-American University Professors Association, Atlanta, GA.

Kim, Jinwung (1989). Recent anti-Americanism in South Korea. *Asian Survey, 29*(8), 749–63.

Kim Kyong-Dong (1986). Sociocultural relations between Korea and the United States. In Robert A. Scalapino and Han Sung-joo (eds.), *United States–Korea relations* (pp. 1–15). Berkeley, CA: Institute of East Asian Studies, University of California.

———— (1993). Korean perceptions of America. In Donald N. Clark (ed.), *Korea Briefing, 1993* (pp. 163–84). Boulder, CO: Westview Press.

Kreisberg, Paul H. (1990). U.S.-Korea political relations: Emerging policy issues. In Robert Sutter and Han Sungjoo (eds.), *Korea-U.S. relations in a changing world* (pp. 65–84). Berkeley, CA: Institute of East Asian Studies, University of California.

Lee, Eun Ho, Kim Hyung-chan, and Yim, Yong Soon (1991). Korea in American kaleidoscope: What Americans think of her. *Korea Observer, 22*(4), 555–83.

Lee, Seong Hyong (1992). American editors' perceptions of Korea. *Sungkok Journalism Review, 3,* 45–53.

———— (1994). U.S. newspaper editorialists' perceptions of North Korea. *Korea Observer, 25*(3), 383–94.

Lim, Hy-sop (1982). Acceptance of American culture in Korea: Patterns of cultural contact and Korean perception of American culture. In Sung-joo Han (ed.), *After one hundred years: Continuity and change in Korean-American relations* (pp. 28–40). Seoul: Asiatic Research Center, Korea University.

Macdonald, Donald S. (1986). Americans' images of Korea: Past and present. *Korea Observer, 22*(2), 213–20.

Nincic, Miroslav, and Russett, Bruce (1979). The effect of similarity and interest on attitudes toward foreign countries. *Public Opinion Quarterly, 43*(1), 68–78.

Oetting, E. R., and Beauvais, F. (1991). Orthogonal cultural identification theory: The cultural identification of minority adolescents. *International Journal of the Addictions, 25*, 655–85.

Parks, R. (1950). *Race and culture*. Glencoe: The Free Press.

Phinney, Jean S. (1990). Ethnic identity in adolescents and adults: Review of research. *Psychological Bulletin, 108*(3), 499–514.

Sue, S., and Sue, D.W. (1971). Chinese-American personality and mental health. *Amerasia Journal, 1*, 36–49.

Takaki, R. (1989). *Strangers from a different shore: A history of Asian Americans*. Boston: Little, Brown, and Co.

Tims, Albert R., and Miller, M. Mark (1986). Determinants of attitudes toward foreign countries. *International Journal of Intercultural Relations, 10*, 471–84.

USA Snapshots: Split decision on Korea. (1994, May 18). *USA Today*, p. 1.

Watts, William (1982). The United States and Korea: Perception vs. reality. In Sung-joo Han (ed.), *After one hundred years: Continuity and change in Korean-American relations* (pp. 41–68). Seoul: Asiatic Research Center, Korea University.

Index